Praise for *Obama on the Couch*

"Frank delves into Obama's youth—his reconciliation of his biracial identity, nontraditional upbringing, and travels—to paint a detailed portrait of a president who is charismatic, well-intentioned, and the ultimate consensus builder . . . [and] returns to key themes regarding race and Obama's relationship with his father, demonstrating how those factors have affected past policy decisions and will probably influence future ones."

—*Publishers Weekly*

"Wonder why President Obama can't fight back? The answer is in this compelling book. Dr. Frank unravels the tragic flaw within a tightly woven man whose unexpressed rage toward both his parents has neutered him as a leader. Aware of his own capacity for destructiveness, he cannot allow himself to retaliate against opponents bent on crushing his presidency. Pass on this book to his advisers. It could lift him out of depression and free him to expose the fractures threatening our country and heal our national split before it is too late."

—Gail Sheehy, author of *Passages* and *Understanding Men's Passages*

"Dr. Justin Frank's brilliant use of psychoanalytic categories to unravel the mystery and enigma of President Barack Obama should be read by every American. For years we have puzzled over how the president elected on a promise of 'change we can believe in' could have become the Democrat who capitulated to most Republican demands—while abandoning and denouncing his political base rather than fighting for the needs of the environment, the middle class, the poor, the immigrants, and the powerless. *Obama on the Couch* demonstrates why this pattern is for our president a necessary response to his own inner needs. Nuanced and measured, Dr. Frank's book is a major contribution to contemporary political analysis."

—Rabbi Michael Lerner, editor in chief of *Tikkun*

"An analyst who can coin phrases like 'obsessive bipartisan disorder' to describe our president is a pleasure to read. But what makes *Obama on the Couch* an important book is Justin Frank's ability to dive deep into the president's eloquent writing about his childhood and emerge with fresh and major insights—unacknowledged rage for the mother Obama claims to idolize, unexpressed despair at his abandonment by his stepfather as well as his father. *Obama on the Couch* is nothing less than a public service."

—Jesse Kornbluth, editor of HeadButler.com

"Dr. Frank's *On the Couch* franchise has reinvented the way we look at political candidates, and I keep asking myself why no one has thought of this before. His latest opus, *Obama on the Couch,* has taken the president apart from the ground up and shown us the real man—half Shakespearean tragedy, half American success story—in a way that other authors could only hope to do. I found myself climbing deeper and deeper into the mind of this most enigmatic and engaging politician—no small feat—enjoying prose at once articulate, engaging, and—the rarest of beasts—occasionally profound. Great work wrapped up in a thoroughly entertaining package."

—Robert Pobi, author of *Bloodman* (to be released May 2012)

"Brilliant. Justin Frank has opened a powerful line of inquiry into the minds of sitting presidents. Using classical techniques of psychoanalysis, Dr. Frank pierces the facades of the high and mighty to delve into their psyches, and he hits the target more precisely and more cogently than any other analyst in America today. *Bush on the Couch* was a triumph of presidential analysis. The arrival of *Obama on the Couch* is a very great gift to the American people, to history, and to Obama himself. Congratulations to Justin Frank for stepping where others fear to tread."

—Michael Carmichael, director of Planetary Movement

$f\mathbf{P}$

Also by Justin A. Frank, M.D.

Bush on the Couch: Inside the Mind of the President

OBAMA
ON THE
COUCH

Inside the Mind of the President

Justin A. Frank, M.D.

FREE PRESS

New York   London   Toronto   Sydney   New Delhi

FREE PRESS
A Division of Simon & Schuster, Inc.
1230 Avenue of the Americas
New York, NY 10020

First Free Press trade paperback edition May 2012

FREE PRESS and colophon are trademarks of Simon & Schuster, Inc.

For information about special discounts for bulk purchases,
please contact Simon & Schuster Special Sales at 1-866-506-1949
or business@simonandschuster.com.

The Simon & Schuster Speakers Bureau can bring authors to your live event.
For more information or to book an event contact the Simon & Schuster Speakers Bureau
at 1-866-248-3049 or visit our website at www.simonspeakers.com.

Manufactured in the United States of America

1   3   5   7   9   10   8   6   4   2

The Library of Congress has catalogued the hardcover edition as follows:
Frank, Justin A.
Obama on the couch: inside the mind of the president /
Justin A. Frank.—1st Free Press hardcover ed.
p. cm.
1. Obama, Barack—Psychology. 2. Presidents—United States—Psychology.
3. United States—Politics and government—2009– I. Title.
E908.F69 2011
973.932092—dc23
2011025377

ISBN 978-1-4516-2063-4
ISBN 978-1-4516-2064-1 (pbk)
ISBN 978-1-4516-2065-8 (ebook)

To Heather with gratitude and love

It is invariably saddening to look through new eyes at things upon which you have expended your own powers of adjustment.

—F. Scott Fitzgerald, *The Great Gatsby*

How children dance to the unlived lives of their parents.
—Rainer Maria Rilke, *Letters to a Young Poet*

What is a family? Is it just a genetic chain, parents and offspring, people like me? Or is it a social construct, an economic unit, optimal for child rearing and divisions of labor? Or is it something else entirely: a store of shared memories, say? An ambit of love? A reach across the void?

—Barack Obama, *Dreams from My Father*

Contents

Introduction   1

Chapter 1: Born Split: Healing the Black/White Divide   11

Chapter 2: Abandoned and Assuaged   37

Chapter 3: Accommodator in Chief   63

Chapter 4: Calming Words   91

Chapter 5: The Only Thing We Have to Fear Is Change Itself   119

Chapter 6: The Achiever   143

Chapter 7: The Company He Keeps   163

Chapter 8: "Their" Obama: Obama in the Minds of His Critics   185

Chapter 9: "Our" Obama, or My President, My Selves   203

Chapter 10: Mission Accomplished   215

Epilogue: O'Bama on the Couch   225

Epilogue, Part Two   233

Glossary   239

Source Notes   249

Acknowledgments   259

Index   265

Introduction

> We must judge men not so much by what they do, as by what they make us feel that they have it in them to do. . . . It is not by what a man has actually put down upon his canvas, nor by the acts which he has set down, so to speak, upon the canvas of his life that I will judge him, but by what he makes me feel that he felt and aimed at.
>
> —Samuel Butler, *The Way of All Flesh*

Recently, as I drove through upstate New York, I was trying to listen to a Beethoven symphony through the chaos of five overlapping radio stations. My frustration grew until I realized that the only way I'd be able to hear "Ode to Joy" was by tuning into the frequency in my own head—the way Beethoven himself must have heard it. Because the competing channels made focused listening impossible, I turned off the radio and continued driving, content for the first time in an hour.

So it is with writing a book analyzing President Barack Obama. It seems that everyone has his or her own personal Obama. He is infinitely complex, the embodiment of one-who-creates-ambivalence-in-all-individuals. There are so many views and opinions that if I start to listen to them instead of to Obama himself—reading and listening to his autobiographical writings and speeches, hearing the discrepancies between his words and actions as president, and paying close attention to his behaviors throughout his adult life and his many repeating patterns of thought—I am lost in any effort to understand him better.

Barack Hussein Obama is unique. He has been "the first" at several moments in his public life—the first black president of the *Harvard Law Review* and the first black president of the United States. In private life he was a firstborn, to a nineteen-year-old white college girl from Kansas. And he has distinguished himself as exceptional in many other ways: by the time he reached law school, one Harvard professor called him the best law student he had ever taught, first out of tens of thousands of excellent students. He is the first person to win the Nobel Peace Prize based on promise, not accomplishment.

But even though we know all of this about him, many of us find ourselves still asking: Who is Barack Obama? Who is this man who suddenly rose to fame in 2004 and rode the crest of an energetic wave all the way to Pennsylvania Avenue four years later? Who, after less than two years in office, passed landmark legislation while he simultaneously dropped like a stone in the polls as his party suffered a crushing midterm defeat in 2010? And who, on May 1, 2011, issued the surprise Sunday night announcement that our Navy SEALs had killed Osama bin Laden, challenging much of what most Americans thought we knew about him?

For much of his presidency, Barack Obama has been a far more closely observed candidate and president than his predecessor. It's also true that he has given his observers much more to work with among his prolific speechwriting, two widely read autobiographies, media accessibility, and open responses to questions; nevertheless journalists, critics, and supporters alike struggle to define him clearly. The scrutiny that has persisted well into his first term reveals more about the scrutinizers than about the subject, however. Birthers cannot relate to him except as an imposter, someone other, black and foreign. He came into office preaching that we all have common ground as Americans, and has been in a maelstrom of controversy questioning whether he is himself a U.S. citizen. His message of unity has been overshadowed by the divisiveness of his very existence. Deep into a first term in which Obama has often seemed adrift and embattled, the question of his identity remains uppermost in the nation's mind—but the answer stays elusive.

More than eight years ago, I began questioning the full and true identity of President George W. Bush, inspired by then-nascent concerns that our president was more disturbed than anyone suspected.

That inquiry grew into a full-fledged exercise in applied psychoanalysis, the discipline pioneered by Sigmund Freud of using psychoanalytic principles to assess the personalities and motivations of public figures. In 2004, I published my findings in *Bush on the Couch,* in which I showed that the psychoanalytic method can shed light on our leaders and how they got to be who they are. The book struck a chord and helped to usher in a new way of assessing and discussing presidential behavior.

Obama on the Couch adapts the model of my first book to provide the deeper understanding of our current president that readers across the political spectrum are hungry for. By helping readers recognize Obama's behavior patterns and illuminating the unconscious thought processes that might be influencing them, the discipline of applied psychoanalysis can profoundly enhance our understanding of Obama's character. Revisiting familiar and emerging details of the president's biography from a psychoanalytical perspective reveals connections between past and present that can reframe recent history in revealing new ways, possibly even helping us anticipate how Obama's attitude may evolve in the future—and what that might mean for our country.

I approach Obama as an admirable and down-to-earth individual who is generally in excellent mental health, especially in light of the challenges he faced in his formative childhood years. Nevertheless, Obama, like all of us, repeatedly demonstrates that his otherwise healthy outlook is not without some potentially troubling blind spots. Left uncharted, these blind spots can undermine his effectiveness as a leader—possibly paving the way for a successor who poses even graver risks to the nation and the world than George W. Bush.

Obama's easily observed characteristics—his abilities to link thinking and feeling, to listen to and assimilate the feelings of others, to transform their input into new thoughts, to have a firm grip on internal and material reality, and to consult both his passions and conscience when making decisions—exemplify strong mental health. They also reveal his personal triumph over a turbulent childhood, and we'll explore how many of his positive attributes—such as his brilliant facility with language, his calm in the face of chaos, and his ability to find common ground and build consensus—in fact developed out of coping mechanisms in response to the challenges he faced growing up.

Though Obama remains an exemplary man, even his most fervent admirers must concede that his performance as president has been uneven, marked by inconsistencies and disappointments that have mystified, frustrated, and discouraged observers on both the right and the left. Among his supporters, a sense of disconnect between the candidate and the president has caused concern about what is driving his choices. As a psychoanalyst I'm fascinated by someone who can be so present yet so absent. His supporters are stuck in the position of cycling between hope and disappointment. Even the satirical TV show *The Onion News Network* chimed in with a "story" that the real President Obama had been kidnapped hours after the election and replaced by an imposter. According to this "breaking news," the real Obama was freed after two years and expressed shock that nobody had suspected anything was wrong—especially since he suddenly acted so differently from his espoused beliefs. He raged, "How could anyone mistake that rudderless pushover for me?" People who like Obama can nonetheless be extremely critical of him as they describe their experience of what he does and how they feel about it, as in shock at how different President Obama is from Candidate Obama.

Obama on the Couch argues that a range of the president's decisions, from his handling of health care reform to his selection and support of economic advisers, has been motivated not just by political preferences but by idiosyncratic unconscious factors that he himself doesn't recognize. At other times he appears to be blind to the circumstances he faces to the point of self-defeat, imposing his personal need for consensus upon the recalcitrant opposition; we'll also look at moments that reveal that despite his emotional health, the president lacks insight into parts of himself where destructive forces gain influence.

In order to understand the parts of Obama's character that remain impenetrable even to him, *Obama on the Couch* considers the work of journalists who have covered Obama's campaign and early administration, including books by David Remnick, Jonathan Alter, Bob Woodward, and others. Obama's books *Dreams from My Father* and *The Audacity of Hope* naturally offer an abundance of material to mine for insight. And his hands-on approach to speechwriting means that his public addresses are more accurate and revealing windows into his motives than those of many other politicians.

The psychoanalytic practice and research I bring to bear on this analysis are heavily influenced by the Freudian model as well as the work of Melanie Klein and her followers. A Viennese psychoanalyst who practiced mostly in England until her death in 1960, Klein expanded upon the Freudian tradition with theories—elaborated throughout this book—about personality formation in early childhood. As a Kleinian, I'm drawn to the numerous events and circumstances from Obama's infancy and childhood, the psychic consequences of which would be felt as he developed his character for decades to come. He faced particular challenges as the mixed-race, ostensibly black child of a white mother, which inevitably made it harder for mother and son to recognize themselves in each other in the critical early stages of his infancy, despite his mother's apparent strengths at being a committed and effective nurturer. Additionally, growing up in a fatherless home, at least after his namesake left the family well before young Barry was two, posed another significant challenge, further complicated by the fact that Obama Sr.'s departure left his son the only black face in an otherwise white family.

In the wake of that departure, Obama's young mother and maternal grandparents, with whom they lived, consciously kept his father alive in his imagination as a positive, idealized figure, a process movingly detailed in *Dreams from My Father,* the title of which alone announces the success of their efforts. His book attests to the power of his mother's mythmaking on another level: Barack Obama is a skilled storyteller and mythmaker in his own right. Over the course of a psychoanalytic treatment the same stories change and have more complex meanings. In the case of Obama's book, however, his stories endure permanently in the form in which they were written, not changing with the advent of his new understanding or unearthed memories.

The potential lasting impact of some of those childhood challenges can't be overstated, and Obama's early childhood experiences deeply influenced his adult perceptions of self and society. I am particularly drawn to the mental attitudes that an individual demonstrates toward aggression. Anxiety about destructiveness—either destroying or being destroyed—gives rise to defenses aimed at protecting the personality; these anxieties shift over time, forming patterns that become character traits. Klein labeled these attitudes the paranoid-schizoid position and the depressive position, and a person can continually alternate between the two throughout childhood and adult life as he seeks to modify his fears that hate or aggression will destroy what he values as good. Our analysis of Obama traces the roots and presence of these two positions past and present, highlighting both his strengths and weaknesses. By revealing when and how he shifts between the two positions, we can make connections that help explain his behavior with his colleagues and family, with his wife and children, with Democrats and Republicans, and with supporters, critics, and the media.

Psychoanalysis is not a linear process; at times its recurring circular patterns more closely resemble a spiral, repeatedly shifting back from present to past to present again. Accordingly, we take as our starting point the present and recent past, especially the president's first years in office, after which even the more casual observers were left with questions, including:

- How does he come across so differently to different people yet remain an enigma to many?
- How does he attract identification from such a wide variety of people yet leave so many of them disappointed?
- Why has someone who campaigned for change so often seemed so tentative?
- What lies behind his exceptional facility with language—and why do his actions so rarely live up to his words?
- Why is he so driven to compromise, settling for positions that leave so few people genuinely satisfied?
- Why is he drawn to charismatic, narcissistic men who ultimately let him down?
- Why does he appear to resist confronting authority figures?
- What is the source of his famous, Zen-like calm, and how and at what cost does he maintain it?

- Does his reluctance to challenge the relentless attacks by his opponents mean that he doesn't recognize the hatred behind those attacks?
- If the president doesn't see red states and blue states, what does he see?
- How was the raid on bin Laden—its planning, execution, and announcement—consistent with his character, and how was it not?

Any attempt to better understand Obama by putting him "on the couch" means that we have to put his supporters and detractors on the couch as well. His supporters in particular have exhibited an interesting evolution. Like any politician, Obama exists in the minds of his supporters as the sum of their countless individual projections onto him. But somehow Obama tapped into one segment of the electorate's yearning to believe that he could be different, and we explore the extraordinary passion that he elicits in so many voters and the cycle of hope and disappointment that it frequently leaves in its wake.

Obama's opponents are equally as passionate, if not more so, about the feelings aroused by their own projections onto the president, causing divisions that profoundly challenge Obama's own drive to heal his psychic splits. Later on, I'll discuss how the Republicans may in fact serve as Obama's best therapists if the vehemence of their opposition grows strong enough to break through his denial about the destructiveness of their intentions. We'll also look at the Tea Party movement, using a psychoanalytical perspective to expose its rigid adherence to the paranoid-schizoid position of fear of the "Other." The more Obama speaks of accommodation, the more anxious and frightened the Tea Party becomes, ultimately justifying murderous aggression in the name of self-defense against its perceived enemies. The party members' paranoid anxiety leads them to conflate thought with action, which tends to encourage acts of violence, aimed at eradicating all perceived evil.

As the toxic divisions between our parties and the rapid and mysterious rise of the Tea Party make clear, it is essential to the health of our nation that we think in a richer way about our leaders and our relationships with them. Thinking about the psychology of leadership and leaders and our relationship to them is an essential component of a healthy body politic. By developing the skills to decode Obama's behavior, we'll improve our ability to make informed choices and keep our democracy vibrant and growing.

My decision to analyze our presidents has its roots in wondering about the ways their psyches and the external and internal pressures they feel influence the difficult job they are trying to do. But what really propelled me in the case of our current president was being struck by what seemed like a disconnect between Candidate Obama and President Obama. I wanted to understand that better, since in this case I don't think it's simply a matter of a politician promising one thing and doing something else. And I was interested in how and why we, by an overwhelming majority, chose Obama to be our leader.

At the end of the 2007 edition of *Bush on the Couch* I predicted that our nation might "search for someone completely different from Bush in the 2008 election, someone not male or white," citing Hillary Clinton and Barack Obama as mother and father figures to choose from. "But simply enlisting an overtly different parent to brush the Bush disaster under the carpet will work no better than changing the Band-Aid on a fracture," I added. "Only a true awareness of our national fracture can lead to real action, carrying us out of our self-imposed ignorance and denial into the painful but clarifying light of day."

President Obama seemed to the majority of voters to carry that message of our need to heal, the need to recognize that the country can unite under shared ideals—and that we are all—Republican and Democrat alike—Americans first. Many Independents and Republicans voted for him, as did the vast majority of Democrats. The tears of joy on election night celebrated that we had actually elected an African-American president. Yet somehow that excitement has died down as his message of common ground has gotten more and more lost. And our national fracture persists and deepens.

Applied psychoanalysis is significantly different from my clinical work. Obama is not in the office with me, so I cannot use two of the fundamental tools of my profession—transference (my patient's thoughts and feelings about me) and countertransference (my thoughts and feelings about my patient). Yet of all the people I know through literature—fiction and nonfiction alike—Barack

Obama has the ability to be with the reader in the moment, whether past or present.

Even a book-length analysis requires omissions that potentially remove layers of detail and some of the genuine richness from both President Obama and my thoughts about him. This limitation reminds me of the first movie Obama took his wife, Michelle, to, *Do the Right Thing*—Spike Lee's meditation on race relations in everyday life—which takes place on the hottest day of the year and ends with a fire that burns down a pizza parlor in the Bedford-Stuyvesant section of Brooklyn. If it were real life, that fire would be merely a brief item on the eleven o'clock news, but the movie tells a rich and complex story about what leads to the fire and the characters involved—something we wouldn't know from watching a simple newscast. In news stories, the forces leading up to a sound bite often get lost, though even there we get isolated glimpses of "different" Obamas that seem illuminating: Obama the candidate, then the president lost in New Orleans or eloquent in Tucson. We build up individual snapshots over time, and hopefully our thoughts and reactions change and evolve to match current events. But even when we pay attention to the twenty-four-hour news cycle, we never quite get to the man behind the man or to the boy inside the man. That is what I hope to provide with this book.

Talking about the boy inside the man puts me in mind of a cautionary note I should include here. Several readers found *Bush on the Couch* anxiety-provoking; it stirred up feelings about their own personal lives and relationships. This could also happen to readers of this book, despite the subject being the psychodynamics of President Obama. Hopefully the experience will be enriching to the reader, despite possible discomfort caused.

Obama invites fantasies of hope, of yearning for something different and better. This book explores the possibilities of understanding him, so the reader can make sense of his or her own experience. President Obama has the power of his office, and we hope to develop our own powers of observation and understanding. Only in this way can we grasp the meanings behind how he relates to and exercises that power. By doing so we can also better understand our own reactions to this complex man.

CHAPTER 1

Born Split:
Healing the Black/White Divide

> There is as much difference between us and ourselves as between us and others.
>
> —Montaigne

> To think clearly about race, then, requires us to see the world on a split screen—to maintain in our sights the kind of America that we want while looking squarely at America as it is, to acknowledge the sins of our past and the challenges of the present without becoming trapped in cynicism or despair.
>
> —Barack Obama, *The Audacity of Hope*

In the most important speech of his political career, then–Illinois State Senator Barack Obama told the 2004 Democratic National Convention that unity was part of what made America great: "There is not a liberal America and a conservative America—there is the United States of America. There is not a black America and a white America and Latino America and Asian America—there's the United States of America. . . . We are one people, all of us pledging allegiance to the Stars and Stripes, all of us defending the United States of America. In the end, that's what this election is about."

That was then. After a year in office, with his first major policy initiative about to be prematurely written off as a failure, now-President Obama attempted to silence his former opponent John McCain at the 2010 White House health care summit by drawing a sharp distinction between their campaign and postelection personae, silencing McCain curtly, saying, "We're not campaigning anymore. The election is over."

There may be one America, but it turns out that there are two Obamas.

When Obama shared his vision of unifying a divided America, and when he differentiated between Candidate McCain and Senator McCain—and in turn between his own candidate and presidential selves—he was evoking one of the most basic tools in infant psychological development that resonates in him still; indeed, it is at the heart of both his agenda for tomorrow and the challenges he faces today. To appreciate this from a Kleinian perspective requires a brief overview of some fundamental principles of infant psychological development. The most basic of these is splitting, a primitive mental process that orders the infant mind, protecting him from overwhelming confusion and chaos. Soon after birth the infant encounters a chaotic jumble of frustration and satisfaction, cold and warmth, anxiety and calm. The infant first attempts to order the chaos by dividing its experiences into good and bad: if the baby is experiencing discomfort or extreme hunger, it links those feelings with the image of a bad mother; if it experiences warmth and satiety, the baby is safe with its good mother.

Our response to our good and bad mothers evolves into a conflict between the desire to exploit the mother—to bite or suck her breast relentlessly—and the desire to preserve her based in need and love. As the infant develops, this conflict becomes the source of a broader anxiety about destroying or consuming the very thing it needs and loves, which expands into the need to manage its innate destructiveness and control its impulses to let bad, hateful feelings overtake good and loving ones. As the young child develops, its ability to create splits as a first line of defense against overwhelming anxiety is central to psychological progress, as is the ability to heal or unify the splits that are mentally created.

Like all of ours, Obama's infancy and childhood included numerous events and circumstances whose psychic consequences would be felt as he developed his character for decades to come. And when Obama spins his crowd-pleasingly vivid images of an America whose racial, cultural, and political divisions have been repaired, he is drawing on his experience healing the splits he had to create to cope with the primitive anxieties of his early childhood. His rhetoric often invites us to identify with some of the splits he has struggled with on a personal level. But as we'll see, Obama's drive to heal his psychic splits is more pronounced than most people's, because of the simple fact that as a biracial child he was born with a fundamental division that he has been trying to heal for his entire life, both within himself and in his relationships.

In retrospect, it seems almost predictable from a psychoanalytic point of view that a mixed-race person would someday attain the presidency, having developed in his pursuit of internal unity the skills of compromise and consensus building that would fuel his political progress. In Obama's case, those skills were further and adversely influenced by the particulars of his family situation—namely, the fact that his parents separated within months of his birth, his mother leaving Hawaii and taking her infant son to Seattle, where she enrolled briefly at the University of Washington, followed by his father leaving Hawaii shortly before she returned there with one-year-old Barry, to pursue a fellowship at Harvard. His father's absence perpetuated a split that could not be healed, twisting Obama's unifying impulse (already stronger than it would be in children of single-race families) into a need that can never be satisfied.

Yet this capacity to contain and heal a split—a process that takes time and continues in some forms throughout life—was well established in young Barack Obama, just as it is in almost all children. The single most important element in any infant's learning to heal splits is the loving connection to the primary caregiver, most often the mother. This is accomplished through regular periods of what is called "break and repair": the mother inevitably has to put the nursing baby down, painfully breaking the connection for both baby and mother, who then returns to repair the damage done. The bad mommy breaks; the good repairs—helping the baby learn over time to tolerate splitting, to manage the experience of having good and bad mommies—and to know that the good mommy will return even when her absence causes him pain. As the baby internalizes the mother's love, splitting lessens in degree and intensity, and the baby develops confidence in his love for her, and in the environment in general.

The image of his mother, Stanley Ann Dunham, which Obama has presented in his memoirs and to his biographers is of a nurturing and supportive mother, at least in his earliest years. Obama's early biographer David Mendell wrote in his 2007 book, *Obama: From Promise to Power,* "As Obama himself will acknowledge, his mother went to great lengths to shore up her son's confidence. She worried that because his father was absent and he was biracial he might fall prey to a lack of self-worth. 'As a consequence, there was no shortage of self-esteem,' Obama told me with a wry smile." Much about the way Obama thinks and communicates indicates that he acquired the skills that derive from the healthy development of the splitting mechanism, a process that good parenting can facilitate. Tolerating ambivalence and ambiguity, for example, is made possible by a healthy splitting mechanism: in the president's case, his capacity for holding conflicting ideas is famously well developed. In describing his core responsibilities as commander in chief to Bob Woodward (who wrote about the president in his 2010 book, *Obama's Wars*), Obama gives special emphasis to the importance of his ability to balance some of the most profound and antithetical truths with which a president must come to terms: "So part of our challenge is reconciling these two seemingly irreconcilable truths—that war is sometimes necessary and war at some level is an expression of human folly." Obama's remarkable capacity to contain such profound opposites is itself different from simple splitting: there is no projection or idealization, and disconnecting them from thought mutes emotions. This expanded capacity is called "dissociation"—something active in Obama since early childhood—where feeling and thought become totally disconnected. It enables Obama to talk in a matter-of-fact way about what for most of us would be highly emotionally charged issues.

The phenomena of splitting and projection help us understand another fundamental psychological structure that this analysis will draw upon frequently. When we split our internal world as well as our perception of the external world into good and bad, we experience pain as a destructive attack from outside the self; this allows us to keep all goodness safe inside. This begins a process of establishing the two opposing attitudes that Klein noted the infant demonstrates toward aggression: the "paranoid-schizoid position," in which aggression is perceived as emanating from outside the self and the infant feels anxiety about being attacked, and the "depressive position," in which aggression is experienced as coming from within the self and the infant feels anxiety about being hurtful in a way that might harm a loved one. These fundamental psychic positions persist throughout life and determine perception of self and other as well as the approach to new experiences.

One way to understand the difference between the positions is to consider different responses to having a fight on the telephone with a friend. A person in the depressive position feels concern for the people he loves and feels responsible if he has injured them in some way; he might say, "I can't believe I just yelled at my friend," feeling guilt and remorse for what he did. Someone in the paranoid-schizoid position might say, "My friend is so abrupt, always hanging up on me," and experience anxiety over the prospect of his friend's telling others about his behavior.

Everyone moves between the depressive and paranoid-schizoid positions throughout life, and we will examine some of Obama's shifts in the chapters ahead. A person firmly rooted in the depressive position takes responsibility and feels genuine concern for others based on self-knowledge of his own aggression and is generally mentally healthy and mature. But a healthy dose of an unhealthy-sounding term—paranoia—is also important in a political leader, and eschewing paranoid anxieties by trying extra hard to see the point of view of an attacker or enemy can lead to a host of problems. Obama often seems genuinely unparanoid and unprepared for the hatred of his opponents—from the irrationality of the Birthers to the noncooperation of the Republicans—despite the evidence before his very eyes. Nor does he grasp the degree to which his opponents—like most people—are dominated by the paranoid-schizoid position of black-and-white thinking; thus, in the bruising and ultimately fruitless battle to win Republican support for health care reform, he failed to see that their rebranding as "death panels" a provision for end-of-life counseling—originally supported by their own party— was evidence of the opposition's inability to face its own destructive- ness or to recognize the essential humanness of the "Other" against which it is opposed.

Though Obama often fails to adequately parry some of his most vehement objectors, he excels in demonstrating compassion and winning hearts and minds. Compassion and acceptance of the "Other" are essential to the depressive position. Obama had to develop these qualities in response to the natural split of being born biracial at a time when racial attitudes in this country were far less evolved and little was known about the psychological impact of a mixed-race heritage. But subsequent studies have shown that biracial children are more prone to experiencing shame and isolation, stemming from the feeling that they don't belong or that there is something wrong with them.

Surrounded by his mother and her parents, Barry was the only black face in a white family after his father's departure. Splitting is writ large in biracial children, who are born with two racial inher- itances, and reconciling that split can pose significant challenges. Biracial people have paradoxical experiences, feeling they don't belong to one particular group while being somehow comfortable in many differently composed groups. The tension between comfort and discomfort can exist within the self: biracial people feel their otherness on a regular basis, constantly facing ambivalence and feel- ing the need to overcome it by identifying with one race or another. They are neither white nor black, but both white *and* black. Obama is both the Other and his own Other; it's like being a stranger from himself and yet totally familiar with himself at the same time. And otherness carries with it specialness, a sense of being different from those around you, whether for bad or good.

Healthy splitting allowed him to feel his genuine goodness inside himself through identification with his white mother. But as he decided to self-identify as black, Obama faced the danger that fully embracing his blackness would risk destroying his deeply loved internal mother. While the biracial person must heal the split along internal racial lines by having his white self get along with his black self, Obama had to bear in mind this other self still existing inside that pushed itself forward when his black self threatened to ignore it.

His mother appeared to recognize the pitfalls of young Barry's circumstances—aware that his black identity might be obscured by being surrounded by his white family—and provided him with many opportunities to keep his blackness as something to be prized and be aware of more often than when he looked in the mirror, promoting the contributions of black musicians to the arts, for example, and teaching her son that "to be black was to be the beneficiary of a great inheritance, a special destiny," he wrote in *Dreams from My Father.* But despite her efforts to shield her son, Obama in his later youth would become deeply aware of shame and its effect on African-American people. We see several episodes in *Dreams from My Father.* The usually socially adept Obama, in his desire to belong to a group, impulsively says embarrassing things—such as criticizing a Chicago community member whose blue contact lenses obscured her brown eyes, and by extension her racial identity. The shame and inhibition that follow such embarrassing interludes may be fleeting, but the feeling of not belonging is a recurring theme in Obama's memoir. At a deeper level we see in Obama's reaction to the blue contacts a projection of his fear of his own desire to belong being so great that it might obscure his essential black identity. He criticized her for wanting to do what he so desperately wished for himself, projecting that desire into her and turning it into something to criticize.

Earlier in *Dreams from My Father,* he vividly recounts a scene from his time in Indonesia, where his mother moved Barry at the age of six to live with her second husband, Lolo Soetoro. His mother got a job at the U.S. Embassy in Jakarta, where, in "the pure and heady breeze of privilege," Barry waited in the library one afternoon while his mother did some work. After finishing his comic books and homework that "my mother made me bring," he focuses on a collection of *Life* magazines:

"I thumbed through the glossy advertisements—Goodyear Tires and Dodge Fever, Zenith TV ('Why not the best?') and Campbell's Soup ('Mm-mm good!'), men in white turtlenecks pouring Seagram's over ice as women in red miniskirts looked on admiringly—

and felt vaguely reassured. When I came upon a news photograph, I tried to guess the subject of the story before reading the caption."

When he comes to an image of "an older man in dark glasses and a raincoat walking down an empty road," he is unable to guess what the photograph is about, his confusion compounded on the following page's close-up shot of the same man's hands. "They had a strange, unnatural pallor, as if blood had been drawn from the flesh. Turning back to the first picture, I now saw that the man's crinkly hair, his heavy lips and broad, fleshy nose, all had this same uneven, ghostly hue."

Deducing that the man in the photo "must be terribly sick," Barry learns from the accompanying article that the subject of the photographs had undergone a chemical treatment to lighten his black complexion. "He expressed some regret about trying to pass himself off as a white man, was sorry about how badly things had turned out," he learns from the article. "But the results were irreversible. There were thousands of people like him, black men and women back in America who'd undergone the same treatment in response to advertisements that promised happiness as a white person."

Barry's response is immediate but remarkably short-lived:

I felt my face and neck get hot. My stomach knotted; the type began to blur on the page. Did my mother know about this? What about her boss—why was he so calm, reading through his reports a few feet down the hall? I had a desperate urge to jump out of my seat, to show them what I had learned, to demand some explanation or assurance. But something held me back. As in a dream, I had no voice for my newfound fear. By the time my mother came to take me home, my face wore a smile and the magazines were back in their proper place. The room, the air, was quiet as before.

When reporters researched the story during the presidential campaign, they couldn't find any such article in *Life* or elsewhere, according to Obama's biographer David Remnick. As a psychoanalyst, I'm less interested in the concrete existence of the story than in its meaning, although the possibility that Obama might have made it up merits comment. If anything, it underscores the fact that these ideas are important to him—most particularly his rage at discovering—at nine years old—that one race could evoke such extreme self-hatred in another. Clearly, a nine-year-old boy is not writing his memoir, so his rage as remembered is at least questionable. But how the story is constructed bears even further analysis.

In the telling of this story we see several themes that recur throughout the memoir (and the life it chronicles): the maintenance of quiet and calm, keeping fears to oneself; using both sleeping and waking dreams as metaphor as well as literal events; and the curiosity and hunger for knowledge and understanding that led him to analyze and invent stories for the pictures he saw in the magazine. That curiosity drives a striking progression from the innocence of a childhood filled with homework and comic books, where race isn't an issue, to the wider adult world of automobile and liquor ads, with their presumably white models of grown-up happiness. Though we don't know the races of the models in the ads, it is implied that the victims of violence he sees on other pages of the magazine are people of color—Japanese victims of retaliatory hatred and the black victim of internal self-hatred.

The experience introduced him to a "newfound fear," the fear of self-destruction. The photograph implied to him that people want so much to assimilate that they will kill off parts of themselves in order to do so. Self-hatred is not just the result of trying to change and blend in; it can derive from the belief that it's better to attack oneself than have someone else do it. In that scenario, the would-be victim identifies with the aggressor and internalizes the aggression, becoming a self-hating punisher instead of attacking someone else. Obama confronts this fact of black American life for the first time in the story of the skin-lightening treatment gone wrong and in the knowledge that there were thousands more like the man in the article. It was a vivid illustration that the black/white split he would become driven to heal can cause even worse, "irreversible" damage if addressed in the wrong way. This is a vital and painful lesson about the adult life before him, a far cry from his homework and comic books, to which he has an understandably visceral response.

Yet his response, though intense, passes quickly, and it's revealing that we don't see the internal process of self-regulation through which the distress is understood and released. Instead, the calm is located in the setting around him—the magazines in the right places, the quiet, still air. What's important to Barry is that he present a calm veneer to his mother, as if he internalized the orderliness of the library. He has taken great pains to present himself this way ever since, as if being "no drama Obama" were second nature. We're left to wonder if his calm exterior actually reflects a comparable internal state or instead seeks to obscure from the world its internal opposite. And if the calm is genuine, the question remains whether it was won by engaging in a variation of the assimilation he was reading about by killing off the fearful and furious parts of himself—a question made more relevant by his relative lack of outrage at some of the disasters he has faced during his presidency, from the BP oil spill to the Tucson murders.

The memory's placement within *Dreams from My Father* also bears examination. His travels to the U.S. Embassy in Jakarta open the chapter that immediately follows his first mention of being aware of his father's absence—musing about why his father might have abandoned the family at a time when he "was too young to realize that [he] was supposed to have a live-in father"—that closes the previous chapter. It is a swift and sudden example of what Obama as president would call "turning the page." The juxtaposition implies a connection between the self-hatred in the magazine and his father's departure—as if young Barry is looking for an excuse to justify his father's decision to leave. More poignant is the possibility that the absence of a black mirroring parent could leave the boy vulnerable to the rage and confusion over black identity that the story reveals.

His response to that article is also a harbinger of further revulsion, this time at himself and his own discomfort at being an outsider, at not belonging. It was less than a year after reading the story that his mother uprooted Barry once more, moving him from Jakarta back to Hawaii to attend the prep school Punahou School, which would help prep him to be "American." At that new school he had a fourth-grader's version of the behavior that had given him stomach knots in the embassy in Indonesia. In his lifelong struggle to belong, at times he puts the need to escape his feelings of being an outsider ahead of empathy and friendship, never more poignantly than in the story of the scene with the only other black student in his grade at Punahou, the plump and friendless little girl to whom he gave the pseudonym Coretta. Barry initially avoids Coretta, but one day at recess they start interacting—teasing, laughing, and chasing each other until they fall to the ground together.

> *When I looked up, I saw a group of children, faceless before the glare of the sun, pointing down at us.*
> *"Coretta has a boyfriend! Coretta has a boyfriend!"*
> *The chants grew louder as a few more kids circled us.*
> *"She's not my g-girlfriend," I stammered. I looked to Coretta for some assistance, but she just stood there looking down at the ground.*
> *"Coretta's got a boyfriend! Why don't you kiss her, mister boyfriend?"*
> *"I'm not her boyfriend!" I shouted. I ran up to Coretta and gave her a slight shove; she staggered back and looked up at me, but still said nothing. "Leave me alone!" I shouted again.*

At that point Coretta runs away, and recess is soon over. But afterward young Barry is "haunted by the look on Coretta's face . . . her disappointment, and the accusation. I wanted to explain to her somehow that it had been nothing personal. . . . But I didn't even know if that was true. I knew only that it was too late for explanations, that somehow I'd been tested and found wanting."

This painful admission is really impressive for any politician to make in print—even if he's talking about his younger self. He clearly defines what he did to Coretta as an act of betrayal and describes feeling shame. Still, he finds a way to conclude with a reversal: "A part of me felt trampled on, crushed, and I took refuge in the life that my grandparents led." Though he is the one who humiliated her, his words indicate that he may have suddenly identified with her feelings of having been betrayed by himself, one part of himself trampling on another.

Obama wrote that he was jolted out of his shame and guilt a few months later by the news that his father was coming to visit from Kenya. It was the first and last time he'd see his father. His apprehension leading up to the visit gave way to bragging rights, as Barry told his classmates that his father was a prince.

Obama had already begun to feel, despite his unusual name and skin color, that he was no longer an outsider. His father's talk to his fourth-grade class was "transformative," he wrote, as measured by the look of satisfaction on even Coretta's face—a look he recalls years later, right before making his own speaking debut at Occidental College. Years after the incident on the playground, Coretta remained a powerful symbol of the divide within himself that he had to heal or risk self-betrayal. She lives on as a shadow to such an extent that I think that we on the left have become Obama's modern-day Coretta—as he turns his back on the deep connection we made in 2008.

The psychological challenge of Obama's biracial heritage both fueled a drive to unify splits and provided an opportunity to develop a remarkable facility for doing so. The normal process of coming to terms with both loving and hating each parent was for him accompanied by a need to come to terms with loving and hating the two races that his parents embodied—and loving and hating both the black and white parts of himself. This was complicated by having a black skin color and features that invited other blacks to comfortably express their hatred of white people to him and the fact that young Obama—who grew up loved and cared for by three white people—was uncomfortable getting too close to those black friends who freely expressed their hatred of whites.

We see in his drive and desire to heal his racial split the roots of Obama's lifelong and well-documented history of bringing people together—from being a community organizer to uniting warring factions as president of the *Harvard Law Review* and into his political career, in which he has operated from the unconscious belief that his hard-won resolution of his internal struggle can be replicated in the world at large. The convention-keynote call for a unified America that put him on the national map in 2004 can be traced directly to his need to heal his internal racial split, which he came close to acknowledging in an interview with Charlie Rose later that year. Asked if "the diversity of [his] own ethnic background . . . [had] made [him] a better political animal," he said, "If you're half black and half white in a highly racially charged environment . . . then you've got to figure out how do you bring all these things together in yourself, but also how do you help bring it together outside of yourself." In the same interview, he told Rose, "I think that these elections are going to be won and lost over the next decade on the basis of who offers a more plausible argument about how we integrate this country along a whole host of lines." It's telling that he sees as his mission the need to "integrate the country," but the split that he is driven to heal politically is not simply between races but rather transcends color: When one of his aunts in Kenya would stereotype different tribes, of which there were forty, he would get angry and say to her, "It's thinking like that that holds us back. We're all part of one tribe. The black tribe. The human tribe."

Representing two races strengthens Obama in many ways. He is able to be at home in many different places just because that split has remained in place: he can be white with whites, black with blacks, Muslim with Muslims, Christian with Christians—and all the while keep a part of himself private and unavailable. This allows him to appear to be comfortable wherever he is because he doesn't completely fit in—and he is the only one who knows it. And the part that does fit in does so completely, as he easily puts the rest of himself in the others' shoes. Audiences marvel at his ease, as described by journalists at his brief visit to Indonesia on November 9, 2010. The BBC newswriter Guy DeLauney was impressed with Obama's "personal touch with great aplomb: reminiscing about the Indonesia he once knew." He added that the "young audience at the University of Indonesia cheered, and much of the rest of the country was charmed. They could perhaps once again think of the president of the United States as one of their own."

His split parts have evolved into different self-states that convince most audiences—and at times even himself—of his total authenticity. Every one of us has different personal, social, and occupational self-states that are genuine self-identities. Obama's identities are there for all to see, yet observers continue to question who he genuinely is. And the elusiveness of his identity, coupled with his ability to address different groups with great conviction and connection, can also get him into trouble—as he saw while telling his Indonesian audience that he felt like he was home drew fire from the right. In that moment he seems all too willing to turn his back on his American self. Obama may be so drawn to assuming different self-states due in part to his being from a broken home, which challenged his navigating the biracial split.

Faced with the isolation of his birth and an extraordinary intelligence and self-confidence cultivated by his mother, Obama set out to resolve his split and turn it to his advantage. Thus he becomes the community organizer whose black colleague John Owens told the biographer David Remnick that Obama "always wanted to be evenhanded in his analysis of things. In that regard, he was able to have stronger relationships with whites more than the average African-American." Nevertheless, in his student days, "he consciously chose politically active black students as his friends because he feared being labeled a 'sellout,'" according to his biographer David Mendell. "In trying to convey an image of being a true black, he would sometimes overreach to gain acceptance among his black peers." Years later, Mendell pointed out, Obama "still had a tendency to overreach in order to fit in with some urban blacks," exclaiming "What's up, brother?" at times that critics deemed "just a little too much."

As skilled as he became at navigating his racial split, Obama ultimately resolved it without actually healing it. Racial splitting is about identity, and the object of mixed feelings—the object of ambivalence, if you will—is one part of the self that may be called the "not me" self. To calm that anxiety, Obama chose in high school to self-identify as black. The effect of this decision was far more than simply mental or psychological: "According to his math and science teacher, Pal Eldredge, the way Barry carried himself changed," Remnick wrote. "'His gait, the way he walked, changed,' he said." The transformation came in the wake of Barry's decision to stop writing letters to his absent father, Remnick reports. "His effort to understand himself was a lonely one. Touchingly, awkwardly, he was giving himself instructions on how to be black." At that point his mother was also absent, far away in Indonesia, having entrusted Barry to the care of her parents in Hawaii, where the black community was a small element of what was a generally racially diverse population. With neither parent available, he was unable to work through his contradictory feelings—love and hate; appreciation and rage—for both parents, limiting his ability to heal the racial split that his black self-identification required. Instead, he developed dissociated self-states that comprised complete personalities and that cohabited without commingling, rather than fully facing his internal conflict of having a white part of him that wants to kill the black part of him, as well as vice versa, as horrific as that sounds. He is able to be comfortable in different places without ever totally healing, which would require putting those parts of him into direct internal conflict first.

One milestone in Obama's resolving the black/white split by self-identifying as black was his decision to change his name from Barry to Barack. Claiming that his father's name was an attempt to heal, he officially decided that he wanted to find a place where he belonged, and he identified that place as the black community. Whereas his father had adopted the name Barry in an attempt to fit in—calling himself Barack in Kenya and Barry in the United States—Obama chose to go by the name Barack to define himself by not fitting in. He remains comfortable with whites, but his most profound community is black. At another psychological level, he has successfully blended black and white both by dint of deep self-reflection and because he had so many varied life experiences in childhood. His capacity to tolerate differences and think about them has become as great a strength as his ability to seem fully at home in widely divergent settings.

Remarkably, the decision to change his name is a turning point that isn't directly addressed in his memoir. However, the change is suggested in an exchange immediately after a scene in which he clumsily tries to question how genuinely black a fellow college student is by suggesting he change his name from Tim to Tom—an exchange that dramatizes the tension of maintaining his own black/white split and the important role that a name can play in his longed-for resolution of that split. At Occidental College, still maintaining his secret white self, "Barry" Obama tried to belong to a black political group of students who didn't know of his mixed-race heritage. He never felt authentic, however, until he met Regina, the black student to whom he revealed his full name, and the one person to whom he felt he didn't have to lie. In the memoir Regina is introduced when the black student who criticizes Barry's Tim/Tom insult censures him for being seen reading *Heart of Darkness*. Barry first defends himself before acknowledging the book's racism to Regina: "The way Conrad sees it, Africa's the cesspool of the world, black folks are savages, and any contact with them breeds infection."

When Regina asks why he's reading it, he hesitates before admitting that

> *"the book teaches me things. . . . About white people, I mean. See the book's not really about Africa. Or black people. It's about the man who wrote it. The European. The American. A particular way of looking at the world. If you can keep your distance, it's all there, in what's said and what's left unsaid. So I read the book to help me understand just what it is that makes white people so afraid. Their demons. The way ideas get twisted around. It helps me understand how people learn to hate."*
>
> *"And that's important to you."*
>
> *My life depends on it, I thought to myself. But I didn't tell Regina that. I just smiled and said, "That's the only way to cure an illness, right? Diagnose it."*

The story continues as Barry tells Regina his real name is Barack and that he was, like her, raised by a single mother. She, in turn, describes her South Side Chicago childhood, a story that for young Obama "evoked a vision of black life in all its possibility, a vision that filled me with longing—a longing for place, and a fixed and definite history." It is a remarkably candid scene, particularly the admission that "[his] life depends on" understanding hate and the description of his yearning for a place to belong. He sees that hatred is based on fear and that he should be his own man, rather than simply calling himself an Americanized or sanitized version of his true self. He can be proud of who he is and not have to instill fear in whites or fear others. This is a central need of his—to explain hate so he can apply reason to it and work toward resolving his black/white split and finding a place he can feel he belongs.

* * *

As Obama's first term in the White House has progressed, it has become ever more clear that he is facing another major internal split that has not been resolved: the split between Obama the candidate and Obama the president. Obama's health care summit remark to John McCain makes clear that he not only recognizes the split between candidate and president, he accepts it. His followers have been less willing to accept what they see as a significant gulf between the man they elected and the man in office. Much has been written, even by Obama's supporters, about his inability as president to live up to the promise he demonstrated as a candidate. This is not lost on Obama; in the aftermath of what was arguably his most presidential action to date—the risky, heroic raid on Osama bin Laden—he was quick to remind *60 Minutes*' Steve Kroft to "keep in mind that obviously when I was still campaigning for president, I had said that if I ever get a shot at bin Laden we're gonna take it," even if it was in Pakistan, as if pointing out a campaign promise he had kept. As we'll see, using Klein's positions as a guide, Candidate and President Obama respond to aggression in significantly different ways. Obama's experience with his biracial split suggests both a level of comfort in containing and sustaining such a split and a history of settling for a resolution that stops short of actually healing such a division. Unlike the biracial split, however, he can't effectively self-identify as only one or the other—as only president or only candidate, especially as the 2012 campaign grows closer.

In the meantime, his lack of resolution is having profoundly and progressively adverse effects on his administration and the country. People who have put their internal splits into perspective can be more decisive because they are not afraid of destroying other parts of themselves. Instead, Obama feels compelled to protect part of himself, which comes out in his worrying about being one-sided or hurting people he has decided against. This informs his impulses to give something to everyone and to make extensive compromises to his own agenda and ideals, from preserving tax cuts on the wealthiest to supporting the military's solitary confinement of suspected WikiLeaks source Private Bradley Manning in 2011. He is more and more disconnected from his espoused principles, from who he is—or from the constitutional lawyer he once was—because of this tendency.

Now, in the second half of his first term, the major choice he appears to have is whether to act like a candidate or the president. As a candidate, Obama had a clear idea of the external source of aggression directed at him—first from the Clinton camp, then from the McCain campaign—and histories of the 2008 presidential campaign have repeatedly cited the purposeful focus of the Obama organization's relentless drive toward electoral victory. Regardless of his compelling calls for unity, Obama was, in Kleinian terms, effectively operating from the paranoid-schizoid position, clearly identifying the opponents to his candidacy and methodically defeating them. His paranoid anxiety served him well in his efforts to fend off attacks from his challengers, who were unambiguously in opposition to him, their aggression clearly sourced from outside the self. Though nominally a senator, his role as an elected official placed so few demands on him that no splitting was required to thrive in his pursuit of a singular purpose.

As president, the situation couldn't be more different. He is no longer in opposition to a single external rival. He is attacked by both the Left and particularly the Right, whose unfiltered animosity toward him is often as pure and persistent as the primal threats and aggression experienced in infancy. And he appears to be profoundly aware of his capacity for destructiveness; hence the tentativeness that is often identified as hesitancy by both critics and (sometimes former) supporters. His degree of power ironically puts him into the hyperresponsible position of recognizing the dangers of using it. His assumption of the presidency has meant that Obama has shifted away from the paranoid-schizoid position that served him so well in the course of the election campaign; now he operates from the depressive position, aware that his aggression may damage fellow Americans—whatever their political party. And because he has evolved into the depressive position, he has to cope constantly with the anxiety that he has the power to destroy the nation he loves.

But this is a false depressive position, embraced to allay his anxiety and fear as it serves his need to see us as one America. Were he not in that state, he could be far more decisive than he has been heretofore. His decisiveness in ordering the Navy SEALs to take out bin Laden is a case in point. There is no ambivalence about bin Laden whatsoever, so having him killed—though clearly bold and risky—does nothing to bring him into the depressive position, which involves ambivalently contending with loving and hating the same person. Obama made that clear to everyone at the end of his *60 Minutes* interview with Steve Kroft. He said, "As nervous as I was about this whole process, the one thing I didn't lose sleep over was the possibility of taking bin Laden out. Justice was done. And I think that anyone who would question that the perpetrator of mass murder on American soil didn't deserve what he got needs to have their head examined."

However, his relationship to his depressive position is still evolving. If it were complete, he would recognize the profound destructiveness aimed at him from many on the right and would not persist in his drive for bipartisanship at all costs. Instead, he manifests only some of the attributes of the depressive position. Obama knows he is president of all the people, which makes it harder to attack individuals or particular groups who attack him. Thus the Tea Party can spew hatred and the Republican Senate caucus can refuse to cooperate, but crushing the Tea Party or giving up on the possibility of bipartisan cooperation goes against his profound urge to heal the splits he sees in the nation. He uses the reality of being responsible for all Americans as a defense against expressing his rage at the Tea Party's destructiveness.

There is another way in which reality functions as a defense: by saying that there are things that he just must do as president, he can sidestep internal conflict while justifying his behavior. The reality of foreign threats merges with potential psychological maneuvers that may allow him to externalize whatever internal murderous impulses he recognizes and redirect them toward Pakistan and Libya.

Domestically, however, he must accommodate right-wing attackers because they are Americans and passionate and deserve his respect. Projections are harder to perceive when they fit with a real situation, and the fact that they are Americans keeps him from facing his own rage and taking a tougher domestic approach. When Obama accuses Osama bin Laden of having brutally murdered so many innocent Americans, his is a tragically accurate assessment; but drone attacks that kill many innocent Pakistani citizens can be subtly overlooked, and Osama bin Laden stays the monster, the only one.

Inevitably, there are other factors at play here, too. Contributing to his accommodating attitude and calm demeanor are character traits developed in his first eighteen years living in Hawaii and Indonesia, where the pace of life was slower, and races and cultures were far more mixed than in the mainland United States at the time. We'll see that his desire for consensus is also fueled by his inability to accept the vehemence of his opposition—a denial that mirrors feelings about his unresolved relationship with his absent father that he can't acknowledge in adulthood. But it's clear that Obama, upon taking office, largely reclaimed the depressive position, mostly giving up his attacks on Republicans and instead becoming tentative and cautious—which has ultimately undermined his authority. In his move away from the kind of partisan presidential politics shamelessly practiced by George W. Bush, he has been so anxious not to attack Republicans that he hasn't fully faced his paranoid fears, as well as the reality of his own hatred. But in going to great lengths to avoid this internal reality, Obama limited his own perspective on the campaign—accepting that it need only be oppositional rather than genuinely transformational. Instead he has redefined hatred by labeling his former attacks against the Republican opposition in 2008 as just part of campaigning and invited Republicans to collaborate as much as possible, even when it wasn't getting him any Republican support in Congress.

Most recently Obama has been more concerned with the split caused by the ballot than by birth. He still at times resembles the candidate elected in 2008, inspiring us with his poetic visions of unity and purpose and still capable of going after an opponent with vigor and focus, the paranoid-schizoid position in action, as he did in the closing days of the 2010 midterm election. But he still muted his confrontational energy, at least toward his domestic opponents, in early 2011. Though his April 2011 speech in response to the Republican budget offered a spirited defense of progressive values and a promise that the proposed dismantling of Medicare was "not going to happen" on his watch, his delivery was far more muted than his language, and he elected to give the speech in the middle of the day when live viewership was minimal at best. Later, when he seemed to challenge Speaker of the House John Boehner in reference to the budget negotiations—"I said, 'You want to repeal health care? Go at it. We'll have that debate. You're not going to be able to do that by nickel-and-diming me in the budget. You think we're stupid?'"— Boehner wasn't present, and the challenge was heard and recorded only because there was an open mike nearby.

But he is more pervasively acting as Obama the president, negotiating the depressive position as he shows both love and hate for his rivals and critics—as well as the institutions behind some of the biggest challenges he has faced, from BP to the banks he saved—aware that due to the broad responsibilities of his office he can't allow himself to inflict the destructiveness that he's capable of. He is both candidate and president, and by switching back and forth, one part of him protects the other part from destruction or from having to be saved by projection: he doesn't have to disavow parts of himself to avoid feeling anxious, because the destructive parts of himself are contained within. And at times he has to project the candidate part into his supporters so he can reject them and keep that part of himself "other." It's his supporters who insist that he not cave in to oil companies, not he. He is trying to compromise, even though he knows full well how destructive continued drilling and draining the earth is.

But the candidate and the president can have very different agendas, requiring Obama to manage yet another significant internal split. There's a reason he often appears to be negotiating with himself, especially on such important issues as health care and the Bush tax cuts: his inner candidate and president not only sometimes have competing political priorities but operate from different mental positions. More often than not, the president's depressive position wins out—as on the day after the 2010 midterm elections when he said, "I have got to take direct responsibility for the fact that we have not made as much progress as we need to make." But even that clear statement was evasive: as an analyst, I'm trained to consider how patients might have said or done things differently in the exchanges they report. In this case, Obama could have taken responsibility for not having fought hard enough and early enough to keep the people in office who really were strenuously supporting his efforts to make changes. He could have said that change is scary to everyone—

even himself—and therefore changes take time. He could have said that the process of change needs to be protected, not destroyed. All would have fallen within his given responsibilities, but in the language of the sound bite, he didn't give any of these specific reasons; in short, he didn't fight.

Nevertheless, Obama has embraced the need to take responsibility more than most politicians in recent memory, and when he makes a mistake he acknowledges it—never more clearly than on that November morning. Ever the healer of splits, he also vowed that day that making progress was "going to require all of us, including me, to work harder at building consensus." The problem with Obama seeming so clear about his personal mistakes and therefore showing the depressive anxiety they represent—namely the fear of hurting others by an action taken, whether willfully or inadvertently—is that he adopts this same position when dealing with Wall Street as well as with Main Street, with BP as well as with the fishermen of New Orleans. He removes morality from the picture, because in his view everybody has a point and he is the president of all. But in so doing he risks betraying his fiercest allies—as he did Coretta—and in 2010 he saw them fall victim to the Republican machine. And he remains blind to one key mistake he made, his failure to explicitly and forcefully label the gangs of nay-sayers for what they really are.

Obama maintains what seems a genuine sense of responsibility to all Americans by taking an antiparanoid stance, but some paranoia is necessary and helpful for a president. For example, he underestimates the level of aggression focused on him, as when he laughed off the depth of the Birthers' hatred in an August 2010 interview with NBC's Brian Williams, saying "I can't spend all my time with my birth certificate plastered on my forehead." And when he finally did move to silence the Birthers, he dismissed their campaign to discredit him as "silliness," rather than the venal destructiveness at the heart of their efforts.

Williams's interview also included Obama's dismissal of Glenn Beck's then-recent rally on the National Mall: "I did not watch the rally. I think that one of the wonderful things about this country is that at any given moment any group of people can decide, you know, 'We want—our voices heard.' And—and so, I think that Mr.

Beck and the rest of those folks were exercising their rights under our Constitution exactly as they should." He spoke about freedom of speech rather than the destructive content of that speech, avoiding the confrontational stance that Candidate Obama might have taken. He has so assiduously managed his own paranoid anxiety over the years that he has blind spots to the dangers posed by people who are stuck in the paranoid-schizoid position, which explains the ease with which he brushes them off and minimizes their threat. And when he does exhibit some paranoid anxiety, calling out BP weeks into the oil spill disaster, for example, his lack of conviction can be seen as a tempering of the paranoid-schizoid position: did anyone take him seriously when he claimed he wanted to find out whose butt to kick?

Still, there is no question that Obama's passion lies in the drive to heal the split he sees as red and blue. And he sees speeches as transformative, no matter what actions are taken. His 2011 State of the Union address presented a litany of references to splits and their healing. He tried to heal the split between family and government by saying we are all in this together: "Every day, families sacrifice to live within their means. They deserve a government that does the same." After living through his mother's sacrifices, it's noteworthy that he asks families to sacrifice but does not ask the wealthy to sacrifice—locking more securely into place the split between rich and poor, something he says he's sensitive to.

In that same speech he also tried to heal splits through belief, referring to our shared faith in the U.S. Constitution—a kind of belief, but one that is associated with action: "We may have differences in policy, but we all believe in the rights enshrined in our Constitution. We may have different opinions, but we believe in the same promise that says this is a place where you can make it if you try. We may have different backgrounds, but we believe in the same dream that says this is a country where anything's possible. No matter who you are. No matter where you come from." The irony is that splits persist, as in the disconnect between saying that "we all believe in the rights enshrined in our Constitution" while tacitly condoning WikiLeaks suspect Bradley Manning's solitary confinement, for example. He also tried to heal the split between past and present, telling Americans—including those supporters who still want him to prosecute members of the Bush administration for crimes against the Constitution—that it is "time to leave behind the divisive battles of the past. It is time to move forward as one nation." This kind of healing is more manic than genuine, brushing under the rug the crimes of the past in the interest of the pressing problems of now.

Finally, repeatedly, he spoke to the need to heal the deep splits in his government that undermine his effectiveness. "Now is the time for both sides and both houses of Congress—Democrats and Republicans—to forge a principled compromise that gets the job done," he said, adding a significant modifier as a reminder that principles don't have to be sacrificed for compromise—yet the split between principle and compromise of principle persists inside Obama as the price he pays, and soon so will America as we know it pay, to satisfy his need to perceive both political parties as united.

And more than once he urged members of Congress to work together, using lofty language for practical goals: "What comes of this moment will be determined not by whether we can sit together tonight, but whether we can work together tomorrow. . . . I believe we can. I believe we must. That's what the people who sent us here expect of us. With their votes, they've determined that governing will now be a shared responsibility between parties. New laws will only pass with support from Democrats and Republicans. We will move forward together, or not at all—for the challenges we face are bigger than party, and bigger than politics."

Unfortunately for him, Obama must now either better manage or integrate the split and differing positions: once the 2010 midterm voters were counted (if not sooner), his efficacy as president depended on his effectiveness as a candidate for reelection, and vice versa. Obama's experience managing and resolving his racial split may serve him here, if he is again able to resolve the split in a manner that empowers him to move forward forcefully. He cannot heal a split without facing the fact that there is a split—that he has repressed his rage at both parents and that the splits are really closer to repressions than to traditional good guy/bad guy splits. He cannot heal until he recognizes this; if he were my patient, I'd try to help him look at his fury and talk about it. On the other hand, he could be so familiar with containing such a profound split that he has developed a false sense of comfort and allowed his impulses to remain in muted conflict with each other, creating an inner gridlock that saps his effectiveness. In a time that demands an effective leader, the stakes for our nation couldn't be higher—and, as we'll see in the next chapter, his personal history may deprive him of an essential ingredient for healing the split and moving America forward.

CHAPTER 2

Abandoned and Assuaged

I saw Adam leave the Garden with an apple in his hand.
I said, "Now you're out, what are you gonna do?"
"Plant some crops and pray for rain, maybe raise a little Cain.
I'm an orphan now, and I'm only passing through."
—Dick Blakeslee

We long for that most elusive quality in our leaders—the quality
of authenticity, of being who you say you are, of possessing a
truthfulness beyond words.
—Barack Obama, *The Audacity of Hope*

Barry Obama was not yet a year old when Barack Sr. left Hawaii
to go to Harvard, turning down a scholarship offer from the New
School in New York that, unlike the Harvard offer, would have
paid enough to support his wife and young son. "Barack was such a
stubborn bastard, he had to go to Harvard," Obama wrote that his
mother told him years later. "'How can I refuse the best education?'
he told me. 'That's all he could think about, proving he was the best.'"
It turns out that Ann's statement to her son was more complicated
than first meets the eye. She was the one who left the "stubborn
bastard" in the first place—and we still don't know why.

But no matter who left whom, Obama didn't see his father again
until he returned to Hawaii for a monthlong visit when Barry was
ten. They continued to exchange letters for a few years after that but
had long been out of touch when Barack, shortly after his twenty-
first birthday, received the phone call with the news of his father's
death—which is the opening scene of his memoir.

Despite the fact that he places this event front and center in his book, whenever he is asked about the significance of his father's absence, he equivocates. "Well . . . I think it had a profound impact," he told CNN, "except, you know, more as an object lesson of what it's like growing up without a father in the house." When I get started with a new patient, I often ask myself "Where's the rage?" in what I'm hearing. This is especially the case with a patient who displays little feeling when describing a significant family rupture or trauma. If a new patient described his experience of being abandoned by his namesake father when he was an infant, I'd suspect that the rage was present but buried; if the mother was white, the father was black, and the son looked more like the father, I'd know that wherever the rage is buried, it's likely fairly deep and substantial.

Obama is at least correct that certain aspects of his adult life offer various object lessons in the long-term effects of growing up as a fatherless son; many elements of the Obama presidency—from the emphasis on consensus building to his conciliatory attitude toward his opponents—can be traced back to the predictable dynamics of a son raised by a single mother. But a closer look at the particulars of how mother and son responded to Obama Sr.'s disappearance reveals how even more facets of the familiar Obama persona and style bear the imprint of a son who not only had no father present but was also discouraged from ever acknowledging or working through the rage—as well as addressing many other questions and feelings—that was an inevitable part of his response to that initial loss and continued absence.

Anyone who loses his father at a young age grows up with what the Harvard psychoanalyst James Herzog identified in 2002 as "father hunger," a deep yearning to get close to a father who isn't there, that can be covered over or expressed in indirect ways. Obama came close to revealing to his biographer David Mendell at least an unconscious role that yearning played in his life. "[Obama] said he derived his personal ambition, arguably the most powerful force in his life, from his father's shortcomings," Mendell wrote. "He also gained his own high expectations of himself from his father's sterling image and talents. Said Obama: 'Every man is trying to live up to his father's expectations or make up for his mistakes. In my case, both things might be true.'"

The absence of the father has a particularly pronounced effect on the son's development involving aggression—how to recognize and handle it both in others and in himself. All sons need to confront their fathers at some point early in their psychic development. When the father is present, the son typically projects his aggression into the father and then fears the father based on this projection. The son competes or fights with the father and then repairs the damage done—a paternal variation on infancy's dynamic of break and repair that helps the son learn how to modulate his aggression. The son benefits further by witnessing the father model healthy aggression, as when one parent stands up to the other or when the father stands up to someone outside the family. This process repeats over time, and the son internalizes his love and rage toward the father. The process is a replay of the shift in mental positions—the son at first having a good and bad daddy, one whom he loves and one whom he fears.

The coming together of those two daddies and their integration into oneself is more difficult when the father is absent. Obama's struggles with his father could only be played out in fantasy (at least until the arrival of his stepfather, with whom Barry lived from ages four until almost ten). When a father leaves, a split occurs in the child's mind; the child's yearnings are projected into the good, idealized father who left, while the pain of everyday life—made more difficult by the lack of a father—is linked to an internal image of a remaining, ever-present hurtful father, whose critical presence can affect his conscience and inhibit his ability to act. But of course the hurtful father isn't present at all; the aggression that the boy projects into him is never modified, and the son's psychic need to confront his father is never met. He thus misses the opportunity to test his aggression through the process of break and repair and never sees his father stand up to anyone, including his mother.

Managing aggression is a problem that is often seen in abandoned children, and studies show that they have more behavioral problems than most other children. Children abandoned by a parent are mystified; explanations of a parent's absence mean very little to young children. As they grow up, they are confused about why their parent left, what that means about their relationship to the parent, whether they had a role in the parent's departure.

Barack Sr. was just too intimidating and too briefly present in young Barry's daily life to have been of help with the process of learning to express aggression through direct confrontation. The impact that the father's absence had on his son was further complicated by the way that the young boy's mother chose to respond to it. Rather than blame her husband for walking out, she went to great lengths to instill in her young son a positive image of his absent father. Barack Sr. was presented as an ecumenical dreamer who was highly intelligent and personally compelling—the proud bearer of a glorious black heritage, particularly African heritage. She invented him in many ways, and he became an internal mythic figure inside which Barry could retreat when he faced disappointment, hurt, or rejection in the real world. He was a present absence, always part of the family, a person for whom Barry yearned in private.

Idealization is a distortion of reality that is necessary for early development, simply because it sustains the split between good and bad that keeps the infant from disorganizing anxiety. Obama's mother made sure—as best she could—that his father would remain a positive presence in his imagination, rather than a frustrating or abandoning one. Having such a positive image of an absent father— an image actively facilitated and supported by the rest of the family—certainly helped strengthen Obama's character. He was spared the image of a hated father being instilled in his head and the corrosive self-doubt and criticism that such an image can entail.

The mother's attitude toward the absent father has a significant influence on the son, who watches how she deals with her own loss, looking to see whether she is bitter or loving, erasing or preserving. At some level, Ann may have identified with her husband's impulse to leave; in subsequent years, she herself would on several occasions initiate prolonged separations from her son, sending him from Indonesia to Hawaii to go to school, then leaving him there to pursue her own studies abroad. Though many abandoned women share their hurt and rage at the abandoner with their children, not so Ann Dunham Obama. Perhaps this was because she contributed to the abandonment, so it was easier for her to resist pointing fingers at her husband. We see traces of her forgiving attitude resonating in the adult Obama's tendency to always find the human side of any opponent—whether that opponent is an obstructionist Republican, an inflammatory newscaster, or an actual foreign enemy. Following his mother's lead, he has maintained his belief in the triumph of compassion over passion, using a reason nourished by attempts to understand what drives the other person's actions. Describing his mother's core beliefs to her biographer Janny Scott, he said, "It was a sense that beneath our surface differences, we're all the same, and that there's more good than bad in each of us. And that, you know, we can reach across the void and touch each other and believe in each other and work together. That's precisely the naïveté and idealism that was part of her. And that's, I suppose, the naïve idealism in me." For Obama, being too politically passionate clouds judgment and leads to impulsivity as well as to sloppy thinking. He takes time to think about the other person—when unconsciously he is actually trying to empathize, albeit unsuccessfully, with his father's reasons for leaving. He cannot risk passionate feelings about his father, just as he reveals in his memoirs and interviews little to no anger toward him.

Obama's mother was thoughtful and protective and fostered his development, and her efforts to shape his image of his father made him a great listener, sensitive to messages communicated whether spoken or not. But neglecting to mention his disappointing behavior made it difficult for the young Obama to imagine the father as a real person. Idealization prevented Barry from experiencing the rage he must inevitably have felt at his father for abandoning him and his family, and he never had to deal with a feared or destructive father. Instead, he had to deal with his own feelings about an abandoning father, a man who put his own needs and ambitions far ahead of his family, and filter his emotions through the lens of his mother's imposed idealization. Though her efforts were well intended, his mother made it even harder for young Barry to experience his own innate aggression, essentially depriving him of the opportunity to work through his rage at his father.

The one time that his father did return, however, was enough to give the ten-year-old Barry a glimpse of the disturbing truth behind the image his mother created. "Fascinated" by his charismatic father's "strange power," he wrote, "for the first time I began to think of my father as something real and immediate, perhaps even permanent." But the family couldn't accommodate the sudden return of Barack Sr. as an authority figure, and tensions erupted when he tried over his ex-wife's and in-laws' objections to forbid young Barry from watching "How the Grinch Stole Christmas" on television instead of doing homework, telling his son, "You do not work as hard as you should." The ensuing argument, which Barry heard from his room behind a slammed door, involved all of the adults, until his grandmother came in to tell him he could watch the end of the program.

> *I felt as if something had cracked open between all of us, goblins rushing out of some old, sealed-off lair. Watching the green Grinch on the television screen, intent on ruining Christmas, eventually transformed by the faith of the doe-eyed creatures who inhabited Whoville, I saw it for what it was: a lie. I began to count the days until my father would leave and things would return to normal.*

It's touching to see young Barry wrestle with the realization that the image of his father that he'd been fed was "a lie," a realization so painful, inciting rage so unbearable, that he projects his insight and reaction onto a cartoon villain (who, unlike his father, really could be transformed by the faith of others). In later years, the myth of his father would be shattered for Obama; the memoir *Dreams from My Father* in a sense traces the process of discovering that his father was an alcoholic and abusive failure as a father, husband, and intellect. (His half brother Mark Obama Ndesandjo was so traumatized by his father Barack Sr.—and what he recalls as the "explosive mixture of drink, maybe disappointment and an inability to understand his own demons that caused the domestic violence we had in our home"—that he "didn't want anything to do with anything that had to do with my father.") As his father's true character emerged, Obama would at least acknowledge disappointment with the man, whose "mistakes" he cited as a motivating force in his own ambitions, offering at least a gesture toward acknowledging that his father was hardly an ideal role model. But there are times in his book when Obama's anger does come out, and when it does, he expresses it as bitterness at male elders in general—before directly settling on his father with a plaint that none of his black friends knew where he belonged: "Where were the fathers, the uncles and grandfathers, who could help explain this gash in our hearts? Where were the healers who might help us rescue meaning from defeat? They were gone, vanished, swallowed up by time. Only their cloudy images remained, and their once-a-year letters full of dime store advice." He needed a father to help him find his place in the world, and there was none to be had. At the same time, his lament is not dissimilar from those of other teenage boys who have longings for their fathers that they cannot express—even when their fathers have not abandoned them. Sometimes the longings are rooted in clinical depression—as was the case of Thomas Wolfe, who wrote, "Which of us has looked into his father's heart?"

But Obama minimizes the extent of his father's destructiveness to himself and to others, dismissing his plight as having "made his share of mistakes and disappointed his share of people in his lifetime." And he speaks of his father with conspicuous circumspection, as in the following remarks, made to a Kenyan audience in 2006, which seem almost willfully remote and unemotional:

In many ways, he embodied the new Africa of the early Sixties, a man who had obtained the knowledge of the Western world, and sought to bring it back home, where he hoped he could help create a new nation. And yet, I discovered that for all his education, my father's life ended up being filled with disappointments. His ideas about how Kenya should progress often put him at odds with the politics of tribe and patronage, and because he spoke his mind, sometimes to a fault, he ended up being fired from his job and prevented from finding work in the country for many, many years. And on a more personal level, because he never fully reconciled the traditions of his village with more modern conceptions of family—because he related to women as

his father had, expecting them to obey him no matter what he did—
his family life was unstable, and his children never knew him well.

Attributing his father's failure to global geopolitical forces and
dismissing his turbulent marriages with the polite and almost per-
functory observation that "his family life was unstable" is consistent
with his typical descriptions of his father, which offer little conscious acknowledgment of any resentment about his absence and
the hardships it imposed on his mother—or the significant role it
had in shaping him as a child. One notable exception to this attitude, according to his biographer Mendell, is that Obama "often
told close friends that he grew up feeling 'like an orphan,'" a remark
that includes a rare public jab at his mother, who ultimately abandoned her son as well. On top of that, one telling passage in *Dreams
from My Father* seemed to escape Obama the memoirist's powerful
self-censor. Describing his fondness for smoking pot in his rebel-
lious teen phase, he wrote, "Nobody asked you whether your father
was a fat-cat executive who cheated on his wife or some laid-off
Joe who slapped you around whenever he bothered to come home.
You might just be bored, or alone. Everybody was welcome into the
club of disaffection." If, in a therapy session, Obama had shown me
his writing about that episode, I would have said to him, "You left
out the example that nobody asked you whether your father was a
failed and bitter alcoholic who put himself ahead of everyone else
in his life—most poignantly ahead of a one-year-old boy who didn't
have a say in the matter." Such a direct comment would hopefully
provoke some anxiety in him—something he appears to be expert at
metabolizing before it gets too much into the atmosphere, so accomplished is he at hiding from himself in a comfortably familiar, dissociated state.

The young Obama's distance from his rage against his abandoning father probably served him well in some respects, tempering the
"disaffection" from which he temporarily sought escape in drugs, as
cited above. Silencing such rage will alter the psychic life of any individual and inevitably limit his sense of his internal world. Obama
wrote that he became aware in Indonesia that the world is a "cruel
place," suggesting that he was developing the ability to see destruc-

tiveness outside himself. But he is so unable to manage his feelings about his father that he must defend against experiencing them in any setting; his silenced rage, in particular, coupled with the lack of a role model in dealing with aggression, fuels the aversion to conflict that now characterizes the president's attitude toward his political opponents.

Though he was clearly willing to step up to a political fight as a candidate and Secretary of Defense Robert Gates gushed that his decision to go through with the raid on Osama bin Laden was "one of the most courageous" he'd ever seen a president make, the list of conflicts that President Obama has avoided is long, familiar, and still growing, particularly as seen by the critics among his former supporters on the left. From their perspective, the five weeks it took to confront BP after the catastrophic oil spill in 2010 was far too long, an echo of the previous summer's delay confronting the Tea Party over the death panels, the misrepresentations of end-of-life counseling, previously supported by Republicans, with which the Tea Party hijacked the debate about health care reform. The reform process also presented missed opportunities to confront the insurance and pharmaceutical industries, just as during the economic crisis and bailout Obama failed to truly take on Wall Street or the bankers and financial firms responsible for the meltdown. He stayed away from forcefully supporting union efforts in Wisconsin in early 2011, offering too little, too late, although he did scold Republican governors for driving away good civil servants by their budget cuts and anti–collective bargaining stance. And when there are legitimate successes, such as the automobile bailout and reshaping GM, he doesn't remind people—and he has fewer surrogates than other presidents.

In late 2010, Obama defied expectations and got his "mojo" back when he passed the 9/11 workers' health care bill, won ratification for a new Strategic Arms Reduction Treaty and repealed "Don't Ask, Don't Tell," all in two weeks. We are left to ask if he must have his back against the wall to get moving. And we must wonder if his need to avoid confrontation, related to his unexperienced rage, prevents him from taking charge in general and using the weight of his office to push bills through *before* things become dire.

In *Revival,* one of the most detailed explorations of exactly how Obama conducts the office of the presidency, *Newsweek* veteran and MSNBC correspondent Richard Wolffe describes Obama's strategy for handling disagreement, which sounds more like avoidance than engagement, characterized by "a steeliness when shutting down even close aides. . . . Senior staff spoke privately of policy discussions that ended with a piercing presidential stare and an icy, abrupt command from Obama: 'Next!'" Later in the book, Wolffe describes what appears to be a rare outburst from the president at the end of the eleventh-hour negotiations between House and Senate Democrats to salvage his health care reform bill, when House Speaker Nancy Pelosi refused to budge in the negotiations to close what by then was only a $15 billion gap in the House and Senate positions:

> *Obama appeared pissed. He clenched his jaw and raised his voice in righteous indignation—an extraordinary sight for members of Congress. "Dammit, folks, this is history," he sputtered. "We're this close to history. We're $15 billion away. This is outrageous. I'm leaving this to Rahm. I'm going to bed. Good night. I'm out of here. You guys can figure it out." He promptly marched out of the room.*
>
> *"Rahm," he said on his way out, "clean it up."*

A reader familiar with Obama's conflict-avoidance style will find the exchange shockingly out of character. In fact, wrote Wolffe, "the presidential walkout was an act, a stage show designed to shock the congressional leaders into action. And it worked. 'I wasn't really that frustrated,' Obama told me later, in the Oval Office. 'The truth was we were very pleased that it was going as well as it was.'" The rage was only a pretense—or, at least in the retelling, was recast as one, the "extraordinary sight" being too much for the president himself to see; either way, he disavowed what would have been a rare and healthy demonstration of understandable anger.

Obama isn't a stranger only to genuine expressions of his own rage; suppressed anger undermines one's ability to recognize animosity in others, as Obama's unexperienced rage at his father has done to him. Thus he is blind to the scale and peril of opposition so extreme that Republicans decided to say "no" to his proposals without even listening to them or rejected their own proposals once he had embraced them, such as the research tax credit they proposed before abandoning it once Obama endorsed it, or refused to offer alternative points of view that could lead to healthy compromise. He is afraid to admit the nature of the Republican threat—describing it to Wolffe, when reflecting on Republican efforts to derail his health care reform bill, as something to evoke appreciation rather than rage. "You have to give the Republicans credit, just from a pure political perspective, that they used every instrument available to them in the Senate to prolong the process in such a way that helped drive down support nationally, that gave everybody a sense that somehow Washington was broken." One way to evade recognition of genuine murderousness is to turn the jousting between them into a game, a sporting event, or in this case into just a matter of skilled legislative process. For someone who campaigned on restoring voters' faith in government, to give anyone credit for convincing the populace that Washington was broken reveals a surprising willingness to see politics as a game, reflecting a remarkable aversion to acknowledging either his opponents' hatred or his own anger. As a result, he fails too often to stand up to the opposition—at once depriving himself of the opportunity to give his anger healthy expression and facilitating the expansion of their hatred.

In addition to denying his rage toward his father, Obama has embraced his father's political philosophy as his own. His father's fantasy—specifically, that reason, if well presented, can neutralize bigotry and prejudice—is the organizing principle of his book and his life, which he must validate in order to keep his father alive internally. The idealized father became the subject of several stories relayed to young Barry by his mother and his grandfather, portraying Barack Sr. as a man with grandiose fantasies about the world and the necessity for shared understanding, for discovering the common factors that make us all human.

Most notable is the story that, according to Obama, members of the family repeated often as Barry got older, "as if it captured the essence of the morality tale that my father's life would become." Interestingly, it is the only family story Obama can remember "that dealt explicitly with the subject of race":

*According to the story, after long hours of study, my father had
joined my grandfather and several other friends at a local Waikiki bar.
Everyone was in a festive mood, eating and drinking to the sounds
of a slack-key guitar, when a white man abruptly announced to the
bartender, loudly enough for everyone to hear, that he shouldn't have
to drink good liquor "next to a nigger." The room fell quiet and people
turned to my father, expecting a fight. Instead, my father stood up,
walked over to the man, smiled and proceeded to lecture him about the
folly of bigotry, the promise of the American dream, and the universal
rights of man. "This fella felt so bad when Barack was finished,"
Gramps would say, "that he reached into his pocket and gave Barack
a hundred dollars on the spot. Paid for all our drinks and puu-puus for
the rest of the night—and your dad's rent for the rest of the month."*

At one level this is a story of courage and confidence, of a father
who "stood up" for what was right. A child needs to idealize his
father, and this story contributed to solidifying Obama's image of
his father as a strong, principled man. It's a story that it was important to Obama to believe; he recounted that after his father's death
someone who had been in the bar that night contacted him and told
him the same story his grandfather had, so impressed had he been
when he witnessed it. The story is about the power of not fighting,
the power of reason over irrational behavior—even over racism—
and how it can lead to a mutually beneficial result. This event would
have made an even bigger impression on young Barry if he had seen
his father act that way in person. It would have given him the example of standing up to someone and dealing with aggression that he
sorely lacked in his formative years. But the fact that young Obama
was not present at this pivotal moment is important on another
level—one of his father's most prized stories is set in a bar, which
highlights, albeit in a flattering light, what Obama Sr. was doing in
his leisure time away from his family. (One can't overlook the fact
that Obama was rewarded for his righteous advocacy of reason with
a night's worth of free drinks.)

Then there is the word "nigger"—something almost conspicuously unexplored in this passage, perhaps because Obama had his
mind on deeper lessons. First, that despite being enraged by hav-

ing been called that, retaliation changes nothing, while words and explanation can promote understanding. A second lesson is that his father had enough self-confidence not to retaliate. The fact that he was confident in his beliefs and authoritative in his speech is what's important, and that is exactly how Obama aims to behave as president and citizen of the world.

The story is joined in the memoir by another of the legends surrounding his father, a tale of how he treated someone who was not fitting Barack Sr.'s idea of honorable behavior surrounding the treatment of others' property. In *Dreams from My Father*, Obama recounts his grandfather, grandmother, and mother all joining forces to recall "the time that my father almost threw a man off the Pali Lookout because of a pipe," a vivid miniature of family life that Obama sketches with the economy, eye for detail—and perhaps imagination—of a novelist or a writer of a sitcom set-piece. The familiar rhythms of television comedy are present as the women keep interrupting his grandfather's attempt to tell the story: when Gramps comments that "Barack was probably on the wrong side of the road" as he was showing another African student around the island, Obama's mother interjects that her husband "was a terrible driver [who would] always end up on the left-hand side." Moments later, she speaks up again, during her father's description of his son-in-law's fondness for the pipe he'd given him for his birthday:

> "Your father was really proud of this pipe," my mother interrupts again. "He'd smoke it all night while he studied, and sometimes—"
>
> "Look, Ann, do you want to tell the story or are you going to let me finish?"
>
> "Sorry, Dad. Go ahead."

His daughter temporarily silenced, and ignoring his wife's attempt to add to the story from the next room, Gramps proceeds between sips from his flask to recount what ensued when the visiting student asked for a chance to puff on Barack Sr.'s pipe—only to discover it was too much for the visitor to handle, resulting in a coughing fit so strong that he dropped the pipe over the railing and off the cliff. When the student refused to climb down the cliff and retrieve the

pipe, Barack Sr. "picked him clear off the ground and started dan-
gling him over the railing!"

> *Gramps lets out a hoot and gives his knee a jovial slap. As he laughs, I*
> *imagine myself looking up at my father, dark against the brilliant sun,*
> *the transgressor's arms flailing about as he's held aloft. A fearsome*
> *vision of justice.*
>
> *"He wasn't really holding him over the railing, Dad," my mother*
> *says, looking to me with concern, but Gramps takes another sip of*
> *whiskey and plows forward.*
>
> *"At this point, other people were starting to stare, and your mother*
> *was begging Barack to stop. I guess Barack's friend was just holding*
> *his breath and saying his prayers. Anyway, after a couple of minutes,*
> *your dad set the man back down on his feet, patted him on the back,*
> *and suggests, calm as you please, that they all go find themselves a*
> *beer."*

Afterward, Barack Sr. acted "like nothing had happened," but his
wife was upset enough that she barely spoke to her husband for
hours, until he tried to dismiss her anger:

> *"'Relax, Anna,' he said. 'I only wanted to teach the chap a lesson*
> *about the proper care of other people's property!'"*
>
> *Gramps would start to laugh again until he started to cough, and*
> *Toot [grandmother] would mutter under her breath that she supposed*
> *it was a good thing that my father had realized that dropping the*
> *pipe had just been an accident because who knows what might have*
> *happened otherwise, and my mother would roll her eyes at me and*
> *say they were exaggerating.*
>
> *"'Your father can be a bit domineering," my mother would admit*
> *with a hint of a smile. "But it's just that he is basically a very honest*
> *person. That makes him uncompromising sometimes."*

Setting aside the possible symbolism of the tale—sometimes a
pipe is only a pipe, so to speak, although the two women's vividly
rendered attempts to commandeer Gramps's storytelling authority
suggest that Barack Sr. might have felt his proverbial pipe was threat-

ened around two such assertive women—the story's comic rhythms can't completely obscure the lie at its core: Barack Sr.'s response to the accidental loss of a pipe is so inappropriately outsized that his motivation for traumatizing his fellow African could not possibly be as simple as a wish to teach a "lesson about the proper care of other people's property," particularly in light of what we now know about the destructive and self-destructive lengths to which his own helpless rage ultimately drove him in his abusive relationships with other wives and children (not to mention his "terrible" driving, which cost him his life). Missing from the narrative is the cruel pleasure Barry's father must have had in frightening the life out of that "chap." The lesson drawn by his father is no more genuine than his mother's misguided characterization of Barack as "a very honest person." He was honest neither with himself nor with Ann when he said that he was just teaching the chap a lesson. He was reveling in his cruelty and in the terrified look on the chap's face. The family's laughter at recounting the story relates to their anxiety and their need to release it through laughter that minimizes the kind of fear Obama Sr. gave rise to.

Nevertheless, his mother remained protective of her son with her false assurances that his father "wasn't really" endangering the man. By recounting Ann's attempt to defuse the scene, Obama reveals her need to protect not just her son but also herself from facing up to her husband's cruelty—something she continued to evade by romanticizing him. Her denial has reverberations to this very day as her son denies hatred in almost a reflexive way. When Bill O'Reilly asked him in their pre–Super Bowl Fox interview in 2011 how it felt to be hated, Obama replied that many presidents—such as Bush and Bill Clinton—had been disliked in the past. O'Reilly called him on his soft-pedaling and repeated, "I said hatred." Obama has more of his mother inside him than first meets the eye, as we see the same kind of hedging that his mother used to mischaracterize his father.

The lie at the heart of the myth of Barack Obama, Sr., is also at the heart of the conflicted attitude—some have described it as betrayal—that Obama has demonstrated toward his father's ideals (and what had appeared to be his own) since he reached the White House.

Obama campaigned on a platform of inclusiveness that would have made his father proud, but since assuming office he has often failed to live up to those ideals. Critics, particularly those on the left, have struggled to understand and explain why Obama has repeatedly let down the people who put him into office and betrayed the ideals he campaigned on—the very "dreams" of reason leading us to a common ground that he inherited from his father. The president's unresolved rage toward his father—the rage that all abandoned children feel—suggests that Obama's betrayal of his father's values is linked to his feelings about his father's betrayal of the family more than forty years ago.

Abused children typically identify at some psychic level with their abusers, in an unconscious attempt to stay connected with them, to figure out what motivated their abuse, and to indulge in a fantasy of controlling them through identification—that is, if you can't beat 'em, become 'em. Obama is dealing with anger at his abuser, the abandoning father, through what is called a reaction formation, a process of evading an unwanted feeling by embracing its opposite. In Obama's case, he evades his anger at his father by living out his father's dreams, a construct that creates the illusion of connecting with, understanding, and identifying with the man who abandoned him. But this is an unrealistic, disingenuous response, because he never faced up to how hurtful his father was and how much rage he felt. This undermines his attempts to live up to his father's dreams. Because his anger toward his father remains unconscious and unavailable, Obama cannot protect what his father stood for in a straightforward way; he won't be able to genuinely claim those dreams until he first feels and works through that anger and hatred. Until then, his pursuit of his father's values is more of a magical, manic grasping after the dreams, which his unconscious will prevent from ever being realized. As a result of his inability to follow through on his promises, he often winds up treating the nation—a body that he often refers to in familial terms in his speeches and writing—like an abandoning father, doing to his national family what his father did to him.

The connection between the nation as family and Obama as its head is one that he seems to make often, if only on an unconscious level. By analyzing two of his speeches made within a year of each other in 2008–2009 we can see that Obama identifies parallels between his roles as president and as father. In these speeches he used the same imagery from the Sermon on the Mount to demonstrate a point about creating a solid foundation. In April 2009, speaking on the economy at Georgetown, he cited the sermon's parable of two men who built their houses on sand and rock, respectively, with predictable results. He exhorted listeners that "we must build our house upon a rock" and "must lay a new foundation for growth and prosperity." Acknowledging that "we have been called to govern in extraordinary times," he shared "a vision of America's future" in which an economically and spiritually revitalized nation that he has been called to govern becomes "that house upon the rock. Proud, sturdy and unwavering in the face of the greatest storm."

The previous summer, in a speech in June at a Chicago church, he drew upon the same imagery, except this time the rock was connected to the family: "of all the rocks upon which we build our lives, we are reminded today that family is the most important." He went on in that speech to speak specifically of the struggles of a single parent in a fatherless family, a rare instance of anything approaching even indirect criticism of his father. He cites "the toll that being a single parent took on my mother—how she struggled at times to pay the bills; to give us the things that other kids had; to play all the roles that both parents are supposed to play. And I know the toll it took on me." He then again positioned himself as the man responsible for the rock—except this time the rock is the family instead of the nation that is now his to lead: "So I resolved many years ago that it was my obligation to break the cycle—that if I could be anything in life, I would be a good father to my girls; that if I could give them anything, I would give them that rock—that foundation—on which to build their lives. And that would be the greatest gift I could offer." Whether or not he realizes it, Obama understands his roles as president and parent in the same terms—he is rock-securing steward of his national and biological families, called upon to serve as the father to both his citizens and his children in ways that his own father wasn't able to serve him.

It's worth noting the lengths to which he will go to avoid commit-ting the same mistakes with his daughters that his father did with him. It's evident that he sees the risk of repeating his father's pattern of some form of abandonment, a risk common among abused and abandoned children when they become parents. In *The Audacity of Hope* he acknowledges the possibility of error: "Of all the areas of my life, it is in my capacities as a husband and father that I enter-tain the most doubt." He was in his second year in the White House when he told CNN, "Without hesitation, the most challenging, most fulfilling, most important job I will have during my time on this earth is to be Sasha and Malia's father." He sees his assignment as father as avoiding the mistakes his own father made with him: "For the most part what I understood from him was an absence, and I vowed that when I became a father one of the most important things that I could be is a presence in my children's lives." He even found a way to joke about it: in a high school commencement speech on May 16, 2011, he said the principal's daughter had gone to a dif-ferent high school because she thought boys would be afraid to talk to her with her mother "lurking" in the hallway. President Obama paused, smiled, and then said, "Which is why my next job will be principal at Sasha and Malia's high school (laugh), and then I'll be president of their college. (Big laugh again.)"

He could also use family duties as an excuse. A few months ear-lier, just weeks before Americans went to the polls in 2010 for the disastrous (at least for Obama) midterm elections, he cut short his appearance at a Rhode Island fund-raiser by leaving as soon as he was finished speaking, telling donors who had paid big money for the privilege of having dinner with the president that he had to "get home because Michelle is on the road, so I've got to be home to tuck in the girls and walk the dog." As he continues as president to work out his ambivalent relationship to his father's ghost, it's clear that he would never dream of treating his daughters the way his father treated him. In his book *Revival: The Struggle for Survival Inside the Obama White House,* Richard Wolffe wrote that Obama even interrupted the final health insurance reform negotiations to attend a flute recital at his daughters' school, one of many such stories from both the campaign trail and the White House. For the most part, he manages the potential conflict gracefully—although he told the Rhode Island audience that his D.C. duties that night would also require him to "scoop the poop."

The image of anyone cleaning up poop is pretty funny—and even funnier when this person is the president of the United States. This joke is Obama's way of defusing the anger of donors who paid a lot of money to dine with him. Moreover, he is reminding them that he's an ordinary man, an ordinary dad who is not just the most powerful person on the planet. He modifies expectations and thereby evades the transference feelings that people in the room must have had— that is, that he would answer tough questions and deal with the nation's angry mood blaming him for its economic woes in the run-up to the 2010 election. Ironically, he wrote in his memoir of being fed up with cleaning up the messes left by other people and then inherited in 2009 a monumental mess to clean up left by the Bush administration, after a long history of cleaning up his own feelings about his childhood family mess. Beneath the humor of the poop remark is a lifetime of unexpressed anger that his own parents not only weren't there to clean up the messes he made, they also weren't there to clean up their own messes.

Obama obviously doesn't want his daughters to feel orphaned the way he has said he felt. And instead of leaving a mess for his kids to clean up, he cleans up the mess left by the dog he got for them as a reward for their patience during his extended absences during the campaign—to compensate for the closest he has come to subjecting them to an absence like he suffered. But the Rhode Island donors likely felt orphaned by his unexpected early departure. And they're not alone; as his disaffected former supporters can attest, Obama has repeatedly failed to express the anger they've felt about some of the problems and challenges he has faced: waiting too long to chastise BP, for example, or leaving the need for gun control out of his remarks after Congresswoman Gabrielle Giffords and others were gunned down by a deranged killer in January 2011, or dismissing as "silliness" the toxic, divisive questions about his citizenship when he finally put them to rest with the release of his birth certificate in April 2011. Though the use of dismissive mockery was effective, he once again evaded acknowledging the degree of hatred continually fomented against him—or the anger that on some level it induces in him. When Representative James Clyburn was spat on by Tea Party protesters on March 20, 2010, after their having been further whipped into a frenzy by some Republican congressmen who spoke at their rally, Obama said and did nothing, leaving it to others when he could have gone on TV and demanded a clear apology from the provocative Republicans who had spoken there.

Unable to draw on his anxiety as a source of information, he has a harder time feeling the anxiety of others unless they show it to him. This is a source of the emotional tone deafness that has often been described by observers, which exposes him to charges of being out of touch with his supporters. Though he can recognize the positive effect of his speeches, he misses the sense of abandonment that his supporters have increasingly developed since he assumed office. Unbeknown to him, his followers often feel as though they are orphaned—that the man upon whom they counted, who unconsciously represented a combined parent to so many, isn't there when he is most needed.

The distance that Obama maintains between himself and his followers serves two purposes, both related to fatherhood. On the simplest of levels, he has managed his internal conflict about his own father by keeping all positive paternal energy directed at his daughters, protecting them from the pain of abandonment by maximizing the love he offers them. He sacrifices the rest of us—as he should, in some ways—to preserve his relationship with his daughters, withholding fatherly love—in the form of attention and fulfilling promises—from his followers in order to hold on to all of it for his children. On some level, he's aware that the myth of his father was a lie and doesn't want to create another absence that Michelle will have to fill, another lie that she will have to sell to his daughters.

His biological family is kept whole and safe and loved, but he starves his national family: at the same time that he tries to avoid duplicating his father's dynamic, at least with his daughters, he is also unconsciously driven to re-create that dynamic, assuming the role of the abandoning and neglecting parent. Because he doesn't allow himself to feel his rage at his father, he directs it toward a safer target, his father's political philosophy and the people who embrace it—namely, the voters who put him into office. As much as he doesn't want to repeat his father's horrendous abandoning mistakes toward his own family, his failure to resolve the original conflict has trapped him in what psychoanalysts call an unconscious repetition compulsion—in this case, the drive to repeat the conflict and pain he felt as a child, probably in the hope that the results will be different. Driven to get inside his father's mind and to answer questions about why his father abandoned his family, he is motivated by a need to express the anger he has displaced from his father onto his followers by repeatedly disappointing them, putting them into the role of little Barry, who kept the myth alive in the face of rejection, seducing and then abandoning them the way his father seduced and abandoned his mother.

When he rejects his followers in this way, Obama is evading what psychoanalysts call the positive father transference, the attraction patients develop toward a therapist into whom they project the attributes they wanted in their biological father. Obama is afraid to fully feel the father transference yearnings he excited in hurt and betrayed Americans who were looking for change. To return to that ugly Tea Party incident, President Obama did not set the kind of limits a father would set on anyone threatening his family. He also didn't confront the Republicans who spoke at the rally—including Mike Pence (the chairman of the House Republican Conference), Michele Bachmann, and Steve King—even though they did not personally spit or hurl hateful epithets. Although Michael Steele, then president of the RNC, and Democrats such as Steny Hoyer did object on Fox News the next day, most did not—and Obama said nothing. If any of those things had happened to one of his daughters, he would not have hesitated to step in loud and clear.

In the romantic phase of his political development, in the ascent of possibility, he reveled in the positive father transference, becoming the father he was waiting for. But once inaugurated, he risked becoming the father he despised, that more realistic father, whom he eventually discovered was destructive, alcoholic, and bombastic, tragically unable to fulfill his grand promises. Obama ducks the transference because for all his understanding of psychology—his own and others'—his unresolved feelings toward his father lead him to avoid an awareness outside his immediate family of how children feel about their father and how important it is for them to feel safe and protected. He wants to avoid confronting in others the vulnerability and lack of protection he felt in his unmet need for a father as a child. He also wants to avoid assuming a key attribute of a healthy father: setting limits on his children as well as on others in order to protect his children. And it's not simply his children or specific members of Congress. He cannot bring himself to protect the Constitution, as evident in his hands-off approach to Private Manning. And then there is standing up to the NRA and its consistent pressure to legalize more and more kinds of guns. Both protecting the Constitution and banning assault weapons would require confrontation with forces totally opposed to him, which he can't bring himself to engage in because it borders too closely on the anger he must avoid at all costs. Other factors are at play here: when he did express frustration with racial profiling after the Henry Louis Gates incident in July 2009, he was savagely criticized in some circles. It appears that he decided not to risk again being called an "angry" black man, even though with this contretemps he used the story about his father—talking over a beer—to heal the rift among Gates, the Cambridge police, and himself.

Although he has lived his life trying not to be like his father, he cannot evade the core ambivalence he feels toward an inner abandoning father. The more he doesn't want to be like his father, the more he ends up being like him in unexpected ways. He never wanted to disappoint his children in the way he was disappointed, yet the rising tide of criticism from his former supporters confirms that he is disappointing many who once had deep faith in him. In some respects this is almost predictable; like a patient with a fear of heights who takes a job on the fortieth floor of a skyscraper, Obama pursued and won a position in which he can't help but disappoint many people. Perhaps he needed an arena that offered the potential of oversized disappointment in order to avoid disappointing his daughters—a protection of his family that claims the nation as collateral damage.

Obama is a family man and, from all evidence, is the consummate father. He had one other aspiration, unspoken but clearly essential in his life story: his struggle to become a man. His unconscious rage, linked with his father's conscious abandonment, made it almost impossible to identify with his father as a man. This is a common problem for children abandoned by their fathers; they look to teachers, other elders in the family, and eventually to public figures with whom to identify. Obama deeply identified with his stepfather, Lolo, as we will see later, as a definer of manly qualities, some of which included not letting others know when you are hurt and keeping other inner thoughts and feelings as private as possible. His search for his racial heritage, though also essential and central to *Dreams from My Father,* was only one motive for learning more about his heritage. He needed to discover who his father really was, even if he couldn't identify with him. And what he discovered made identification even more difficult—and helps us understand his difficulty in sustaining his rhetoric either by repeating it enough or by converting it to action. If he effectively achieved manhood, in his mind, by becoming president, he would be that much harder pressed to act like a man and take charge of our country—to be a man and not just play the part of one. There have been times I've thought Obama identifies with the idea of who a president should be, rather than bringing his own convictions to the office and molding it into his own vision of what he seeks to accomplish. But on a closer look, he does have his own vision, though closely aligned with elements of his father—and that is the vision of common ground, of this being one nation, indivisible. If he were hoping to have fully grasped manhood by playing the role of president, however, he is finding it tough sledding because the presidency is an idea and a duty to which one brings one's own needs and desires. He did bring to the presidency a clear view that he was going to get bin Laden— and that he was going to try to make that happen. And he did; by the spring of 2011, it appeared that he was doing more and more to make this *his* presidency.

But the gap between the soaring rhetoric of the 2008 campaign— and the occasional White House speech that rises to the linguistic occasion—and the remote, out-of-touch persona he has developed in office persisted, although he did give several personal interviews on television before Father's Day 2011 as well as one for *People* magazine about Sasha and Malia and his being the father he never had.

Mostly, however, he inspires everyone with a great idea or speech, and then he goes quiet and at times seems to disappear, perpetuating a cycle of being a person who excites and then rejects, much the way his mother did with him—and perhaps the way his father did with his mother. Also contributing to his tendency to go quiet is his having only a partial identification with his father; because his identification with his father's great oratorical gifts feels false and incomplete to him, he retreats in disbelief after a powerful, transformative speech. It's clear from a psychoanalytic perspective that Obama's thoughts are too often dominated by the desire to live out what he sees as his father's dreams, at the expense of knowing the nightmares his father caused in others—including his mother. Those nightmares resurface after a great speech, and the dangers of more complete identification with the man his father became block his capacity for follow-up.

He has to keep the myth of his father alive, no matter what. One way is to insist that despite our differences—both within our nation and between nations—we have more in common as humans than otherwise. And what he went on to say in "A New Beginning," his June 4, 2009, speech in Cairo about American relations with the Muslim world and then elsewhere is that what we have in common are hopes and dreams for our children, for our security, and to live in peace with our neighbors. But what he omits is that we also have aggression in common, as part of human nature. And that is why we have laws—not because they are natural but because they help protect us from what is natural.

As a candidate, author, and orator who wrote and spoke his way into office more than any president in memory, he grasps the power of his language and sees that it calms people and excites them— the way Barry witnessed his father exciting and "transforming" his fourth-grade class and heard his father's persuasive skills repeatedly mythologized by his family. But his subsequent relative unavailability as a father figure and as a leader suggests that he doesn't fully understand or trust the power his language has on people, how it lives inside them as a means of satisfying elemental needs—and how much it inspires them to believe that promises made will be promises fulfilled. He wants to elicit specific responses with his words, but he doesn't want to accept the transference that those responses naturally lead to. It would mean being too much like his father, a risk he dare not take.

In this light we can begin to see Obama as an almost tragic figure—a man who loves his children and talks lovingly to them but who cannot allow himself to be swallowed up by his flock, by the primitive needs of the child part of a frightened populace. He either doesn't recognize his transferential power and therefore is unable to lead from genuine strength, or he feels it but, consciously or unconsciously, chooses not to use it. He does address the adult in each of us, talking about health *insurance*; simultaneously, he evades addressing our childlike needs by not talking about health *care*.

Then suddenly he used his transference power by ordering the raid on bin Laden. He became the recognizer and protector of the vulnerable feelings many of us had. He became our paterfamilias, though in his speech announcing the raid he quickly backpedaled into his more familiar emphasis on American unity. After a long period in which his fatherhood in the public arena had been limited to rhetoric without action, he was suddenly standing taller, and the American people were feeling fathered by this president for the first time. But as brilliant as he is, as great as his capacity for reason and understanding is, he didn't feel comfortable, even at that moment, with continuing to share the masculine part of fatherhood with us for too long a time.

CHAPTER 3

Accommodator in Chief

I wanted to nudge history forward in the way a child would when wishing to make a flower grow more quickly: by tugging at it.

I think the art of waiting is something that has to be learned. We must patiently plant the seeds and water the ground well, and give the plants exactly the amount of time they need to mature.

—Vaclav Havel

I find his "I'll stand up for your rights soon, or next week, or in two years" to be tiring and unconvincing.

—Christopher Durang

In his 2010 best seller, *Obama's Wars,* the veteran journalist and author Bob Woodward offers a blow-by-blow account of the decision-making process behind the 2009 resolution to send 30,000 more troops to Afghanistan. In so doing, his book makes a key contribution to our knowledge of Obama's thought process and our analysis of it. The tale Woodward tells—and it's one that continues to repeat itself in Obama's presidency—is one of costly compromise. As he deliberated between the various arguments about troop surges— the liberal contingent, led by Vice President Joe Biden, who wanted to limit the troop increase to 20,000, and the military leadership's call, supported by Secretary of State Clinton, for 40,000 or more— Obama took months, called countless meetings, and considered multiple reports to conclude that the solution was essentially to split the difference.

But Woodward, and his sources who participated in the decision process, recognized that there was more than politics at play here, as the president often seemed motivated more by the pursuit of unity than anything else. "Grappling for consensus, [Obama] noted the general agreement on the difficulty of defeating the Taliban and the importance of protecting Afghans," wrote Woodward. "'The fact that we agree on these pillars of a strategy belies the notion of huge divisions among the team here and it provides a basis for moving forward,' Obama said, overlooking substantial disagreements. Biden and chief counterterrorism adviser John Brennan, for example, were not on board." Obama himself tells Woodward that he felt he needed to "get everybody in a room and make sure that everybody is sing- ing from the same hymnal." And when they did finally strike a com- promise, Woodward noted, "in an unusual move, [Obama] said, 'I want everybody to sign on to this—McChrystal, Petraeus, Gates, Mullen, Eikenberry, and Clinton. We should get this on paper and on the record.' Even those sophisticated members of Obama's inner circle of military advisors are so unused to metaphor coming from the White House that they responded as if there would be a signed contract, as if he wanted actual signatures on a document." The mili- tary leaders had their own ideas about what was really going on in the mind of the son of two broken homes: "Clearly, the vice chair- man of the Joint Chiefs concluded, the president had picked 30,000 in order to keep the family together," reported Woodward. But just how much did Obama sacrifice to preserve family unity? Despite all of his efforts to build consensus and reach a compromise, Wood- ward concluded, "the military was getting almost everything."

Obama was never able to reassemble his families of origin, which were twice disbanded through abandonment and divorce. But he subsequently developed a long history of striking compromises to heal fractures: mending a rift between benchwarmers and play- ers on his high school basketball team; uniting opposing factions when presiding over the *Harvard Law Review*; helping the disen- franchised come together as a community organizer in Chicago; even naming as secretary of state his chief Democratic rival for the presidency. He attributes this penchant for getting along in a frac- tured world to dreams he inherited from his father, which he tried to make reality by helping disparate people appreciate what they had in common.

We think of compromise as an essential element of living peacefully in relation to others, but the act of compromise has a vital internal function as well. An individual strikes a balance between conflicting parts of the unconscious—the desire to get what he wants, the desire to please the person he loves, and the desire to do the right thing. Constructing an internal compromise among different wishes allows a person to satisfy a demanding conscience that will give him relief from self-criticism, as well as get something else he wants—a positive response from the person with whom he is compromising, which helps him tolerate the feelings of loss and resentment for not having his way entirely. He also gets the added bonus of feeling good about himself for having rejected the selfish impulses that would otherwise have impeded compromise, thereby silencing any criticism from his conscience.

His role as a compromiser helped young Barry find a constructive way to strike the internal balance he needed to excel in life—namely, by repressing his own considerable hurts, rage, and the destructiveness they fueled. Contributing to his effectiveness in the art of compromise was his well-honed ability, learned perhaps from his mother, to see some good or common ground in the worst of situations. This, too, served an internal function, helping him to deny the destructiveness of others as well as his own, further protecting himself from the external and internal rage against which he felt compelled to defend himself.

Obama has spoken and written frequently and passionately about the primary value that he places on unity. This was perhaps never clearer than in his spotlight-claiming 2004 Democratic National Convention keynote address, in which he stated that a senior citizen struggling to pay for prescriptions "makes my life poorer, even if it's not my grandparent," just as "an Arab-American family being rounded up without benefit of an attorney or due process . . . threatens my civil liberties." He then tied his sense of connectedness to the rest of us to "that fundamental belief—I am my brother's keeper; I am my sister's keeper—that makes this country work." To cement this bond even further, he contrasted the sense of unity he was celebrating with the forces that work against it, warning, "Even as we speak, there are those who are preparing to divide us. They are the spin masters and negative ad peddlers who embrace the politics of anything goes."

Critics who say that Obama has no strong belief system—typified by the syndicated columnist Richard Cohen writing in *The Washington Post,* "Who is this guy? What are his core beliefs? The president himself is no help on this score"—overlook the fact, evident in his remarks above, that he believes that Americans have more in common than they sometimes act as though they do. He does have a strong belief system that includes an insistence on mutual respect and on the importance of listening to other points of view, and a clear ideology that Americans have far more in common than they realize. He rightly sees himself as being an American more than a Democrat and treats Republicans as if he believes that seeing themselves as Americans first is a trait they share—despite the persistent and escalating Republican attacks on him in his first two years in office. Majority Leader Mitch McConnell and other Republicans have stated publicly that they are more interested in preventing Obama's 2012 reelection than anything else—which makes them Republicans first, Americans second. Obama's tenacious hold on his belief in the illusion of common ground indicates that it functions as an *idée fixe,* a guiding principle he clings to regardless of evidence to the contrary. In this respect, rather than the pragmatist that he presents himself as, he is truly an ideologue, albeit in pragmatist's clothing. But the belief that we are fundamentally more united than divided serves as a blind spot for him, as well, undermining his efforts to foster a unity that could be realistically attained. Thus he courted Republican votes for health care reform for so long that he began to lose support among his Democratic base. And he closed his speech about the BP oil leak with a comment about fishermen of various religious backgrounds praying together—reducing the effectiveness of the speech's understated and overdue attempt to connect with the populist anger toward the perpetrators of the disaster.

On a conscious level, Obama attributes this belief in the power of American unity to his parents, whom he cited in the 2004 convention keynote: "My parents shared not only an improbable love; they shared an abiding faith in the possibilities of this nation. They would give me an African name, Barack, or 'blessed,' believing that in a tolerant America, your name is no barrier to success." But unconsciously it's not so simple, and though his trademark pursuit of unity and compromise is certainly linked to his parents, it's not as straightforward as a deliberate desire to enact the principles he attributes to the values he believes they once embodied.

As we now know, Obama's parents' love turned out to be as impermanent as it was improbable. There is little known, said, or written about what went wrong in their marriage. Obama omits a key detail in his account of the separation, never mentioning that his mother moved him from Honolulu to Seattle in his first year, leaving her husband behind in Hawaii months before he left for Harvard. The omission is revealing, as if he wants to minimize or deny how much there is known about the breakup, particularly if it implicates his mother. Nowhere is there any record of young Obama asking what made his father leave, and the passage in *Dreams from My Father* in which he comes the closest to wondering why he left—or at least suggesting that it might be natural to wonder—is typically couched in a discussion of larger cultural issues, including the belief in the united, tolerant nation of possibilities without barriers that he would so eloquently celebrate decades later. After relating vignettes of his grandfather discussing young Barry with racially unenlightened tourists—telling some that the black child they're watching on the beach is the great-grandson of King Kamehameha while telling another of his mixed Kenyan/Kansan heritage and proudly proclaiming him as his own—Obama concluded that "race wasn't something you really needed to worry about anymore" in the view of his grandfather, who assumed that "the rest of the world would be catching up soon" to the enlightened Eden of 1960s Hawaii.

There was only one problem: my father was missing. He had left paradise, and nothing that my mother or grandparents told me could obviate that single, unassailable fact. Their stories didn't tell me why he had left. They couldn't describe what it might have been like had he stayed. Like the janitor, Mr. Reed, or the black girl who churned up dust as she raced down a Texas road, my father became a prop in someone else's narrative. An attractive prop—the alien figure with the heart of gold, the mysterious stranger who saves the town and wins the girl—but a prop nonetheless.

Looking back, Obama recognized that his father "may have been complicit in" the creation of this image, citing an article published at the time of his father's graduation, which Barry discovered when he was in high school. Depicting his father as "guided and responsible, the model student, ambassador for his continent," the article was as much a record of where Barry came from as the birth certificate and vaccination forms that he found it folded among. Obama Sr. claimed to have experienced no racial discrimination, though he sensed it occurring between ethnic groups. His summation of what the rest of the world can learn from Hawaii—involving "the willingness of races to work together toward common development, something he has found whites elsewhere too often unwilling to do"—provided young Barry a clear statement of an objective that would drive his political career.

Despite the dose of political DNA, however, what struck Barry most about the article is what was missing:

No mention is made of my mother or me, and I'm left to wonder whether the omission was intentional on my father's part, in anticipation of his long departure. Perhaps the reporter failed to ask personal questions, intimidated by my father's imperious manner; or perhaps it was an editorial decision, not part of the simple story that they were looking for. I wonder, too, whether the omission caused a fight between my parents.

I would not have known at the time, for I was too young to realize that I was supposed to have a live-in father, just as I was too young to know that I needed a race. For an improbably short span it seems that my father fell under the same spell as my mother and her parents; and for the first six years of my life, even as that spell was broken and the worlds that they thought they'd left behind reclaimed each of them, I occupied the place where their dreams had been.

I'm struck more by what Barry left out than by what his father omitted. At its simplest level, the omission of mother and son from the article was because they weren't there; according to the timeliness offered by both David Remnick and Janny Scott, the separation had already taken place. Barack Sr.'s omission may even have been because his father forgot he was his father or that he had married Barry's mother. Barry is the one who fails to acknowledge that separation, that having "left paradise." It was he, the son, who was thrown out of the nuclear-family paradise by his parents' separation, which Obama characterized as his father's departure. He went on to say, in a way, that his mother didn't give him what he needed: she didn't give him his father. Instead she gave him a myth, a prop, and a romantic vision and narrative; she was either unable to keep the actual man around, to prevent him from his wanderlust, or unwilling to keep their young family together by moving to graduate school with her husband and infant son. Without engaging in the completely natural process of looking for an explanation of why his father left, Obama the memoirist did portray Obama the young abandoned son's discovery of the article as raising questions around the edge of the larger issue of his father's departure, wondering why he and his mother weren't mentioned, whether his father knew at the time that he was never coming back, and whether the article (but, interestingly, not his departure) caused a parental fight (which presumably would not have been the first fight between them). Although those questions suggest that the issues were on his mind, he betrayed neither anger nor blame toward his father, whom he once again depicted as an almost passive object of larger cultural forces—concluding that he had fallen under "the same spell" that had removed his mother and grandparents from "the worlds that they thought they'd left behind" into a world of racial tolerance.

Later in the book, Obama returned to the question of his parents' marriage, during his mother's visit to New York after Barack had transferred from Occidental to Columbia. After having avoided her during most of her New York visit, he asks her directly about their marriage. It is at that moment that she tells Barack not to be angry at his father or blame him for leaving. In fact, it is the second time she has told him not to be angry at his father, the first time being when Barack was Barry. Then she said, "You shouldn't be mad at your father, Bar. He loves you very much. He's just a little stubborn sometimes." She now admits that she divorced him, not vice versa—although she manages to add "bastard" to change what she had earlier said about him, that he was "a little stubborn." Still, as an accommodator she always tries to protect her son's view of his father, though he doesn't offer any plausible explanations from her about why she divorced him. In fact, she may also be protecting herself from her son's view of her. If that was the case, it worked, as he continued to write about her love for his father. He wrote about how her chin trembled whenever she talked about him—as though she were about to cry. And again he reassured the reader—and himself—that their love was real. He mentioned overtones of sexual passion only once in his book—implicit in his description of his parents in what seems to be a postcoital scene, the day after his father forbade him to watch the Grinch on TV: "I knocked, and my father opened the door, shirtless. Inside, I saw my mother ironing some of his clothes. Her hair was tied back in a ponytail, and her eyes were soft and dark, as if she'd been crying. My father asked me to sit down beside him on the bed, but I told him that Toot needed me to help her, and left."

He didn't use the word "improbable" again, but he did say that very few Americans could ever understand the depth of his parents' love. At its deepest level, his need to accommodate is aimed at validating his parents' shared love for each other, as something deeper than a marriage forced upon his father by her pregnancy. It is universally—or almost so—difficult for a son to speak or write about his mother's sexuality for a variety of emotional reasons. But for all Obama's description of his mother as a naive woman, the recent biography of Stanley Ann Dunham by Janny Scott says otherwise. According to the people Scott interviewed on the subject of Ann's relationships with men, there was always an erotic component—and there were intense affairs after Lolo, always with men of color. One younger man Ann is said to have described as looking like Mike Tyson. How much of her behavior was a repudiation of her own parents remains for others to assess. But Obama's description of her in his interview with Scott was of someone taken advantage of because "there was a sweetness about her and a willingness to give people the benefit of the doubt, and a sort of generosity of spirit that at times was naive." He further said that she was at times "taken advantage of" because of those qualities. One can see that he might simply prefer to keep his mother as a naive "poster child" for liberal causes than a woman who pursued erotic liaisons in far-off lands at the expense of raising her son. His sustained view of his mother and father as having a perfect black-and-white union of love may be used to bolster him against this other aspect of his mother's life—and act as an added force behind his dreams of creating bipartisan harmony. He wrote, "What I heard from my mother that day, speaking about my father, was something that I suspect most Americans will never hear from the lips of those of another race, and so cannot be expected to believe might exist between black and white: the love of someone who knows your life in the round, a love that will survive disappointment."

But if she were to blame for the breakup, then Barry would have had to redirect his anger at his own mother. The fact that he didn't mention that she initiated the separation suggests that the anger he feels toward her is beyond either his consciousness or comfort level. But Ann's divorce from Barack Obama, Sr., set into motion a series of dislocations that deepened the sense of instability in young Barry's family life. First she met and married Lolo Soetoro, another University of Hawaii student from abroad; she and her son joined her new husband in his native Indonesia in 1967. The environment was decidedly more hostile to her child than Hawaii had been. Friends she met in Jakarta "were floored that she'd bring a half-black child to Indonesia, knowing the disrespect they have for blacks," her acquaintance Elizabeth Bryant, another American living in Jakarta at the time, told Janny Scott. Bryant recalled walking with Ann and Barry while Indonesian children were taunting and throwing rocks at the boy. When Bryant offered to intervene, Ann stopped her. "No, he's O.K.," Ann said. "He's used to it." Her seemingly casual reaction to her son having more than epithets thrown at him helps us further question his own inconsistent regard for the deep parental transferences so many Americans feel about him and their desire that he pay closer attention to their severe plights—rather than giving speeches about the Middle East, which is rapidly becoming to American poor and homeless the national equivalent of the Indonesian villages that took Barry's mother's attention away from her son. This vignette helps us again think about why Barry never told his mother about the *Life* magazine article.

Four years later, she sent Barry back to the United States to live with his grandparents in Hawaii, where he attended Honolulu's finest prep school from grades five through twelve. Barry was alone with his grandparents for a year, until his mother left her second husband to return to Hawaii in 1972, now with her two-year-old daughter, Maya Soetoro. According to some reports, the marriage failed because Lolo wanted to have more children and Ann wanted to continue her academic career. Maya later wrote that her mother might have left because she "really got a voice," acquired both a professional and feminist language, and started to "demand more of those who were near her." Still, family life occupied her for just another five years, and she returned to Indonesia to continue her anthropological fieldwork in 1977, leaving Barry alone in Hawaii with his grandparents once again.

His relationship to his mother, especially his denied rage, adds yet another layer to his passion for consensus building. We've seen how Obama's compulsive need to heal splits is driven by his two central inner cracks, as it were, between his white and black selves, as well as the crack that kept running through his desire for an intact family. But at another level, his desire for consensus is more than an outgrowth of the need to heal—it is in itself a defense aimed at covering over his deep unhealed rage at his mother. She was domineering, seductive, and abandoning. No man could stand up to her; or at least Obama never saw his mother ever solve a problem with a man. Separations became solutions. Though he makes references to not wanting his parents' restless, wandering lifestyle for himself or his family, Obama has never expressed any public anger toward his mother for uprooting or abandoning him and has conspicuously understated her role in that process. David Remnick, in his book *The Bridge: The Life and Rise of Barack Obama,* observes that "Obama is not always easy on Ann Dunham," which he sees as "part of the drama of" *Dreams from My Father:* "his obvious love for a woman who is intelligent, idealistic, brave, and engaged with the world but also, at times, maddeningly naïve and frequently thousands of miles away." By contrast, Obama's father, who was a present absence and an angry self-indulgent phantom who interacted directly with Barry for only one month, was the "singular object of the narrator's imaginings, at the center of a young man's quest to claim a race and a history."

Obama's anger toward his mother definitely crops up in *Dreams from My Father*, most notably in an exchange that took place in Hawaii after she returned from her Indonesian fieldwork. When she confronts her son, now a high school senior, about an acquaintance's arrest, he tries to explain to her "the role of luck in the world, the spin of the wheel," and attempts to dismiss her with a smile and reassurances not to worry.

> *It was usually an effective tactic, another one of those tricks I had learned: people were satisfied so long as you were courteous and smiled and made no sudden moves. They were more than satisfied; they were relieved—such a pleasant surprise to find a well-mannered young black man who didn't seem angry all the time. Except my mother hadn't looked satisfied. She had just sat there, studying my eyes, her face as grim as a hearse.*
>
> *"Don't you think you're being a little casual about your future?" she said.*
>
> *"What do you mean?"*
>
> *"You know exactly what I mean. One of your friends was just arrested for drug possession. Your grades are slipping. You haven't even started on your college applications. Whenever I try to talk to you about it you act like I'm just this great big bother."*

When Barry tries to tell her he might not go away to college she cuts him off, telling him he can get into any school he wants to, as long as he puts in some effort:

> *"Remember what that's like? Effort? Damn it, Bar, you can't just sit around like some good-time Charlie, waiting for luck to see you through."*
>
> *"A good-time what?"*

"A good-time Charlie. A loafer."

I looked at her sitting there, so earnest, so certain of her son's destiny. The idea that my survival depended on luck remained a heresy to her; she insisted on assigning responsibility somewhere—to herself, to Gramps and Toot, to me. I suddenly felt like puncturing that certainty of hers. Letting her know that her experiment with me had failed. Instead of shouting, I laughed. "A good-time Charlie, huh? Well, why not? Maybe that's what I want out of life. I mean, look at Gramps. He didn't even go to college."

The comparison caught my mother by surprise. Her face went slack, her eyes wavered. It suddenly dawned on me, her greatest fear. "Is that what you're worried about?" I asked. "That I'll end up like Gramps?"

She shook her head quickly. "You're already much better educated than your grandfather," she said. But the certainty had finally drained from her voice. Instead of pushing the point, I stood up and left the room.

Though he stopped short of acknowledging it, Obama the memoirist may have recognized the anger he felt toward his mother as an adolescent and perhaps even as an adult. He described treating his mother, at that moment, the way he would treat any white woman—a remembered way of unconsciously equating all whites he must have been angry at with his mother when writing the scene years later. But he resisted any more explicit or conscious expression of anger—both in the actual exchange and in its retelling. Bitterly describing himself as her failed experiment, even silently, speaks volumes about the neglect he felt as a result of her other experiments—the anthropological fieldwork that she abandoned him to pursue and the two marriages that in their failure twice cost him familial stability and the presence of a father figure. Instead of confronting her, the high school senior Barry evaded the truth—something understandable in a teenager who didn't want to make his feelings public and found it safer to hide them behind defensive contempt, and to leave the room to protect her from his fury.

Years later, he again evaded his feelings in the retelling, delinking himself from his genuine anger at her, but the anger comes through nonetheless, particularly in his choosing to follow the vignette with a postscript about his mother's lifelong, skillful manipulation of guilt and the pride she takes in it. In the next section of the memoir, Obama returns to the late-night college scene from which he had been remembering the above exchange in flashback while listening to a Billie Holiday record after a party:

> Billie had stopped singing. The silence felt oppressive, and I suddenly felt very sober. I rose from the couch, flipped the record, drank what was left in my glass, poured myself another. Upstairs, I could hear someone flushing a toilet, walking across a room. Another insomniac, probably, listening to his life tick away. That was the problem with booze and drugs, wasn't it? At some point they couldn't stop that ticking sound, the sound of certain emptiness. And that, I suppose, is what I'd been trying to tell my mother that day: that her faith in justice and rationality was misplaced, that we couldn't overcome after all, that all the education and good intentions in the world couldn't help plug up the holes in the universe or give you the power to change its blind, mindless course.
>
> Still, I'd felt bad after that particular episode; it was the one trick my mother always had up her sleeve, that way she had of making me feel guilty. She made no bones about it, either. "You can't help it," she told me once. "Slipped it into your baby food. Don't worry, though," she added, smiling like the Cheshire cat. "A healthy dose of guilt never hurt anybody. It's what civilization was built on, guilt. A highly underrated emotion."

Guilt means feeling bad for hating or hurting the person whom you love; when Obama's mother jokes about putting guilt in his baby food, she is touching on something serious about controlling his anger at her. We relieve our guilt by disguising the anger we feel toward our loved ones. By manipulating his guilt, she played a role in his inability to find a way to express his anger toward his mother directly to her.

On close examination of the text, there is clear evidence that Obama did express anger at his mother—not directly but in the form of contempt for her emotional vulnerability. He wrote several times about her chin "trembling" whenever she talked about his father. His subtle use of contempt—not so subtle when read closely—is a way of obliquely and patronizingly expressing his anger at his mother without having to confront her directly.

Obama has spoken and written frequently and powerfully about the profound love and gratitude he felt for his mother, celebrating her values in the 2004 keynote address, attributing his success to the work ethic she instilled in him through 4 A.M. preschool tutoring sessions when he was in Indonesia. But something must have damaged their relationship. Dunham's biographer Janny Scott wrote that his mother, "for whom a letter in Jakarta from her son in the United States could raise her spirits for a full day, surely wondered about her place in his life. On rare occasions, she indicated as much—painfully, wistfully—to close friends." Indeed, between her alternately abandoning him and then pressuring him when she was present, he had obvious reasons to be angry with her. And some of his anger toward his father and in response to the serial dissolutions of his families was likely displaced onto her. He was a little clearer about both his resentment toward her and his discomfort expressing it when speaking to Scott, who asked him about the "serial displacements" of his childhood. The "critical distance" that Scott noted is made clear in his likely unconsciously referring to himself in the third person:

> "I think that was harder on a 10-year-old boy than he'd care to admit at the time," Obama said, sitting in a chair in the Oval Office and speaking about his mother with a mix of affection and critical distance. "When we were separated again during high school, at that point I was old enough to say, 'This is my choice, my decision.' But being a parent now and looking back at that, I could see—you know what?—that would be hard on a kid."

But the positive maternal input made it harder for him to express his own rage at her, so instead he mocked her in public and defied her in secret by drinking and smoking and by studying only hard enough to get by. And in failing to fully express her own rage at having been abandoned by Obama's father, she left young Barry without a model of confrontation or of resolving conflict. One form of protection from his powerful mother was to retreat into himself and then internally mock her by referring to himself as her "experiment." He didn't observe parental quarrels and thus could never establish an internal father who could protect him from his powerful mother. The seeds of accommodation were planted. Though she set limits on her son when he was young and tried less successfully to do the same when he was a teenager, she evaded conflict, choosing to induce guilt rather than express her rage.

Obama's mother set no example for how to deal with conflict that young Barry could use to manage his unexpressed rage toward both his father and his mother. This difficulty he has standing up to attacks—not that he saw them as a child—continues to reverberate on a profound unconscious level today. Observers of Obama's first two years in office have repeatedly wondered why he refrained from taking on the Republican opposition with the same vigor with which he pursued the Democratic presidential nomination and then the presidency. Then he stood up in his April 13, 2011, speech at George Washington University in favor of raising taxes where necessary and not exclusively cutting Medicare, but reforming it. Within the week he started making noises about standing up again, this time to eliminate tax breaks for big oil. But without a history of experiencing direct confrontation, that standing up to big oil was short-lived, as he still prefers to remain outside domestic fights and function as a community organizer helping others negotiate their battles. So he sat down again, deciding to increase drilling in Alaska and the mid-Atlantic, where our policy was to do no offshore drilling before 2018. Though he still speaks against oil tax exemptions, his actions do not.

Once president, on key issues from health reform to the stimulus, time and again he has sacrificed his agenda in the pursuit of Republican support that has continually failed to materialize. But rather than express his anger at Republicans or acknowledge the extent of their destructiveness, he has repeatedly evaded conflict with the opposition by moving his position closer to theirs without acknowledging that theirs wasn't moving in return. Some may regard this as political compromise, but that falsely implies that he has received much in return. Others have dismissed it simply as political weakness, branding him the "conciliator in chief," a term used by the MyDD blogger Charles Lemos, the pollster John Zogby, and others. But this quip overlooks the considerable strength he has demonstrated elsewhere in his political skill set. Instead, for a better explanation we must look to his unconscious motivations, where we find that he is more accurately labeled as the "accommodator in chief," burdened by a psychological condition known as "pathological accommodation."

Accommodation is something we all learn in childhood, one of five problem-solving methods identified by the mediation expert Kenneth W. Thomas in *Handbook of Industrial and Organizational Psychology*. In *accommodation*, one individual gives up what he or she needs in order to do what the other wants, a lose/win scenario. This is perhaps a step up from the lose/lose nonsolution of *avoidance*, in which the conflict is not acknowledged, but avoids the potential benefit of *competition*, in which there's the possibility of being the winner and brings far less reward than the win/win scenarios of *compromise* and *collaboration*.

The term "pathological accommodation" is used to describe persistent accommodating behavior that continues in the absence of any evidence that it will be rewarded with even partial victory or satisfaction. Rather than the pursuit of competition, collaboration, or compromise, pathological accommodation is a preemptive negotiation against the self, a self-inflicted strike against one's own needs and values that are sacrificed to preserve another person or relationship. It expresses a deep unconscious need to protect the self against inner chaos and disintegration in the face of the overwhelming anxiety and mental anguish that the individual—again unconsciously—anticipates in response to a threat to that other person or relationship.

Pathological accommodation is closely associated with the work of Dr. Bernard Brandschaft, who in 1985 identified the condition in children who deny their own beliefs and needs in an attempt to please their parents. This is particularly powerful in the dynamic between a single parent and his or her child: the child of a broken home may defend against the pain of losing one parent—or the anticipated pain of losing the second parent—by taking on the belief system of the parent who remains. The child's need to appease is most often driven by fear and results in extreme difficulty in directly confronting aggressors in adulthood.

Brandschaft's is a fairly recent construct, but it builds upon other terms that have been used previously for these similar psychic processes. In the 1930s, the psychoanalyst Helene Deutsch coined the term "as-if personality" to describe people who seem to be genuine but are in fact putting on a false front of which they themselves are not fully aware. Subsequently, the psychoanalyst D. W. Winnicott described what he called the "false self," which he felt arose from the child's feeling a need to protect his mother from his own anger at her, thereby protecting himself from experiencing that anger by consigning it to his unconscious mental life. Both of these are consistent with what we observe in Obama, who appears to be unaware of the gap between what Deutsch would identify as the false front he presented as a candidate and the persona he has manifested as president. And the unexperienced maternal anger that Winnicott cites is at the heart of the dynamic that Obama's pathological accommodation seeks unconsciously to preserve: he defends against the symbolic loss of his mother that would occur if he truly acknowledged and felt his rage at her. He can't even acknowledge that his mother may have set his parents' separation in motion, let alone how he feels about it. This helps us understand the indirect put-downs he occasionally reveals in *Dreams from My Father*.

Brandschaft also wrote that the development of the child's ability to question and stand up to authority is compromised by parents who selectively exclude family information—as Ann did about Barry's father. We see Barry doing the same thing as he grows up, excluding expression of feelings from his mother—keeping himself separate. But a second and fundamental point is that whatever information is given is often twisted in a way to be rewritten or reframed. The amused spin his mother and his grandparents put onto their story about Barack Sr. teaching the "chap" a lesson is a good example of denial of sadism—something that teaches a child to distrust his own emotional reactions. The narrative that his mother fed him was not only factually selective—she left a lot out—it was also emotionally obfuscating, making it difficult for her son even to consider that his father was being cruel. She preferred to portray him as brilliant, sensitive, and clever, with an inclusive and ecumenical worldview and a personality ruled by reason. According to Brandschaft, the internal configuration of pathological accommodation developed in childhood remains in place, though dormant, into adulthood, but can be reactivated in adults in situations of severe stress. Though Obama previously gratified his attachment needs through promises of possibility and progress, culminating in the loving and powerful response he got from so many during the 2008 campaign, it is wholly understandable that the burdens of the presidency could be activating this deep-seated internal configuration, forcing Obama to sustain the dreams from his father that he once needed to cling to in order to survive.

Other unconscious needs drive his pathological accommodation, the source of which can't be reduced to one factor. First, he protects the memory of his father from his unexpressed rage by accommodating his mother's estimation of the man. His accommodation tendency also serves to keep alive and well the dreams he inherited from his father, protecting against the painful realities of how unconnected his father was to him, realities that would emerge if he abandoned his father's vision of a world where reason transcends prejudice. Still, as each accommodation he makes to the Republicans chips away at that vision, he is able to give indirect expression to his fury at his mother by betraying the idealistic and enthusiastic supporters of his 2008 campaign, particularly the youngest generation of voters, onto whom he had projected the image of the vulnerable young Barry, who was betrayed by both of his parents.

Because our inner world is richly populated with important people from our past, as well as with different feelings about those people, we can make multiple projections onto the same person or people and vice versa; in my consulting room projections sometimes occur in rapid succession. Thus we see Obama projecting himself, his mother, and his father onto his supporters—all in different ways. He hates being pushed by supporters who want him to make good on his promises of universal health care and care for the poor— something that represents his mother and how she pushed him to study harder. It is as though he feels he is the Left's experiment, the United States' first black president. When he abandons the Left, as he ignores it often, he is replicating his father's behavior—though at times he also seems to project his incurably naive mother onto those same supporters, his most ardent followers, at whom he feels he can express anger and annoyance and not risk losing their support. He is more comfortable attacking his supporters because they have nowhere else to turn; they can withstand his dismissive behavior, so he thinks, and will never abandon him. He is more comfortable attacking them because they remind him of both of his parents, whose idealism was more selfish than genuine, especially since it was clearly more important to them than the needs of the little boy they both abandoned.

It's well known that Ann relied on food stamps for part of Barry's childhood and that the final year of her life was made harder by her having to fight to receive health insurance benefits—a fight that helped inspire her son to spearhead health care reform. She thus clearly fits the profile of the sort of individual who is served by the social safety net that progressives are fighting to keep intact. However, to hear Obama talk about it today, he remembers that neediness in almost judgmental terms, revealing an unconscious and somewhat negative connection among his mother, the underprivileged, and the Left that champions their cause. When asked by Ann's biographer Janny Scott to identify her "limitations as a mother," Obama first describes her as "a very strong person in her own way . . . resilient, able to bounce back from setbacks, persistent—the fact that she ended up finishing her dissertation." Remarkably, the strengths that he enumerates—which are really just one strength, stated three different ways—he clearly links to her professional life, rather than her motherhood. But then he continues:

> Despite all those strengths, she was not a well-organized person. And that disorganization, you know, spilled over. Had it not been for my grandparents, I think, providing some sort of safety net financially, being able to take me and my sister on at certain spots, I think my mother would have had to make some different decisions. And I think that sometimes she took for granted that, "Well, it'll all work out, and it'll be fine." But the fact is, it might not always have been fine, had it not been for my grandmother. . . . Had she not been there to provide

that floor, I think our young lives could have been much more chaotic than they were.

Although the safety net he's speaking of is familial rather than societal, the clear implication is that she needed it due to her "limitations" and, worse, took it for granted in ways that forgave if not encouraged irresponsibility and ensuing chaos. It's unlikely that he is conscious of the contempt that he conveys, but it's easy to see how that would extend to those who land in today's safety net and their champions on the left.

Accommodating the opposition is another form of abandoning the people who support him or work for him. At great political and personal sacrifice, many senators and congressmen supported Obama on health care despite relentless Republican opposition in their home districts. But Obama did not help them during their reelection campaigns, leaving them to fight their own fights—much the way he was left by first his father and then his mother.

Though he didn't direct his rage at his parents in his memoir, Obama did reveal some of the anger, and other attributes, that unconsciously pointed him toward pathological accommodation. He admitted at times feeling trapped in his black skin for a variety of reasons and described his "withdrawal into a smaller and smaller coil of rage, until being black meant only the knowledge of your own powerlessness, of your own defeat"—a rage that ended up buried beneath his need to accommodate, to get along, to understand and make sense of things intellectually, which spurred the development of his ability to reason things through and see others' points of view as a further defense against experiencing that rage. He traced the evolution of learning to keep his mouth shut in order to survive, which was driven by his realization that he couldn't easily join in with his other black friends in their hatred of white people. After all, his mother and his maternal grandparents raised him lovingly. Ever understanding, he wrote, "It was as if whites didn't know they were being cruel in the first place. Or at least thought you deserving of their scorn." This implies that he knew they were being cruel. And though he felt the sting of their cruelty, he also made excuses for it by saying that they didn't really know what they were doing.

Then, he described his discovery that he could turn his own rage off and on at will: "Our rage at the white world . . . could be switched on and off at our pleasure, [so] maybe we could afford to give the bad-assed nigger pose a rest. Save it for when we really needed it." But elsewhere he wrote that he "had no idea who my own self was. Unwilling to risk exposure, I would quickly retreat to safer ground." The paradox screams out from the pages—he claims he can control expressing his feelings, turning them on or off, and therefore not risk exposure, and in the same passage says he didn't have a clue about who he was. And then there is the "pose" problem—a problem either way: he could pose either as a "bad-assed nigger" or as a reasonable young black man who could get along well in the white world. So his unwillingness to risk exposure is about control, about protecting his different selves; he doesn't want to expose his rage before he knows where it comes from.

What is important in this analysis of Obama is the question of whether or not he can remain in touch with his rage. He has sudden outbursts that we've all seen, but then he seems to retreat to a quiet and almost detached space. As president, when a particular issue links to his internal world, he can speak about it and be articulate—as in the celebrated April 2008 speech about race and the January 2011 Tucson speech about the recent killings there, as well as the April 2011 defense of Social Security when he presented his deficit reduction plan at Georgetown. All these issues have to do with civility and respect and the danger facing us when they are lost or compromised, which makes his anger more palatable or justified to him. But to express rage directly, or to clearly perceive it in others, is something against which he is so deeply defended that he doesn't know his own feelings—although there are reports that he does occasionally get outraged at black men who criticize from the left, who see him as a betrayer. He has learned over time to control his aggression—which is not the same as controlling his rage per se. He has the lifelong experience of a black person getting along in a white world. Posing makes him feel less genuine; conscious posing is a way he has of maintaining contact between what seem to be otherwise indigestible unrelated selves. He can evade when necessary, and for a black man smarter than most of his white classmates in a historically white institution such as Harvard Law School, being able to float between those selves is a good survival technique.

This kind of self-awareness made Obama fear directing his rage against the one person he most loved and depended upon: his mother. In that sense, pathological accommodation has its roots in the depressive position. Obama's fear of destroying his internal and beloved mother is so great that he can't own his aggression against her. His refusal to acknowledge the depth of his rage at the woman upon whom he ultimately depended has led to serious difficulties managing confrontation; at times I think he confuses being enraged with having an internal killer, that he'd destroy the good mother living inside. The safest place to let out aggression is on the basketball court, where elbows are free to fly. By ordering bin Laden's death he gratified that murderous bit in a good way, directing it far away from his mother onto someone we all agree is evil.

And we do see his comfort with having killed bin Laden, in contradistinction to his continued fear of confronting the angry Republican attacks. The more one holds back one's aggression, the bigger the explosion when it is expressed. Obama has lived a life in which the safest place to let off steam is playing ball, but holding it in too long leads to an inner confusion among anger, rage, and murder, making his contained emotions feel out of proportion. Holding back his frustration at Republicans makes it easier for him to confuse his legitimate frustration with feelings of murderous rage. But having a not-Republican to kill allows everything to work out, and bin Laden certainly served that purpose.

Meanwhile, his unconscious fear of this rage seeing the light of day has led to the pattern of preemptive appeasement that we see in his repeatedly accommodating his Republican rivals. The psychoanalytic term for this process is "reaction formation," the oversimplified version with which we are all familiar being "Kill them with kindness." Not only does he preemptively appease Republicans, he is cool and even understanding when attacked by them. This modifies his sense of his own power, diminishes it. He ends up behaving as if he were suffering from a false sense of insecurity.

Obama's diminished expectations for himself make his impulse to help diverging groups find areas of common ground all the more powerful. But those efforts to create unity through compromise (or ultimately accommodation) aren't driven simply by politics. Observing how his pathological accommodation has played out in office, we see that Obama is operating under the influence of a psychological conflict described here for the first time: "obsessive bipartisan disorder." His first two years of dogged pursuit of evasive Republican support in the face of unwavering and hostile opposition is best understood not as naiveté or faulty political strategy but as the sometimes puzzling outward manifestation of a fundamental organizing principle of his psyche, which he must protect from challenge in order to maintain his sense of calm and self.

This isn't to say that bipartisanship is on its own either pathological or a disorder. There's certainly a powerful resonance for many of us in response to Obama's dream of one America, of common ground between warring parties, and of the triumph of patriotism over divisive hatred. But bipartisanship is politically expedient only when it gets results, when both sides compromise and give in order to get something they both want. And when an otherwise effective individual continues to pursue an object or result after every attempt is rejected, that pursuit is seen as acquiring the attributes of an obsession, in that it appears to be a self-destructive pattern motivated by unconscious drives. From a political perspective, the outward manifestations of Obama's obsessive bipartisan disorder—the one-sided compromises, rebuffed advances, and unexplored inquiries into Republican and financial-industry malfeasances—may seem only like ineffective policy, but in fact, Obama's internal force compels him to sacrifice effective policy to sustain an unconscious ideological belief system. And, after all, he has passed more new legislation than any Democrat since LBJ, so some may argue that he's right to be obsessed; he certainly cites his legislative accomplishments when attacking the Left for being too unrealistically demanding. He can justify his emotional condition by pointing to legislation he has passed—albeit at the price of continued tax breaks for the rich and massive gifts to medical insurance companies. As I stated earlier, reality is a defense that he uses effectively; like many smart people, he can justify his behavior based on material facts and brilliantly defend his actions while completely disregarding or projecting unconscious fantasies so clearly and totally that they are impossible to detect.

Observers who share Obama's background in community organization might also see nothing pathological about his approach. His relentless pursuit of compromise is certainly consistent with a community organizer's mind-set—indeed, is perhaps more reminiscent of a chief organizer than a chief executive—as is his vision of living in a community that tolerates difference and continues to grow. But even a community organizer can't be effective when one segment of the community is as uncooperative as the Republican leadership's insistence in late 2010 that preventing Obama's reelection was a higher priority than governing. Seen in its full and unprecedented destructiveness, which in early January spilled over into violence in Arizona with the tragic killing of six innocents and the serious wounding of Representative Giffords that some found shocking but close observers saw as inevitable, the Republicans' position is dangerous not just to the Democrats but to our very democracy and transforms Obama's vision of community into a misleading fantasy. It is also a violent reaction against Obama's vision that includes having people respect one another—enough to accept that a black person could indeed be president. Racial hatred is not exclusive to Republicans, to be sure, but the criticism that disappointed Democrats level at Obama—at least the part of the criticism that isn't racist, which we'll later see is present in many of the attacks on Obama—is not hate-based the way it so clearly is on the part of a majority of Republicans. The Left is also critical of him, attacking him for "selling out" to big corporations. Many on the left are fed up. But the destructive murderousness just isn't there, despite overwhelming frustration and a sense of betrayal.

Given the extent of the danger the Right poses to the republic, trying to accommodate individuals committed to his destruction is unhealthy, yet Obama persists despite the urgency. Rather than seeing the danger, he disconnects from himself—something that started in a palpable way with the broadsides he got on health care reform, when he seemed to switch off after being accused of promoting death panels. The old fears of annihilation, as adumbrated in that magazine article when he was nine, reared their ugly head, and he retreated into himself. Once perceived as a strength and capacity to be above the fray by driving the opposition crazy, his calm demeanor is more accurately understood as a kind of paralyzed dissociation. Those pundits who think he was clever to bring out his birth certificate to refute Donald Trump may be right, as well as those who think it was tactical and shrewd to let Congressman Paul Ryan's budget proposals be hoisted on their own petard. That seems less consistent with Obama's psychological profile than with a tendency toward wishful thinking on the part of his supporters, who can't bear to think that their hero has blind spots or, even worse, character defects.

Behind that persistence, we see at work factors that trace back to Obama's drive to heal his racial split, to deal with his father's departure, and to manage his unspoken rage at both parents. Obama's bipartisan disorder is fueled in part by a need to reconstitute his family of origin, as well as to integrate his black and white selves. He wants a family more than anything, a defense against visiting the murderous feelings against his father—or at least against finding out whether they in fact exist. His search for family is displaced onto his relentless pursuit of compromise and his choice of the community organization model for his presidency so far. The fantasy of a restored family also rehabilitates his diminished and disappointing father and defends against his visiting his repressed, murderous feelings against him. He is relentless in that pursuit, despite having created with Michelle a deeply connected and loving family of his own. He wants, and keeps trying, to do the same with the American people.

Obama's need to accommodate is equally relentless; he mentions what people have in common every chance he gets. You can hear it everywhere from his truly great speeches to his minor spontaneous remarks: he sees what we have that unites rather than divides us all. He still sees it in his family, as well. Visiting his half sister Auma in Kenya in 1988, their conversations often turn to dreams—mostly to her dreams. She had dreams not that different from his:

> *Sometimes I have this dream that I will build a beautiful house on our grandfather's land. A big house "where we can all stay and bring our families, you see. We could plant fruit trees like our grandfather, and*

our children would really know the land and speak Luo and learn our ways from the old people. . . . It would belong to them."

"We can do all that, Auma."

She shook her head. ". . . All I can do when I think this way is to get mad at the Old Man because he didn't build this house for us. We are the children, Barack. Why do we have to take care of everyone? Everything is upside down, crazy. I had to take care of myself."

There is a vacuum—a male vacuum—in this family. And Barack still denies his anger at his father—despite his earlier dig at his father's letters that were full of what he called "dime store advice"— and finds it easier to describe his half sister Auma's rage and hurt. It's ironic that a person who clearly hates having to clean up other people's messes got elected president to do that very thing. He thus accommodates to evade rage, to evade the kind of clear thinking that Auma seems able to do. She doesn't let up, however, saying to her half brother, "'That's why I keep coming home. That's why I'm still dreaming.'" She needs to come home to remind herself of that rage.

What is this process, and does it not apply to all of us at one time or another in our lives? We dream—and Obama calls those dreams audacious and worth pursuing. And that message inspires. Unconsciously, however, it's hard not to call those dreams a variant of denial, as we see in people who deny evolution and science or who deny the realities of global warming. In those cases we can see the cause, even—that this kind of denial is a response to overwhelming fear of facing facts. Recently several psychoanalysts in Great Britain described this kind of hopeful dreaming as the attraction to nonthought, the unconscious avoidance of thinking. It was easy to see that thinking provoked anxiety in the nuance-averse George W. Bush, but it's harder to talk about Obama as someone attracted to not thinking, other than his insistence on accommodation. Obama's impulse to accommodate comes so automatically that it is a form of thought avoidance, which to him justifies his need to seek common ground whenever possible. Because he believes he can convince the Republicans that they share enough common ground, he thinks there is nothing to fear in their attack machines. This confidence that we have such a great possibility to get along is a bulwark against the overwhelming fear that there really is murder in the air. He runs after the Republicans while looking over his shoulder to shush (or worse) the Left for fear that it will interfere with his accommodation efforts.

Attraction to thought avoidance is based on fear; in his case it is fear of taking charge because he has been clinging so long to accommodation as the way to get things done that he avoids thinking clearly about the necessity to stand up against the opposition or to own the powerful influence he has over his followers through the dynamic of transference. Evading the acceptance of the power of transference is something I see in beginning psychiatry students, who often fail to understand how important they are to their patients, because it creates too much anxiety and too great a sense of responsibility. It may be the same for beginning presidents. Adding to this dynamic in Obama's case is the difficulty of acting as a father figure when he must evade so many of his feelings toward his own father. He doesn't have an internal model of a father figure, so he clings to other presidents to define what a president is and does. Hence his admiration for President Ronald Reagan, whom he saw as "transformative"—the same word he used to describe his father's speech to his fourth-grade class.

Perhaps he thinks his office alone explains his power. Though the presidency confers transference power regardless of who occupies the office, Obama seems to be unsure of a power that history suggests others saw in him long before he became president and that he was able to use to his advantage as far back as his college days. And although unconscious identification of Obama as a father figure inevitably varies greatly among individuals and groups, he often seems unwilling or unable to provide the father figure that the nation has been looking to him to become. It's hard to be a father figure if one has never felt anger at one's own father. But then he killed bin Laden, someone so apparently unlike his father that he didn't have to threaten his discomfort about killing someone he cared about. And he had people to care about during the process: he said on *60 Minutes* that he was so concerned about the well-being of the SEAL team that he would not go ahead with the mission unless there were clear contingency plans for their safety should the initial assault misfire. He managed to have no internal conflict, as he clearly indicated in the same interview. He was protecting his American family by killing off its greatest sworn enemy.

Obama is capable of being decisive, as we've now seen from the bin Laden raid, but he can't manage to confront the destructive hatred directed against him here at home. By evading that part of his personality, Obama is doing all of us a phenomenal disservice, giving the nation an accommodator in chief when it needs a decisive commander.

CHAPTER 4

Calming Words

Tell all the Truth, but tell it slant—
Success in Circuit lies
Too bright for our infirm Delight
The Truth's superb surprise
As Lightning to the Children eased
With explanation kind
The Truth must dazzle gradually
Or every man be blind
—Emily Dickinson

The greatness of our democracy is grounded in our ability to move beyond our differences.
—Barack Obama, Cairo, June 4, 2009

Barack Obama owes his political career to his words. It's hard to imagine Obama as president without his prior renown as an orator and memoirist. His speeches made him a national political figure long before he assembled a record of accomplishments commensurate with his reputation. His books made him a household name and a wealthy man, the first president since John F. Kennedy to become a best-selling author before publishing his presidential memoirs.

Though it made scant impression when originally published in 1995—readers showed little interest in the artfully rendered memoir of the first black president of the *Harvard Law Review*—*Dreams from My Father* defied typical publishing sales patterns to become a multimillion-copy phenomenon almost ten years after publication, in the wake of his 2004 convention keynote address. Its style and

91

construction were closer to the publishing norm, however, employing many of the conceits favored by memoirists in the category's 1990s heyday, including the use of composite characters, conversations reconstructed with improbable accuracy, multiple points of view, and sudden, almost cinematic shifts in time and place, all designed to shape the reader's emotional response. In short, he told a story to create an experience for the reader—a process that included sometimes modifying the truth or facts in ways consistent with the genre convention in order to enhance the impact and effect he desired his story to have.

Obama's storytelling prowess and priorities are hardly surprising in light of his childhood, which was shaped by the myths and tales his mother and grandparents spun about his father: stories that were "compact, apocryphal, told in rapid succession in the course of one evening, then packed away for months, sometimes years, in my family's memory," he wrote in *Dreams from My Father*. By that point, his mother had begun seeing the man who would become her second husband, and young Obama "sensed without explanation" that the old photos had been removed from public display and put into storage. "But once in a while, sitting on the floor with my mother, the smell of dust and mothballs rising from the crumbling album, I would stare at my father's likeness—the dark laughing face, the prominent forehead and thick glasses that made him appear older than his years—and listen as the events of his life tumbled into a single narrative."

Obama recounted the unlikely tale of his father's journey and parents' marriage with the studied simplicity of myth:

In 1959, at the age of twenty-three, he arrived at the University of Hawaii as that institution's first African student. He studied econometrics, worked with unsurpassed concentration, and graduated in three years at the top of his class. His friends were legion, and he helped organize the International Students Association, of which he became the first president. In a Russian language course, he met an awkward, shy American girl, only eighteen, and they fell in love. The girl's parents, wary at first, were won over by his charm and intellect; the young couple married, and she bore them a son, to whom he bequeathed his name. He won another scholarship—this time to pursue his Ph.D. at Harvard—but not the money to take his new family with him. A separation occurred, and he returned to Africa to fulfill his promise to the continent. The mother and child stayed behind, but the bond of love survived the distances. . . .

There the album would close, and I would wander off content, swaddled in a tale that placed me in the center of a vast and orderly universe. Even in the abridged version that my mother and grandparents offered, there were many things I didn't understand. But I rarely asked for the details that might resolve the meaning of "Ph.D." or "colonialism," or locate Alego on a map. Instead, the path of my father's life occupied the same terrain as a book my mother once bought for me, a book called Origins, *a collection of creation tales from around the world, stories of Genesis and the tree where man was born, Prometheus and the gift of fire, the tortoise of Hindu legend that floated in space, supporting the weight of the world on its back. Later, when I became more familiar with the narrower path to happiness to be found in television and the movies, I'd become troubled by questions. What supported the tortoise? Why did an omnipotent God let a snake cause such grief? Why didn't my father return? But at the age of five or six I was satisfied to leave these distant mysteries intact, to be carried off into peaceful dreams.*

Obama the storyteller described himself as *swaddled* in stories and words, a direct nod to the psychological function that can be performed by language, as it contains our thoughts and anxieties to make them manageable. Notably, it wasn't until years after reading the *Origins* myths that he raised questions about the circumstances of his own origins and the connections between the plight of the tortoise and the threat of the snake and his own uncertain future. Until then, the words had been enough to keep him from wondering why his father didn't return. Consciously or not, he understands that language can have a powerful effect distinct from its meaning— an awareness that Obama the best-selling memoirist leveraged with enormous skill and impact. Now, as president, Obama still resides inside words, just as he, as a child, lived inside stories woven by his mother. But now he plays the linguistic role of the parent as well, swaddling his national family in language and stories. His words can be very comforting, inspiring, and even seductive. But as we'll see, he uses language to create emotions that can obscure meaning, doing as president what he did so well as memoirist. This is a hazard of being governed by a writer to which we should all pay heed.

The practice of swaddling gives us useful insight into the role language and story played in Obama's childhood and how he uses them today. The mother swaddles the child to calm it. Binding its fragmented selves into something whole is not only calming; it can be inspiring and confidence-building. It was so for our young president when he was a small child. And it is thus for us, as he swaddles us in order to soothe and unite our fragmented selves and nation into something whole—to wrap us in a blanket of hope. Swaddling is about containing, to be sure, but it is also about the assertion of authority implicit in a parent's ability to bind the infant together, an unconscious awareness of how fragmented the life of an infant must feel. The mother's understanding of this is often instinctive; it was likely even stronger in the case of Obama's mother, who remembered her own fragmented past, which had included periods living in California, Oklahoma, Texas, Kansas, and Washington, in addition to Hawaii. She also didn't want her son to have any sense of the fragmentation she was feeling in her own unstable marriage.

In terms of early psychological development, swaddling is linked to what's known as the "containing function"—the process by which a baby's distress is modified and alleviated by the mother's thinking and feeling about what is bothering her baby and then taking appropriate action, of which swaddling is but one example. The mother contains the baby's discomfort, and the baby makes a link between its mother and the relief she provides. In this way the baby begins to modify its preconceptions and internalize the capacity for thought; as the process of assigning meaning to its experiences starts to evolve, the baby associates the phenomenon of meaning with the comfort it received simply by having its mother contain and relieve its chaotic discomfort.

Word swaddling, to give this practice a name, offers the possibility of containing, but without assigning particular meaning. In the infant's preverbal state, the mother's words soothe through the tone and emotion conveyed within by the sounds, far more than any meaning in the words. With time, the mother's use of words to describe experiences helps create meaning. Giving words to feelings is an ongoing process in the infant-mother relationship, and as the mother creates her thoughts and conveys them to her baby, the baby over time internalizes her words and links them to his own feelings—giving them meaning. Through her own reverie the mother can sense what the baby is feeling and take the appropriate action: when she thinks the baby is hungry, she feeds it; when she thinks the baby is wet, she changes it. Over time the baby internalizes this interactive process and develops thoughts that can be used to create further meaning, and so on. This back-and-forth process can be easily observed when spending time with a mother and her infant—particularly if the mother is especially verbal, assisting the baby as it builds up an internal conceptual world. How the mother feels about her baby's cries leads to having thoughts about their meaning; but the mother's internal state also contributes to her interpretation of those cries—so if Ann were angry with her husband for having left her, she might have heard Barry's cries as expressions of rage rather than of need. Staying in tune is easier for a mother when her internal world is stable and when she can rely on having an internal couple to help her care for her baby. Part of the reason for Ann's keeping the myth of Barack Sr. so present in young Barry's life is that it helped solidify her own internal world as well.

Naturally, the capacity for connecting language and meaning eventually develops and takes on special resonance for a child who remembers his mother's storytelling practice as a calming influence as powerfully as Obama does. Language is still related to the containing function. A word contains a meaning, and a meaning can contain a word; there is an internal interaction between word and meaning much the way there is between container and contained and between mother and infant. Ann was reportedly quite the storyteller; Obama's half sister Maya also wrote about their mother's incredible storytelling prowess and how central that experience was to her own childhood. For young Barry, swaddled in words and stories, language and his mother's use of it became the container for his anxieties, first the typical fears and discomforts of an infant, then the particular concerns of a young child whose father has disappeared but remains present in stories. Looking into the face of a mother who didn't look like him, as she spun tales to keep his absent father present, young Barry learned that language could ward off irrational forces within himself and give him the means of reaching out, connecting, and explaining the inexplicable sorrow of loss, just as his mother showed him. Transforming her own anxiety about her abandonment into thoughts and words that soothed her child, Obama's storytelling mother created the model for the use of language that he has used for the rest of his life, calming himself and his listeners by creating an "ordered universe" with his words and thoughts.

His mother also used words to convey excitement, as an expression of her enthusiasm—something that was very much part of her. When she decided to marry Lolo and move Barry to Jakarta, she enthusiastically gathered information about their new country and started working on learning the language. By then Barry was almost six and understood clearly what she was saying—but the maternal tone of excitement would have been reminiscent of earlier experiences before words had additional, nonverbal, associative meaning to him.

As an adult, Obama has been successful at managing his internal anxiety by transforming it through words and thought—writing, thinking about and discussing issues, using anxiety as a source of information—a signal to the self to pay attention to whatever is causing the anxiety rather than as something to be evaded or avoided at all costs. In this way language still performs a calming function by making anxiety into something useful instead of something to be denied or evaded, converting feelings into thoughts that can be effectively used on the very emotions producing the anxiety. This process unconsciously links Obama to his first model of soothing containment, further enhancing the soothing capacity of language by centering him in relationship to his mother, the word swaddler, with whom he reconnects by using the gift of language that she lavished on him. He has a patient way of explaining things at times, much the way a mother explains something to her child. We see both qualities in his March 24, 2009, press conference at the height of the financial-crisis panic, when he patiently explained how AIG was different from a bank and thus "more problematic" to regulate; then, moments later, when the reporter Ed Henry twice asked why Obama had waited so long before criticizing AIG. He said, "It took us a couple of days because I like to know what I'm talking about before I speak." Clearly he was annoyed, but even then he was like an annoyed but patient parent.

Obama's mother used language like music with her young son, creating a melody to help salve his wounds. She read to him, talked to him about his father, and her song helped him keep his balance, preventing him from being too depressed or too enraged when asking about his father's having left the family. She anticipated his questions and sang enough to keep that melody going inside him, surrounding him with an internal protective shield. But there was a delinquent part to the song, because the words—though beautiful—were ultimately hollow, unable to cure his yearning with anything real and palpable. And the song meant even less than it appeared to, as she herself would later abandon him to do her field research, sending him back to his grandparents while keeping her other child with her.

Despite the music in Ann's song for Barry's father, the gap between her words and the truth created dissonance as well, and Barry had to find out the truth for himself. And though he did try in some ways to define who his father was in order to differentiate fact from fantasy, he was only partially successful. One way to manage a discordant but beautiful song is to reverse roles—to become the singer instead of the listener. In adulthood Obama has become the singer of his mother's soothing song, helping to salve the wounds of a troubled nation. And like his mother, he offers a song whose words often mean less than the melody, leaving many of his supporters as full of yearning and longing for a leader as he was for a father. This behavior is an early part of mourning, becoming identified with the lost mother and singing us her song. But there is also an element of aggression bound up in the song, namely, telling her he knows the hollowness of the myths she fed to him and that he recognizes he is giving the American people something akin to what he was given.

Still, when he wrote about his mother in the 2004 edition of

Dreams from My Father, which was originally published just months before her death in 1995, Obama used words to convey love in as poetic and caressing a way as any reader is likely ever to encounter:

> *I think sometimes that had I known she would not survive her illness, I might have written a different book—less a meditation on the absent parent, more a celebration of the one who was the single constant in my life. In my daughters I see her every day, her joy, her capacity for wonder. I won't try to describe how deeply I mourn her passing still. I know that she was the kindest, most generous spirit I have ever known, and that what is best in me I owe to her.*

His writing evokes in me not just empathy for him and the absolute loss of his first north star but also makes me feel that he knows me and knows how I felt about my own mother. I feel understood by him, just as I understand him. Thus his words are both containing and contained; they communicate deep emotional meaning of the kind that has its earliest source inside the mother-infant nursing couple.

The passage and its impact on the reader show just how fruitful and supportive that early dynamic was for Obama. As he unconsciously transfers his feelings to the reader, Obama echoes the process between mother and infant by which the infant receives both love (the contained) and the ability to think about that love (the container), a capacity that over time evolves into his own ability to reflect and process thoughts that are also freighted with feeling. People who have spent time with Obama often describe this phenomenon in one way or another, observing how good a listener he is, how responsive he is, how he thinks in such a rich way about what is conveyed to him verbally or even by a nonverbal glance. There's every indication that he is this way with his children, too—passing along a deep capacity for connection that he developed from within the same dynamic with his mother from which his linguistic gifts were born.

The reader of his memoir can trace his development of these gifts in tangent with his acquiring the insight and skills to wrestle with the issues he was facing. Demonstrating his acute appreciation for words and their power, for example, he wrote: "*Miscegenation*. The word is humpbacked, ugly, portending a monstrous outcome: like *antebellum* or *octoroon,* it evokes images of another era, a distant world of horsewhips and flames, dead magnolias and crumbling porticos." Attentive to the danger of sloppy word usage and the sloppy thinking that went with it, he defined words carefully, using them to make himself think as deeply as possible about the challenges he faced. For instance, he realized in high school that the term "white folks"—which he and his black friend Ray used—made him uncomfortable: the phrase evoked for him a loving image of his "mother's smile," but upon reflection he saw that the phrase typically connoted distrust. But he did not back down when confronted—at least as he wrote about it. He shot back at his high school basketball coach, "There are white folks, and then there are ignorant motherfuckers like you," after the coach tried unself-consciously to distinguish between "black folks" and "niggers."

In time, his appreciation of the power of language expanded beyond how he used it in relationship with himself to how he used it with others. The critical juncture in this process—indeed, in retrospect, a critical juncture in the history of our nation—occurred when he made his public speaking debut in his sophomore year at Occidental College. The occasion was a rally during which Obama was supposed to make a few opening remarks; but his speech was only meant to be a bit of agitprop to launch the theatrical demonstration against apartheid. As he spoke, he would be carried off the stage by students in paramilitary uniforms, as if they were in Johannesburg.

Prior to the day of the rally, Obama had a transformative conversation with a fellow black student, a girl named Regina, in which they openly discussed their families in a way Obama had yet to really do with anyone. In talking about the struggles her mother faced as a single mom, she invited him to be open about himself for the first time in his life—using real words with real meaning as he talked about his own chaotic family life. Interestingly, this is almost the first time in the entire book that the fact of his having a single mother is presented. His recollection of this moment with Regina allowed him to set the scene of the speech at the rally, during which he describes how thinking about his father's voice allows him to find his own.

He began the memory with a moment of disingenuously casual uncertainty: "Let's see, now. What was it that I had been thinking in those days leading up to the rally?" His role in the carefully choreographed rally was minimal, but the meaning he assigned it was not:

I was only supposed to make a few opening remarks in the middle of which a couple of white students would come onstage dressed in their paramilitary uniforms to drag me away. A bit of street theater, a way to dramatize the situation for activists in South Africa. I knew the score, had helped plan the script. Only, when I sat down to prepare a few notes for what I might say, something had happened. In my mind it somehow became more than just a two-minute speech, more than a way to prove my political orthodoxy. I started to remember my father's visit to Miss Hefty's class; the look on Coretta's face that day; the power of my father's words to transform. If I could just find the right words, I had thought to myself. With the right words everything could change—South Africa, the lives of ghetto kids just a few miles away, my own tenuous place in the world.

These thoughts put him into what he describes as a "trancelike state" when he reaches the stage before a restless crowd of a few hundred.

"There's a struggle going on," I said. My voice barely carried beyond the first few rows. A few people looked up, and I waited for the crowd to quiet.

"I say, there's a struggle going on!"

The Frisbee players stopped.

"It's happening an ocean away. But it's a struggle that touches each and every one of us. Whether we know it or not. Whether we want it or not. A struggle that demands we choose sides. Not between black and white. Not between rich and poor. No—it's a harder choice than that. It's a choice between dignity and servitude. Between fairness and injustice. Between commitment and indifference. A choice between right and wrong . . ."

I stopped. The crowd was quiet now, watching me. Somebody started to clap. "Go on with it, Barack," somebody else shouted. "Tell it like it is." Then the others started in, clapping, cheering, and I knew that I had them, that the connection had been made. I took hold of the mike, ready to plunge on, when I felt someone's hands grabbing me from behind. It was just as we'd planned it, Andy and Jonathan looking grim-faced behind their dark glasses. They started yanking me off the stage, and I was supposed to act like I was trying to break free, except a part of me wasn't acting, I really wanted to stay up there, to hear my voice bounding off the crowd and returning back to me in applause. I had so much left to say.

He is followed on stage by Marcus and Regina, but whereas he "should have been proud of them," he distances himself from the entire effort, returning to "the outside again, watching, judging, skeptical." In his self-critical assessment, he and the protesters "suddenly appeared like the sleek and well-fed amateurs we were. . . . The whole thing was a farce, I thought to myself—the rally, the banners, everything. A pleasant afternoon diversion, a school play without the parents. And me and my one-minute oration—the biggest farce of all."

When Regina later offers her congratulations, he responds with dismissive sarcasm, resisting her observation that he was so effective because he "spoke from the heart."

"Listen, Regina," I said, cutting her off, "you are a very sweet lady. And I'm happy you enjoyed my little performance today. But that's the last time you will ever hear another speech out of me. I'm going to leave the preaching to you. And to Marcus. Me, I've decided I've got no business speaking for black folks."

"And why is that?"

I sipped on my beer, my eyes wandering over the dancers in front of us. "Because I've got nothing to say, Regina. I don't believe we made any difference by what we did today. I don't believe that what happens to a kid in Soweto makes much difference to the people we were talking to. Pretty words don't make it so. So why do I pretend otherwise? I'll tell you why. Because it makes me feel important. Because I like the applause. It gives me a nice, cheap thrill. That's all."

"You don't really believe that."
"That's what I believe."

It's impossible to read this account today and not think of other "transformative" speeches that Obama has delivered in the decades hence. Years from now, we may learn what memories resurfaced for Obama in the moments before his 2004 keynote or 2009 inaugural address—or learn at least what he wants us to believe he remembers resurfacing, from the point of view of the presidential memoirist. When Obama eventually does write his presidential memoir, it will no doubt be the best-written presidential memoir ever published. But it's unlikely that it will show him as freely associating to such revealing effect as moments like this one in *Dreams from My Father*.

Revisiting the memories of his father and Coretta, the only other black Punahou student in his fourth-grade class, whose friendship he betrayed, Obama reveals that much of the "transformative" healing he hopes to accomplish through his speech is personal and internal. He seeks to repair the damage he did to Coretta with his eloquence, just as his father's words did when he spoke to their class—and in so doing, he seeks to repair the damage he did to himself, back when trampling on the girl's feelings left him feeling trampled upon, too. His shame and guilt were enormous. He seeks also to identify with his father—again attempting to repair damage both to his father and to himself. But the reparation is magical and indirect, dependent upon the power of words to heal without the risk or exposure of direct apology or amends—a harbinger of the magical faith in language he will express in subsequent years. At one level, however, writing about his feelings was all he could do to repair the damage to Coretta, perhaps in the hope that she might someday read what he wrote.

This is, of course, a lot of psychological weight to put on what was supposed to be a demonstration, nothing more to him than theater, and at some level Obama—either in the event or looking back on it—recognized the grandiosity of his fantasies, as he is too precise a writer and thinker to suggest that "with the right" anything that "everything could change." The trancelike state that he described was an altered self-state, as if he had climbed inside the words he was about to say—living inside them and swaddled once again by their carrying so much possibility that he actually believed his grandiose dream. He is describing a living reverie, suddenly interrupted by a plan he appeared to forget once he got started.

It seems as though he didn't exactly know what Regina was referring to when she later complimented his speech. Already emptied out from within those grandiloquent words, he felt ashamed and like a fraud. Not only that, he had a link to his father and the emptiness of his words—something that led him to deflect Regina's praise in a self-hating way. This set up the denial of the impact that the speech had on him that he explained to Regina after it was over. Despite his need to undermine the authenticity of the moment, something clearly got to him on that stage, and he needed to undo what he had done, to unconsciously disparage the powerful moment of finding his voice. But after it was over he felt as if it weren't his voice, that he wasn't authentic. Feeling inauthentic also protected him from feeling carried away by the thrill of having so much power over others. Given what he wrote about his thoughts before the speech, he seems to have suddenly become confused with his father and had to devalue the entire experience. He yearned to identify with the idealized father, but once he succeeded in doing so he faced the other side of his ambivalence, his awareness of how hollow his father's words ultimately were—because they were hollow to him growing up, full of "dime store" platitudes. By the time Obama was in college, his father's words meant less and less to him, a feeling that coexisted with his having once felt them as transformative—at least to fourth-graders.

Inevitably, it wasn't simply the act of speaking that held meaning but the particular words that were said, few though they were. There was indeed "a struggle going on," as he repeatedly told his listeners. The struggle was going on inside—and had been for a while—having to do with dignity and self-respect. He is as much speaking to his own fear of not belonging that led him to sacrifice Coretta's dignity, and his own, in order for him to join the bullies. This fear remains an issue for him to this very day; he is unconsciously torn between needing to belong and needing to do the right thing—a dilemma complicated by the fact that both his parents tried to do the latter when at times they devoted themselves—in different ways—to their own dreams rather than to the here-and-now needs of their son. They were doing what they felt was right, what was true to themselves. The irony is that they ended up marginalized by most of the world, including by their son, as in when he describes them as hopelessly idealistic liberals. Though he was ostensibly supposed to be acting, he found himself giving voice to his inner struggle to become authentic. He "had" the audience before he was grabbed from his trance. Since he had been in an altered state, his sense of what had happened became less real and he couldn't understand or even tolerate Regina's positive reaction.

We're left to ask what really scared him, whether it was truly and simply the jarring disconnect from his audience that he suddenly perceived as disinterested, along with the trustees who "chuckled" at the gathering. The presence (or rather present absence) of his parents in the story suggests that they are part of the explanation—that he was scared to sound like his mother or afraid of sounding more powerful or persuasive than his father. Perhaps he felt that his grandiosity was exposed, he forgot it was only theater, that he was only playing the role of an activist—an auspiciously ironic beginning to a lifetime of public speaking and a career in activist politics. The fact that he suddenly realized he was pretending certainly limited the extent to which he could attain the sense of authentic belonging that he sought and underscored the limits of the reparative power he yearned to invest in his words. The struggle going on shifted between living inside a rhetoric that conferred a sense of power and belief and being aware that his words were just that, words he used to prove himself legitimate and more mature than he felt inside.

Words are vehicles of understanding that allow the listener to transform thought into action. Witnessing one's words inducing action in a listener can be a significant confidence builder for the speaker, just as the reverse can have the opposite effect. In his public speaking debut, Obama experienced both results; he saw and heard his immediate impact on the crowd but concluded that his words' long-term effects were minimal (the students quickly return to playing Frisbee, for example). He went into the event with an unrealistic assessment of his words' and voice's potential. He thought that in using them he could live up to his father's transformative gifts, give his "own tenuous place in the world" a surer foundation, solve the intractable conflicts in South Africa, live up to the wildly overstated expectation that "with the right words, everything could change." We see here the roots of his almost magical faith in the power of his words, uttered from a trancelike state, savoring the intangible connection he makes with the audience despite the brevity of his remarks. "I knew that I had them, that the connection had been made." The action he induced in his listeners in this case was the act of connecting, establishing a pattern that would continue for years to come.

Investing words with magical attributes is a form of the deluded belief that wishing makes it so. Since words are precursors of action, magical language presupposes that saying something is the same as doing it; thus saying something out loud makes it a fact. The example famous among analysts is the patient who asks, "After my analysis, will I be able to play the piano?" The analyst says, "Yes, if you remove the emotional barriers to doing it." The patient says, "Good, I always wanted to play the piano." Obama addresses this in his postdebut speech conversation with Regina, to whom he says, "Pretty words don't make it so. So why do I pretend otherwise?" Not surprisingly, his answer to his own question—"Because it makes me feel important. Because I like the applause. It gives me a nice, cheap thrill"—misses the mark. It also represents the sudden appearance of self-hatred, of putting himself down after what he initially felt was a psychological breakthrough. This offers a glimpse of a tendency we still see today—that after he gives a powerful speech that affects crowds, he tends to keep a low profile on the content of that speech, at the risk of undermining the long-term impact of his message. It seems almost automatic, most dramatically in the aftermath of his race speech in Philadelphia in 2008, after which he seemed to avoid the topic of race. In his college experience, Regina liked his speech and felt it was strong, but he pushed her away because he felt he didn't have genuine passion behind his words. His race speech in

Philadelphia was far more than just words, but even so, he retreated after that, confusing pretty words with substance. What he didn't realize was that just because his words were pretty it didn't mean that they were without substance. As a psychoanalyst there is a technique called "working through," which means repeating an accurate interpretation regularly over time. Obama needed to repeat in future campaign speeches, with whatever variations he needed to use, his ideas about race and about separating people from their prejudice. By doing so he would have internally separated himself from his father, rather than reverting to his father's once-a-year communication pattern.

Obama learned about pretty words from his mother, who taught him by example that pretty words do in fact make something true or real—at least until they're proven wrong. The source of magical thinking is an unspoken understanding parents have with their young children, as when they give a flashlight to a frightened child so he can scare away all the monsters; in adulthood, Obama indulges in the same magical thinking and use of language that his mother did in spinning myths about his father. Though the thrill he gets is far from cheap, he's right that it makes him feel important—as important as an infant is to his mother. Thus he connects with his primary model of the power of magical thinking, which was guided by his mother's belief that providing positive examples of her abandoning husband would ensure that he live inside the mind of her son in a fresh and vibrant way, changed from who he actually was into someone far more loving and benign, someone whose dreams were valid and worth pursuing and whose heavy drinking, womanizing, and abusiveness receded from awareness.

It was from stories about his father that Obama learned the power of using words to reach into the preconceptions of others and effect change. Those stories contained and stimulated the imagination of a young boy, who could thus imagine possibilities while at the same time being calmed in the face of genuine hatred. They gave Obama his first experience with the hypnotic power of narrative and how it could put one into a kind of blissful trance—the trance recalled by his Occidental College debut. Obama recounts that each story told by his family was "seamless, burnished smooth from repeated use."

This is where the orator learned the beginning of his trade, at the feet of two, maybe three—his grandmother Toot also participated—spellbinding storytellers.

Obama's adult expression of magical language is seen in his conflating words with action, something he does more often as president than he did as a candidate. His words urge his followers to work for him, but as president he has seemed to equate saying something with getting it done—as if talking about ending tax breaks for the rich were the same as doing it. In one sense his words are his actions; whenever there is a tough situation, he gives a speech, relying on his rhetoric to save the day. He has a magical relationship to the oratorical process itself. Sometimes it works, as in his generally well-received speech in Tucson after the January 2011 shootings. He united the nation in mourning and in condemning the violence of that day—but that is not the same as denouncing hateful rhetoric or promoting gun control. At the time, however, the speech served the purpose of an emotional equation between sentiment and act—something mothers and fathers often achieve with their bedtime stories.

But sometimes his words fail him, as they did in his long overdue response to the Gulf oil spill on June 15, 2010, almost two months after the rig's mid-April explosion. In the weeks after the spill, we waited for Obama to speak with the magical healing effect he has brought to past speeches and then were disappointed when he hid behind citing others' credentials, telling the nation that "just after the rig sank [he] assembled a team of our nation's best scientists and engineers to tackle this challenge, a team led by Dr. Steven Chu, a Nobel Prize–winning physicist and our nation's secretary of energy," then pointing out that the cleanup effort was being led by "Admiral Thad Allen, who has almost forty years of experience responding to disasters." He then concluded his unconvincing show of anger with an ineffective call to unity through prayer—substituting prayer for action, thereby treating it as a kind of action. Perhaps, by expecting more, his audience also conflates words with action—awaiting the magical change—and he counts on his supporters doing that as a way to satisfy them and, by extension, himself.

It's understandable that Obama might conflate words with action. In many respects, his words are his most visible and effective actions: writing books that would eventually make him wealthy and famous—almost magically so, since his first book was all but forgotten until it became a big-money best seller almost a decade after publication—and giving speeches that made him even more famous and powerful. For Obama, oratory is action—he induces his audiences to construct him as a container for their dreams and experiences the power of his language when they do. He's aware of his effectiveness as a speaker; when Senator Harry Reid complimented him on it, as Reid reported in the 2009 edition of his memoir *The Good Fight,* Obama simply and quietly replied "I have a gift, Harry." But the notion of the "gift" of effective oratory also leads directly to the tendency to imbue language with magical powers: the essence of his effectiveness is a gift, something bestowed on him, rather than a skill or a practice.

His belief in the power of his words as action can also be glimpsed in Richard Wolffe's account in *Revival* of the development of his 2008 campaign slogan and catchphrases, in which he describes the pollster Joel Benenson's observation that Obama resisted having to repeat words, phrases, and passages from previous speeches, as if his having spoken the words once was action enough. Believing in the magic of his words and in the "gift" of his ability to deliver them, he seems to sometimes forget that words are the end result of a long process of writing, editing, and refining that gives them their power, enabling them to more closely substitute for action—and views them as powerful actions in and of themselves. At the same time, by calling it a gift, he seems humble in the face of genuine power. He is also able to deny to others the amount of work put into crafting a good speech, like the classroom stars we all remember who gave the impression—perhaps falsely—that they didn't spend much time studying.

The moment when Obama's tendency to conflate words and action revealed itself most clearly may have been in his Oval Office address in which he declared the end of combat missions in Iraq. After telling the American people that "Through this remarkable chapter in the history of the United States and Iraq, we have met our responsibility," he concluded. "Now it's time to turn the page." It's not surprising that Obama would see U.S. history as a series of "chapter" divisions. Ever the author, consciously or not, he seeks to contain all of the controversy, misconduct, and tragic loss of life and treasure of the war he successfully ran against in the same basic organizational unit within which he contains his life story in his best-selling memoirs. But beyond containing history in a chapter, he wants to incite action in the form of turning the page. He's using a common metaphor to encourage us to move on, of course, but he's doing so by asking us to replace one set of words with another. This is made even more interesting by Obama's ambivalent relationship with the phrase. When the McCain campaign suggested that it was time to "turn the page" on the economic crisis in early October 2008, Obama pounced on the remark: "We're facing the worst economic crisis since the Great Depression, and John McCain wants us to 'turn the page'?" The idea that progress could be as simple as turning the page—as replacing one set of words with another—was grounds for attack in early October. But by the end of the month, Obama was telling voters with a straight face that on election day they "can turn the page on policies that have put the greed and irresponsibility of Wall Street before the hard work and sacrifice of folks on Main Street." Two years later, he's turning the page on the war that was so central to his election—and its origins and monetary scandals that he won't investigate now that he is president. The conviction with which he unapologetically adapted the phrase and its conflation of language and action is astonishing, suggesting an audacity of trope so pronounced that it must be unconscious.

The substitution of words for action is familiar to astute Obama observers and points to a significant dynamic underlying his entire approach to language that is as pervasive as it is instructive. The psychoanalyst Wilfred Bion distinguished between "the language of substitution," in which words are used to evade their genuine meaning rather than express the feared emotional truth that lurks below the facile use of symbols, and "the Language of Achievement," in which words are used to formulate thoughts and draw conclusions and serve as a prelude to action rather than a replacement for it.

The Language of Achievement fosters growth and involves the capacity to manage emotions, serving as a prelude to action or genuine understanding by linking reason and love. When he said in his

April 13, 2011, speech on the deficit at George Washington University that the Republicans' plan to use vouchers for health care was unacceptable, he was thinking and feeling, using reason and love to make clear where he stood. There is a receptive element in the Language of Achievement that is characterized by listening with an open mind. Finally, the Language of Achievement invokes shared process, an admission that the speaker is unable to accomplish change on his own. Obama is expert at this; hence his continued clarity about the legislative process as a central force for change—as well as his regular e-mails encouraging his supporters to participate by lobbying their representatives on particular issues. The language is the opposite of magical, as it doesn't say "Follow me and I'll make it all better." It is a mature language of respect for the intelligence and autonomy of his audience.

The language of substitution, on the other hand, serves to obfuscate, allowing the individual to deny his own emotional experience—protecting him from serious anxiety, paranoia, suspicion, and pain by replacing feelings with things. The speaker provides what's needed, and the pain of uncertainty is averted. Though this undermines the analytic process in the consulting room, the language of substitution can be helpful to a leader who needs to inspire confidence. This can, however, lead to jumping to conclusions or typecasting those who disagree or even obstruct. Obama's press secretary, Robert Gibbs, was practicing the language of substitution when he characterized the liberal wing of his party as the "professional Left," a term that attacks observation and thought, dismissing the disagreeable and limiting the possibility that growth can be promoted by the loudest critics of the Republicans and their destructiveness. This is the antithesis of the Language of Achievement, because the administration saw the Left as a thorn in its side rather than a spur to action in the best sense of the word. Dismissing the Left as persecutory converted suggestion into whine, obfuscating the Left's experience of itself, turning critics into something they were not.

Obama still uses the Language of Achievement the way a patient might do in an analytic relationship—tolerating the uncertainty of not knowing (called "negative capability") and being open to working on uncertainties with genuine dedication. Obama asks us to do that indirectly, by letting us work with him on change—reminding us that change takes time and patience. His e-mail system, asking supporters for their help and thoughts, is part of that interactive process. It is this process that underscores the Language of Achievement in the best sense. However, it is hard for the public to accept, since we elected a president to do the changing for us, the way some people go to a therapist so he or she can make it all better. That is looking for the language of substitution—for the other person simply to make it better—and unfortunately, Obama can't always practice what he preaches. While he ignores attacks from the Right, he has shown great impatience with the Left, as when he passively condoned the impulsive firing of Shirley Sherrod from her Department of Agriculture post after the NAACP condemned as racist remarks she had made that were posted out of context in video clips online. On the one hand, he says attacks from the Right don't bother him; on the other, words from a black woman are seen by his administration as actions justifying reaction. The irony is that words experienced as actions cannot be shifted into words simply to think about and mull over. Obama himself created an atmosphere that helped convert Sherrod's words into something that could not lead to thought but that required action. This is an ironic sensitivity, most likely a holdover from his youth, a hatred of how he felt when he was accused of not being black enough.

The Sherrod firing was a clear example of the language of substitution in which action replaced thought, and her words were treated as if they were hostile actions. Unfortunately, he applies this attitude to his critics only rarely; his inaction on the Tea Party cries of "death panels," for example, was a failure to link feeling and fact, an inability to accept the potential for destructiveness before him. He appears unwilling or unable to think about and act against the destructive attacks on his policy initiatives made by Republicans. His action in this case was fragmented and based on the fear of seeming to protect an intemperate black person rather than sitting and thinking about it.

This is a bigger issue than how Obama thinks and uses words. The way in which American society currently deals with conflict is so destructive for us because it limits us to the realm of a language of substitution in which words are taken very literally, rather than as representations of so much more. We tend to latch on to words because of how evocative they are. The danger of negative evocation is so great in an environment in which his words are so quickly pounced upon by the media that Obama is virtually under siege to eschew the language of achievement. If he wants to think about Egypt or wait for European involvement before attacking Libya, he is pounced upon for being weak and indecisive. Disapproving the pace of Obama's response to Egypt, the *Newsweek* columnist Niall Ferguson compared him unfavorably to Otto von Bismarck (who 125 years earlier literally defined Africa by European spheres of influence), asking where Obama's "grand strategy for America" was. Obama knows that a grand strategy substitutes action for thought, invites specific knee-jerk reactions to specific situations. But the more he keeps quiet, the more action language takes over. Nowhere is this more apparent than in domestic policy, when relentless attacks on language kept us out of the realm of imagined possibilities and simply moved everyone into the realm of practical possibilities, such as passing an extremely watered-down version of health care legislation. The idea of transformation, of taking in a problem and transforming a reaction into something new and different, is contained in the Language of Achievement. But Obama chooses substitution, the practical result, rather than the dreams that he says guide him. Success becomes a simple matter of having passed a bill, more meaningful than what the bill actually accomplishes.

In the language of substitution, words become things in themselves. They begin to lose meaning, or at least the intended meaning, and instead come to symbolize the notion of meaning. This goes to the heart of Obama's agenda, as he wrote in *Dreams from My Father*:

> *In 1983, I decided to become a community organizer.*
>
> *There wasn't much detail to the idea; I didn't know anyone making a living that way. When classmates in college asked me just what it was that a community organizer did, I couldn't answer them directly. Instead, I'd pronounce on the need for change. Change in the White House, where Reagan and his minions were carrying on their dirty deeds. Change in the Congress, compliant and corrupt. Change in the mood of the country, manic and self-absorbed. Change won't come*

from the top, I would say. "Change will come from a mobilized grass roots."

That's what I'll do, I'll organize black folks. At the grass roots. For change.

Long before he could know that his chorus of change would carry him into the White House, Obama was treating the word as a concrete object, emptying it of its meaning—at least of the meaning once ascribed to it by a naive undergraduate, as recalled by a more seasoned memoirist a decade later. In a vivid illustration of the language of substitution, change, the action for which he would later call, is introduced as a rhetorical device, something about which he would pronounce. The passage is remarkable for opening five consecutive sentences with the word "change." By the time the reader gets to the fifth instance, "change" has, ironically, become a constant—the opposite of its ostensible meaning. Its final use, at the end of the next brief paragraph, is almost a punch line, the author's conviction drained out of his empty rhetoric, replaced by unrealistic hope that he could accomplish his lofty objectives, turning a language of possibility into the acts themselves, to instigate changes as easily as he could "pronounce" about them. As his pronouncements sputter to a tentative close, all pretense of conventional grammar discarded and replaced by tentative sentence fragments, "change" has evolved into a mere container for his idealism—an instrument of denial that obfuscates his uncertainty that he will be able to effect the change at the heart of his mantra and mission.

The paragraphs that immediately follow in the memoir further reveal the author's awareness that even he realizes that "change" has become a container for something other than the vigorous call to action of his initial pronouncement:

And my friends, black and white, would heartily commend me for my ideals before heading toward the post office to mail in their graduate school applications.

I couldn't really blame them for being skeptical. Now, with the benefit of hindsight, I can construct a certain logic to my decision, show how becoming an organizer was a part of that larger narrative,

starting with my father and his father before him, my mother and her
parents, my memories of Indonesia with its beggars and farmers and
the loss of Lolo to power, on through Ray and Frank, Marcus and
Regina; my move to New York; my father's death. I can see that my
choices were never truly mine alone—and that that is how it should
be, that to assert otherwise is to chase after a sorry sort of freedom.

But such recognition only came later. At the time, about to graduate
from college, I was operating mainly on impulse, like a salmon
swimming blindly upstream toward the site of his own conception. In
classes and seminars, I would "dress up these impulses in the slogans
and theories that I'd discovered in books, thinking—falsely—that the
slogans meant something, that they somehow made what I felt more
amenable to proof." But at night, lying in bed, I would let the slogans
drift away, to be replaced with a series of images, romantic images, of
a past I had never known.

Without explicitly saying so, Obama describes how his call for
change illustrates the language of substitution. He sees both the
idealism in his litany of change as well as the grounds for skepticism
about its efficacy. He acknowledges that the deliberate structure
of the serial invocations of change in his writing here, but also in
his repeated discussions in classes and seminars at the time, belies
the impulsiveness behind them. He reveals how his efforts to incite
others to change contain his own history, memories, and dreams and
admits that slogans lack the meaning they're assigned.

As already suggested, Obama's overreliance on the language of
substitution can have significant impact on his governance—both
on his style and his effectiveness. If language replaces action, action
takes a backseat. But the above passages indicate that that concept
of the language of substitution can help us understand his attitude
toward the most vital, far-reaching promise he made during the campaign. As we'll see in the next chapter, getting deeper into Obama's
true feelings about the nature of change is an essential step toward
understanding him as an individual and as a president and how he
might be more effective. A simple example of language butting up
against material reality is his January 22, 2009, promise to close the
prison at Guantánamo within a year. He also promised to have all

suspects tried in U.S. civil courts, and he said there would be no indefinite incarceration. All those were ideas about changes he was going to make, as if they really could happen. Members of his administration believed him, as did some members of the public, but he was at some level not that different from the way he was in 1983 when he wrote about becoming a community organizer: "There wasn't much detail to the idea." But when using the language of substitution in talking about change, one doesn't need details because change itself is the ideal, the goal, the reality within our reach.

In the Language of Achievement, he needs to work with others to actually make change. But, as *The Washington Post* reported in March 2011, it is clear that most of his supporters who ended up working for him feel that they are underutilized and have no access to him or to policy makers. Practicing the Language of Achievement has to do with tolerating uncertainty while reaching toward new possibilities. It requires cooperation—and not just from Republican obstructionists. It requires an administration working together. And it requires that Obama himself deal with uncertainty, rather than pronouncing impossible realities. The most recent critique of the Obama administration is that change is no longer a "we" process but an "I" process. And it's clear that his language doesn't contain possibilities the way it once did, certainly not the way *Dreams from My Father* does.

There is one more irony to the relationship between substitution and achievement, and that is that substitution doesn't just substitute pseudoaction for genuine thought and prelude, it also employs abstraction to obfuscate affect, to reconfigure genuine feelings—as Ann did with little Barry. This is a different kind of substitution, but also a kind of action to replace uncertainty caused by strong feelings. The ideas of change and then the detailed structure of those ideas devitalize the emotional reality, the essence. Wilfred Bion did not address this, but the philosopher Søren Kierkegaard did years earlier. And what he wrote in 1846 still holds true and has a significant bearing on both Obama's presidency and character: specifically, that when intelligence is valued over all else, ideas replace reality and then become the new reality.

To return to the psychoanalytical concept of splitting, there is a split in such instances between thought and feeling—something we see hinted at by Obama when he poetically describes, in *Dreams from My Father,* being so moved by a church sermon in Chicago that he didn't realize he was crying until a boy in the next pew handed him a tissue. He has, over his lifetime, perfected those kinds of splits in order to protect himself from being dismissed or attacked as an angry black man. So he is on the horns of a psychic dilemma. When he keeps the split well in place, he keeps passion out of his reactions—as when he failed to support striking government workers in Wisconsin. We saw both sides of the split at the press conference held the day after Henry Louis Gates was wrongfully arrested in Cambridge for breaking into what turned out to be his own house; Obama first gave a balanced answer to questions about his response, acknowledging that neighbors as well as police had been doing their civic duty, but then spontaneously went off message and spoke about racial profiling. I was impressed by that, but it brought down numerous hailstones from the Cambridge police as well as from the right, and after that he went back on his tightrope. And when attacks break through that split he sometimes becomes testy, as Bill Maher described him when joking about his press conference revealing his "long form" birth certificate. Obama clearly conveyed his annoyance, revealing that the Birthers' attacks—which had been given too much credence by the media—had in fact gotten under his skin. It took years of the Birthers' hounding him for that to happen, however, so defended is he against the danger that his affect might alter or even derail the supremacy of his thought processes.

Abstract thinking is so powerful a factor in his life that it may not simply be the transformation of internally metabolized passion and feeling but an override of emotion by replacing it with thought. If that is the case, ideas become things in themselves, devoid of the passion they once gave birth to. Thus Obama can claim the very thing he rails against: an "us-them" claim to a higher reality. His reality about change is greater than what he calls the Left's impotent calls for wholesale change. Kierkegaard said that abstraction "transforms the real task into an unreal trick and reality into a play." One of the most nefarious techniques of the Republican opposition, which is apparently lost on Obama, is the blurring of play and reality—perhaps not surprisingly, due to his difficulty distinguishing theater from real rhetoric at a turning point in his life. The reality of the Wisconsin union battle in 2011, for example, was not a play and not about some abstract idea of balancing the budget. The abstract idea of balancing a budget is destructive of reality if it doesn't take into account the genuine suffering of the millions of Americans facing unemployment or foreclosure, just as an abstract interpretation of a patient's pain robs him of his genuine experience—and also robs the analyst of sharing that experience. But the blurring strategy worked well enough to discourage Obama from sharing their experience. Words swaddled him when he was a child; the striking union members in Wisconsin needed some swaddling, too, from their leader, but he was conspicuously silent. That was a missed opportunity to use language as he does best, because words actually do help and can have deep meaning and effect, especially when coming from as gifted an orator as Obama. But words alone do not suffice. As we will see, change involves passion and exhortation and commitment. Obama as president seems averse to that kind of speech, which came easily to him as a candidate—the very kind of speech that was required in 2011 to support the unions' efforts against midwestern governors who wanted to destroy them. Obama could have pointed with pride to Wisconsin citizens locally initiating recall efforts, but we heard no passionate oratory for these domestic protesters confronting authority in this country akin to the words he had for protesters abroad in Tunisia or Egypt.

It's not just mass domestic protests he doesn't encourage with his soaring rhetoric. When running for president, Candidate Obama championed whistle-blowers: "We only know these crimes took place because insiders blew the whistle at great personal risk. . . . Government whistle-blowers are part of a healthy democracy and must be protected from reprisal." But now his rhetoric has changed, as Mark Klein, who heroically exposed government wiretaps done by AT&T, told Jane Mayer in the May 23, 2011, *New Yorker*: "The Bush people have been let off. The telecom companies got immunity. The only people Obama has prosecuted are the whistle-blowers." Championing personal courage is conditional, it seems.

CHAPTER 5

The Only Thing We Have to Fear
Is Change Itself

> Inevitably we resist change and turn back with passionate
> nostalgia to the stage we are leaving. Still, we fulfill ourselves by
> choosing what is painful and difficult and necessary. . . . In short,
> organic development is a hard paradox.
>
> —Lionel Trilling, *The Liberal Imagination*

> The recurrent configuration is of an explosive force within a
> restraining framework.
>
> —Wilfred Bion, *Attention and Interpretation*

Nowhere in the language of politics does the unconscious express
itself more powerfully than in the political slogan, the short phrase
that, through constant repetition, comes to function both as a symbol
of an individual and as a container for the voters' projected hopes
and aspirations for a politician and for their shared relationship
moving forward. The effectiveness of a political slogan draws on
echoes from voters' childhood willingness to believe their parents.
Even in adulthood, one of the most important sets of fantasies
that survives from childhood is the belief in authority—a belief
that has its roots in parental authority but that can be activated or
manipulated to attach to any sort of authority figure. As a result,
we unconsciously assign our presidents and candidates to the office
with parental authority, intensifying our response to when they live
up to our expectations and when they let us down. Our unconscious
needs, which stem from open-mouthed childhood hunger, to take

things in from parents and teachers, extend to a belief in authority, and that results in our giving leaders the benefit of the doubt and defending them against criticism by others.

These factors make political slogans unusually powerful containers, and we are unconsciously predisposed to embrace and defend them—as well as, by extension, the candidates and leaders they symbolize. But what are we truly embracing? The conscious mind regularly overlooks the essential truth that negatives are not recognized by the unconscious—that is, that the unconscious doesn't understand "no," "not," or any of their variations. Thus, every absolute statement carries its opposite within it; in the case of a political slogan, we must question whether the candidate in fact unconsciously means the opposite of what he so often repeats. It often ends up that a candidate or politician who defines himself by what he is not is disclaiming a part of himself that he is trying unconsciously to deny or disown—not necessarily to fool the voters but to keep his own self-awareness unconscious.

That is how George W. Bush let us know ahead of time that he was in fact a divider, not a uniter, despite claims to the contrary—just as Richard Nixon, in an utterance that wasn't actually a slogan but was repeated (at least by others) as often as one would be, revealed that he was indeed a crook. But the absence of a negative doesn't mean that the unconscious isn't hiding something else other than the opposite of what a candidate is saying.

We see this "something else" in a candidate talking about an aspect of himself that enhances his perceptions of the world around him. John Edwards's concerns about two Americas ultimately revealed that he was unconsciously far more concerned about protecting his own double life than lamenting his nation's. Ironically, it may be because Edwards knew about both Edwardses—his own psychic split between long-suffering family man and secret lover—that he perceived this particular aspect of an America that was not only economically split but psychologically split as well. For example, most Americans who don't live in New Orleans have forgotten all about the devastation of that city's already impoverished Ward 9—in fact as well as in feeling.

* * *

When Obama promised "change you can believe in," he was doing more than offering some unknown transformation that we are hard-wired to want to have faith in. He was unconsciously giving us a glimpse of what change does—and doesn't—mean to him. Though he wasn't presenting something that we "couldn't" believe in, per se, he was sending us a kind of unconscious warning that the change he touted might not come to pass—particularly when it was being promised by someone whose linguistic reassurances are based as much in myth as in fact. The refrain was also designed to do what he had learned language was for—to offer comfort and reassurance, to counteract both his own opposition to change and the natural resistance to change that exists in everyone.

At a deeper level, President Obama ultimately chose the slogan of change—something actually recommended to him by his advisers—because it fit with core issues in his own psyche. During his adolescence, he changed from seeing himself as biracial to declaring himself to be black. When he was about thirteen, he stopped telling friends he had a white mother. Very close friends knew, of course, but he let most people just assume that his genetic makeup, and therefore his racial identity, was wholly conveyed by his skin color. Because he had such internal conflicts about change—change he could believe in, to put a fine point on it—his sensitivity to the conflicts people have about change was greatly heightened. As the biracial author Shelby Steele wrote in 2008's *A Bound Man,* "What seems clear is that Barack Obama is a man who truly wants to be black, a man who is determined to *resolve* the ambiguity he was born into." This is change he can believe in—or can he really?

Richard Wolffe's detailed account of the development of Obama's slogan reveals that the emergence of the phrase was not without resistance.

Take the defining line of the Obama campaign: Change We Can Believe In. The same slogan appeared on the same plastic banner at almost every campaign event of the extended primary contest. But it didn't emerge until the late summer of 2007, some six months after Obama announced his candidacy, after months of hand-wringing by Axelrod and his team. "It's my least favorite thing," said Axelrod.

"We all struggled with it." The idea first came from Jason Ralston, a member of the media team handling the campaign's ads under the superconsultant Jim Margolis. But the candidate didn't much like it because it conveyed nothing about his position on what he called "the issues." To Axelrod and Plouffe, it was imperfect but it spoke to their rationale for believing in Obama and signing up to one more exhausting election. "It was good because it went to a lot of the character questions," said Axelrod. "We were running against the inauthenticity of Washington. We were appealing to everyone's sense that we needed real change, not phony change. But it took several months before we finally persuaded ourselves that we had to have it."

Once they were persuaded, it was far too much trouble to dream up—and agree on—a new slogan. So the candidate, and the campaign, stuck at the same message week after week, month after month. It was a repetition that Obama hated, even when the lines were his own. Early in the campaign, Margolis and pollster Joel Benenson urged Obama to repeat the lines from his breakthrough convention speech in 2004, about uniting red and blue America. "He didn't want to do it," said Benenson. "He thought everybody had heard it. But we tested it in polls and ads and people were crazy for it. They said, 'I've been waiting for somebody to say this.'"

Wolffe's account reveals an obvious irony—that the people behind the slogan about believing in change didn't initially believe in it and then decided it was too much trouble to change the slogan—which makes it harder, if not naive, to take the meaning of the phrase at face value. They don't believe they can change the change slogan. And it's clear that the slogan became a container for more than just candidate Obama's attitudes toward change and belief. Thus it may be too simplistic to dismiss the phrase as an obfuscation of its exact opposite—"change we can't believe in," for example, or "stasis we can believe in," although both describe some of what the Obama presidency has offered. But Obama's decision to follow his advisers' instructions to repeat "the same message week after week, month after month," indulging in "a repetition [he] hated"—a decision that embodies neither belief nor change—begs the question of just what his attitude toward change really is. In his 2011 State of the Union address, Obama presented a vision of change very different from the campaign slogan. Change was introduced as something to be endured, if not feared; evoking a bygone time of economic and vocational stability, he announced, "That world has changed. And for many, the change has been painful." He went on to detail the painful change:

> *I've seen it in the shuttered windows of once booming factories and the vacant storefronts of once busy Main Streets. I've heard it in the frustrations of Americans who've seen their paychecks dwindle or their jobs disappear—proud men and women who feel like the rules have been changed in the middle of the game.*
> *They're right. The rules have changed.*

Look closely at the change he describes, and a theme comes quickly into focus: Obama's bleak 2011 vision of change is rooted in abandonment, replete with images of people and places that have been abandoned by their jobs, paychecks, employers—people whose very way of life has drastically changed. This, of course, brings to mind the fundamental change in Obama's life that had a significant impact on everything that followed and sowed the seeds of his outlook on change that would start in childhood and reverberate for years to come. Obama approaches change from the position of someone who had change forced upon him by his father's abandonment, a rupture that was followed a few years later by his mother's breaking up their second family with Lolo in Jakarta and then—speaking of forced change—abandoning Barry as well by dropping him off in Hawaii to live with her parents so he could attend an American private school. Just prior to being moved back to Hawaii, young Barry read the article about a man obsessed with change, the drive to change from black to white. Quite understandably, change is something that young Barry learned to fear at a very early age.

It's not abnormal for children to resist change. Our natural resistance to change is related to the deep need to control anxiety, to keep the personality cohesive, preventing unconscious chaos and fears from breaking through, and to protect against loss of the familiar. Despite being open to many things, children have a naturally conservative predisposition that helps them to grow and develop, creating an internal psychic organization so they can better manage their thoughts and feelings and convert impulse to reflection. The child develops a little more internally each time that conversion happens, creating a more solid psychic foundation.

Against this developmental backdrop, enjoying change is an acquired taste. The child first learns to tolerate change from the actions of the caretaker. The daily actions of infant care—picking up, putting down, changing diapers, disrupting feeding, resuming feeding after the disruption—are elements of change that occur without overt notice throughout the weeks and months of early development. Mostly those changes are positive, with bad moods modified by maternal care. The infant develops a sense of mastery, of control over his emotional highs and lows, and a capacity to tolerate frustration. Having predictable patterns of feeding, behaving, living is part of what helps the child develop a stronger inner capacity to manage change, to deal with the unexpected. One of Obama's core strengths as president stems from his attitude toward change and his approach to dealing with the unexpected: more than any president in memory, Obama's deliberative style in thinking things through—such as his decision to work with European nations in bombing Libya—helps reduce the dangers of unintended consequences.

The lessons about the dangers of change that Obama learned from his father's disappearance were reinforced when his second father figure left his life. Whereas the infant Barry was too young at the time of his father's departure to retain conscious memories of the rupture, the various changes to his family and living situations that involved his stepfather, Lolo, were very much part of his conscious experience. Obama's father left Hawaii before Barry was one, and Lolo came into his life when Barry was four. Lolo was at the house playing with Barry every night in those early years before he was called back to Jakarta before Barry was six. Lolo was very present in young Barry's life for six years, including Barry's time in Indonesia, and Obama wrote poignantly about him in *Dreams from My Father*. His portrait of his stepfather is loving, if not effusive, demonstrating the role he played in his development. Lolo was someone he respected and who taught him an appreciation for practical things in life, but also, more significantly, he gave him a model for how to manage his emotions. He learned that to be a man meant not revealing his own feelings and never letting anyone know he was hurt. We see this lesson in action when Obama writes about not telling his mother about the deep laceration that he suffered in his arm from climbing a barbed-wire fence—an injury that Lolo also dismissed, further suggesting that Barry was emulating his stepfather's attitude of the stiff-upper-lip approach to pain and injury. Obama took a similar approach when he didn't reveal to his mother his feelings about the disturbing *Life* magazine photos, which "permanently altered" his vision, introducing a brand-new awareness of race that he kept to himself.

For children, change is fraught with a sense of loss of the familiar, and Ann's decision to remove Obama from his stepfather and return him to Hawaii must have been a crushing loss for the fourth-grader, though he gave it little attention in his memoir. Lolo, though taciturn, was very respectful of young Barry and answered any and all questions thrown his way—very unlike how private he was with Ann. If there were any modeling of parental relationships for Barry, it must have been that keeping quiet was preferable to facing Ann's sharp criticism and moral judgment. I think that he learned that behavior from watching Lolo and that it confirmed his later decisions not to be open with his mother. His stance in that regard is the opposite of his emphasis on unity as president. Interdependence is fine for others, but not necessarily for him. His return to Hawaii was yet another change for the better, at least according to his mother.

One way to manage the loss of Lolo was through identification, an unconscious attempt to keep the missing person around by becoming like him. Identification with Lolo could also have been an act of defiance against his mother, who permanently separated them, by becoming the very person she eventually came to detest. Lolo jettisoned his revolutionary ways once he returned to Indonesia, and Ann rejected him for making moves that Obama has subsequently mirrored, such as embracing Jakarta's wealthy business communities, particularly the oil industry, which won Lolo's support for offshore drilling as he became more loyal to power than to rebellion.

* * *

The lessons Obama learned from Jakarta and Lolo are that the world is a cruel place and one should do one's best to manage within that world, without disclosing too much about how one feels. Obama wrote that Lolo's "knowledge of the world seemed inexhaustible . . . elusive things, ways of managing emotions I felt, ways to explain fate's constant mysteries." We see here the genesis of Obama's trademark calm. Though it has numerous sources and serves multiple psychological purposes within his defensive character structure, it remains a central and visible element of his personality today, and Lolo is the most evident model for the practice and benefit of managing emotions, certainly more so than Obama's volcanic father, whose volatility was celebrated in family legend, or his easily tearful mother.

At the same time, Lolo introduced Barry to the exotic dangers of life in his new home: he made a show of having a chicken killed in front of the boy on his first day in Jakarta, fueled his fascination with the solitary warrior-hero monkey god Hanuman, encouraged him to defend himself from other boys by teaching him how to box, and cautioned Barry that he wouldn't have enough money left for himself if he gave too much to the poor—advice he arguably still follows as president today.

He wrote:

> With Lolo I learned how to eat small green chili peppers raw with dinner (plenty of rice), and, away from the dinner table, I was introduced to dog meat (tough), snake meat (tougher), and roasted grasshopper (crunchy). Like many Indonesians, Lolo followed a brand of Islam that could make room for the remnants of more ancient animist and Hindu faiths. He explained that a man took on the powers of which he ate: One day soon, he promised, he would bring home a piece of tiger meat for us to share.

The adult Obama's delight, years later, in recalling the attributes of the local delicacies offers a glimpse of the impression Lolo made on the boy, even as he distances himself from his boyish enthusiasm by stepping back to view Lolo's spirituality through an adult's analytical lens that identifies "more ancient animist and Hindu" influences that a child would never articulate.

But Indonesia was also a scary, unstable place, far from the paradise of Hawaii. Obama wrote that his mother was horrified by what she was learning about the regime change that had preceded their arrival and that directly impacted Lolo's fortunes, freedom, and general outlook. Too young to appreciate the particulars of what was going on, Obama adopted his mother's point of view to lend a historical and cultural perspective to the disquiet he sensed. She was frightened by "the notion that history could be swallowed up so completely, the same way the rich and loamy earth could soak up the rivers of blood that had once coursed through the streets . . . ; the way people could continue about their business beneath giant posters of the new president as if nothing had happened, a nation busy developing itself."

Unlike his parents' breakup, however, the pain of the dissolution of Lolo and Ann's marriage was not lost on young Barry. Again filtering childhood impressions through the adult perspective, Obama noted that Lolo's attitude toward his mother had changed in the period between their introduction in Hawaii and their arrival in Indonesia: "It was as if he had pulled into some dark hidden place, out of reach, taking with him the brightest part of himself." Lolo was very much a product, if not a victim, of contemporary events, and his response to them took a toll on his marriage to the idealistic Ann. She would ask Lolo what was wrong, and Lolo wouldn't say—and in this way Barry also learned not to talk to his mother. There were things Lolo just didn't want to get into with his new wife—perhaps including his having switched sides from revolutionary to a man on the side of power. And Obama went further, implying that Lolo, in his revolutionary days, had been beaten, perhaps even tortured, by the new regime. Young Barry asked about Lolo's various scars, but his stepfather never admitted to any pain. Still, Barry understood enough to observe that power had "yanked [Lolo] back in line just when he thought he'd escaped," adding that "Lolo had made his peace with power, learned the wisdom of forgetting"—although some of this forgetting was accomplished with the aid of alcohol, which by some accounts he drank to excess.

Leading up to their separation, however, there were further hints of discord between his mother and Lolo. He snapped at her for her constantly pestering him with her questions, much as she did her son. Obama downplayed those contretemps; his account of their marital tension is noticeably tame, writing that her "tone alters slightly" when she remembers Lolo's obstinacy or that "such arguments were rare." But the tension clearly left an impression on him, and he felt that most of it was expressed through his mother's worrying about Barry becoming disconnected from his American possibilities. She became obsessed with his education, concerned that he was too exclusively exposed to Indonesian culture; this led to 4 A.M. studies before the school day began, his mother tutoring him so that he would learn English, read English, and speak like an educated American. He eventually came to see himself as the pawn in a struggle between Lolo and herself for influence and power—which ultimately led to his being shipped back to Hawaii to live with his grandparents to go to school. Though he never addressed it—he had, after all, been shown that hiding one's fears and feelings is the manly thing to do—the whole experience had to have sharpened the young boy's sense that change can be disruptive and must have left him feeling at least partially responsible for the rupture.

Once back in Hawaii, away from the stepfather with whom he shared dark skin, young Barry was faced with the unusual disjunction of being raised in an all-white family but seeing a black face staring back at him when he looked in the mirror. That kind of identification change, from preconception—*I am white like my mother and grandparents*—to shock and realization—*I am black*—took place on microlevels every day. There wasn't much he could do about the subsequent changes to his family configuration, and there's no evidence in his memoirs that he complained about or resisted the departures and moves that shaped his childhood and youth. There are multiple explanations for this propensity to silence in the face of change: a learned response to his feelings of helplessness as an abandoned child; a desire to protect himself from what he sometimes suggests was undue intrusiveness by his mother; a passive expression of the resentment he felt toward his mother rooted in his blaming her for his father's departure; and an identification with Lolo, for whom silence was manly.

The change imposed by being abandoned by both parents sensitized him to the dangers of change and launched an unconscious association between danger and change that continues today, despite his campaign-slogan exhortations to the contrary; indeed, it is this fear of change that makes hope such an audacious attitude. His fear of change is deeply unconscious and denied by him consciously. Instead he flirts with danger by flirting with change. He wants change, argues for the audacity of hope, but shies away from the audacity of action. His first two years in office, he promised, then pulled back from change—sometimes suddenly and inexplicably—until he finally did what was necessary for action, as when he extended tax cuts to the wealthiest Americans to get things done in a flurry of activity in the lame-duck weeks of late 2010. He has become known for his caution even when advocating change.

Many observers recognized the December 2010 burst of productivity as reminiscent of the way Obama delays action until the eleventh hour and then pulls it out at the last minute, a pattern rendered with particular detail in Wolffe's account of his writing of his Nobel Prize acceptance speech. A derivative of magical thinking from childhood, this approach leads him to flirt repeatedly with the dangerous, unplanned part of change—how it will go and what will happen after you make it. The pattern is pervasive enough to take the form of a repetition compulsion, an unconscious drive to relive the trauma of his abandonment by pushing himself closer to the dangers of the unknown and then, at the last minute, choosing either a safer approach or, driven by the fantasy of saving the day, a dramatic compromise to get something passed. We all have core issues that we revisit over our lifetime, and Obama's conflict about change is one of his. Each time he repeats this struggle, he is drawn to revisiting familiar conflicts yet hopes to achieve a different result—hence the term "repetition compulsion." This approach-avoidance attitude helps reinforce his denial of his fear of change, thereby making him feel stronger.

Not surprisingly for an individual who has learned that he can exponentially expand his power by claiming to believe in the very change he fears, Obama maintains his power and sense of himself as a calm, fearless person by not revealing the anxiety he experiences. I have learned in my years of practice how important it is for patients themselves to say aloud what they are thinking and feeling. The importance extends beyond the obvious value of assigning names to thoughts and emotions to the process of owning them by stating them in their own voices and words. If I accurately identify a thought or feeling in an interpretation I offer, patients will respond with something along the lines of "Yes, I know." But when they say they know, they are in fact psychically tying up a thought in a bow and then burying it almost immediately. Speaking thoughts aloud makes them more real; allowing others to articulate those thoughts makes them less real and easier to deny.

Denial can take other forms as well, including hiding from view, which describes Obama's approach to his nicotine addiction. Obama's denial about his smoking required that he hide his habit from the public and the press, vividly conveyed in his biographer David Mendell's account of following the campaign car during the 2006 Senate campaign and observing cigarette butts being tossed from the rear windows as the convoy traveled the Illinois highways. Though keeping his nicotine addiction out of public view helped maintain his cool image (to himself and others), indulging in it within such proximity of the press again flirted with the danger of discovery, allowing Obama to repeat the compulsively exciting— but relatively benign—tension between risk and antirisk. Of course, by hiding his smoking he's been able to deny not only that he relies on a chemical crutch to manage his anxiety but that he has enough anxiety that he has to go to such lengths to manage it. This protects himself from scrutiny and avoids his having to see in the eyes of the other the looks that verify that he does indeed still regularly feed a nicotine addiction in order to manage his fears. He grew up around men—Gramps and Lolo—who used alcohol to manage their anxieties, and he later learned that his father used alcohol for the same purposes. Cigarettes, unless you pay attention to the surgeon general's report, don't cloud thinking—something very important to Obama that he not impair, despite his brief flirtation with pot and beer as a teenager.

Obama hides his smoking to dissociate himself from his addiction and the anxiety that it attempts to manage. In psychoanalytical terms, *dissociation* also describes the phenomenon of managing anxiety by disconnecting thought from feeling. Dissociation is in the eye of the beholder: Is Obama the dissociated president who is so out of touch with the aggression of a Republican leadership dedicated to destroying his presidency that he gave away the store to sign a few nice-sounding but watered-down bills at the end of 2010? Or is he the realist who compromises with Republicans by continuing their no-tax demands in order to pass legislation he regards as important for the nation? Fortunately, we don't have to answer the question one way or the other to use the concept of dissociation, and its causes and functions, to shed meaningful light on the way Obama handles fear in general and fear of change in particular.

His dissociation needs go deeper than simple fear of change; change for him meant abandonment, especially loss of mother. He dissociates from his rage about that, as well as from his experience of having his own needs killed off by her behavior. After all, in high school he called himself her "experiment." Dissociation serves to evade the intensity of that experience, and Obama began to dissociate again after having been attacked in 2009 on health care. I think he was shocked and felt defenseless—even though he was in charge and had Democratic support in both Houses. He became slightly disconnected after that, though occasionally rallying himself as he did with his "teach-in" on health care in February 2010. But change and catastrophe are not far apart for him, despite his reassuring posturing to the contrary.

To the extent they are familiar with it at all, most laypeople think of dissociation as an emotional shutdown in the wake of trauma or injury. In fact, there are multiple manifestations of it, and dissociation need not be caused by abuse; it may result from a desperate need to avoid facing some painful reality, such as a loss or an emotional hurt. In child development the process of dissociation involves matters of privacy, of keeping parts of the self off limits to parental inquiry—of becoming a genuinely separate person. But in the most familiar dissociative response state, the individual develops a split-off consciousness in which memory of the traumatic event must be denied in order to avoid psychic collapse and unbearable pain. This process represses the capacity even to think about that trauma, manifesting itself, when under duress, in a more generalized paralysis of thought, as in the case of President George W. Bush, whom one could observe actively dissociate in press conferences or in that now-famous image of him staring off into space after being told of the 9/11 attacks. Such paralysis serves to protect the individual from collapse and panic, but also renders him unable to think or function. A second extreme form of dissociation that also describes an immediate response to a sense of danger involves disconnecting thought from affect in order to protect against overwhelming anxiety; the person who does so often has hyperintellectual reactions to deeply emotional situations, allowing him to respond with supreme calm. A third kind of dissociation, not involving paralyzed or devitalized abstract thought, is evidenced by a manic grandiosity that wards off the reality of impending danger—a kind of upbeat "what, me worry?" attitude that we commonly define as denial. We saw this in Obama's interview with Bill O'Reilly when he said clearly that being hated didn't affect him, just after he had suddenly glanced askance as if struck in the face by the question.

Dissociated states may be chronic, like living in a fog or trance, similar to Obama's altered state at his first foray into public speaking at Occidental. These states are subtle and exist in people who otherwise are psychologically healthy and who appear calm and centered. Their ability to disconnect thought from feeling may make them intellectually nimble, able to respond quickly to questions that would leave others drawing a blank. And chronically dissociated people have often been that way for a very long time, traumatized Holocaust survivors being classic examples.

Obama's dissociation is chronic and subtle. He dissociates himself from the full force of his rage and, by extension, his fear, including the fear of change that he has worked so hard to obscure. The inability to confront or connect with his rage and fear stems from the early trauma of the initial disruption of his childhood—the disappearance of his father, which instilled rage he can't express and fear he can't acknowledge. In the wake of this signal event, he doesn't project his fear and rage into others the way people with a more healthy (or unhealthy, as in the case of some, like many members of the Tea Party, who aggressively project their fears onto others) measure of paranoia do, making him less able to see how destructive many Republicans and most media critics actually are and how much he should really fear them.

Obama's dissociation is so subtle that few see it lurking underneath his dream of an America united in purpose. He sees a common ground of purple majesty when he should be seeing killer red. In his pledges to find common ground in the immediate aftermath of the 2010 midterm elections, when Republicans reclaimed control of Congress, Obama demonstrated a relationship with Senate Minority Leader Mitch McConnell and Speaker of the House John Boehner that reflected dissociated thinking rising to the level of a psychological version of the rare neurological condition known as Anton's syndrome. Anton's syndrome describes the condition in which patients deny their blindness despite objective evidence of visual loss and moreover support their stance through confabulation, inventing memories they treat as fact. It is a rare extension of cortical blindness in which, in addition to the injury to the occipital cortex, other cortical centers are also affected, with patients typically behaving as if they could see. Obama acts as if he sees the hatred from the right and that it doesn't bother him—as when he took a South Carolina congressman's outburst accusing him of lying during the 2010 State of the Union address entirely in stride. But he clearly is blind to it, or he would do more than simply appease. Part of his job is to remain above that kind of attack, but though he certainly couldn't respond during the State of the Union, he could have said far more afterward, just as he could have responded quickly after Representative John Lewis was spat upon by members of the Tea Party. Is he just trying to be blind to it? What makes his relationship to the vitriol interesting are the occasional breakthroughs to consciousness, when he spontaneously exclaims how beaten up he feels, as when he churlishly complained in September 2010 that the Republicans "talk about me like a dog." But for the most part, as in his interview with O'Reilly, who had to repeat the word "hate" to keep Obama from substituting "dislike," he acts as if in a trance when it comes to dealing with people like Boehner and McConnell.

On an emotional level this indicates that Obama cannot interpret what he thinks he sees; he now sees leaders of the party of "no" but seems to be blind to the malevolence that drives them. Internally blind to his own hate, Obama is also blind to the depth of hatred he needs to see but can't. His postmidterm cordial invitation to Republicans to join him in the White House and on the golf course leads one to question whether his dissociation from his own rage has left him so blind to the Republicans' destructiveness that he can't even recognize that he *doesn't* see it, too unconsciously fearful of the internal change that would inevitably result if he let go of the bipartisan fantasy to which he clings. We're left to wonder what he saw when he looked across the nation in early 2011 at so many Republican governors aggressively trying to dismantle workers' unions. Governor Scott Walker of Wisconsin led the other midwestern Republican governors into a union-bashing frenzy based on claims that pensions and medical care for workers are breaking state budgets. While it turned out that those allegations were false—Wisconsin has one of the most solvent state budgets in the country—the attacks did not let up and fostered recall efforts from angry voters who felt lied to by their governors. President Obama was relatively mute on the subject, though he did state that civil servants should not be singled out for budget cuts. It's as if he doesn't anticipate the consequences of his anticonfrontational nature.

But there is a positive aspect to the blind spot caused by Obama's denied fear and anger. Because he is without much fear (or at least outward expression of it), he is less susceptible to being overwhelmed by the opposition. He is able to think without having to block and parry. He can take the time to argue and debate because he sees the world as bipartisan purple—a mix of red and blue—employing his worldview to temper any danger. By denying his fear the way his father denied the murderous hatred he undoubtedly felt in that apocryphal bar scene so often recounted to the young Barry, he enables himself to think and reply in a measured and intelligent way and to use modified anxiety to spur further thought. Although his father's direct nonviolent confrontation won over the racist, the son remains calm in a way that frustrates his sworn enemies, who hope that their attacks will evoke an emotional response that indicates they have succeeded in getting under his skin. By using this approach, he provokes irrational behavior and outrageous reactions from some of the opposition, making them easy targets of ridicule. Newt Gingrich was such a target on *Meet the Press* on May 15, 2011, when David Gregory played a recent video of him equating Obama with Nazis.

Obama acknowledges his lack of fear in *Dreams from My Father* in a passage introduced by his observing changes for the worse in the Chicago neighborhood in which he was working as a community organizer. The plight of the kids who lived there haunted him with a sense that "an invisible line had been crossed" in the neighborhood, a place "where police or press rarely ventured until after the body was found on the pavement, blood spreading in a glistening, uneven pool . . . [where] prison records had been passed down from father to son for more than a generation." He feels the change one evening when he sees "four tall boys walking down a tree-lined block idly snapping a row of young saplings that an older couple had just finished planting in front of their house." He sees the change in "the eyes of the young men in wheelchairs that had started appearing on the streets that spring, boys crippled before their prime . . . eyes so composed, already so hardened, that they served to frighten rather than to inspire."

He discusses the possibility that "some, if not most, of our boys were slipping beyond rescue" with a lifelong South Sider named Johnnie.

"I ain't never seen it like this, Barack," [Johnnie] would tell me one day as we sat in his apartment sipping beer. "I mean, things were tough when I was coming up, but there were limits. We'd get high, get into fights. But out in public, at home, if an adult saw you getting loud or wild, they would say something. And most of us would listen, you know what I'm saying?

"Now, with the drugs, the guns—all that's disappeared. Don't take a whole lot of kids carrying a gun. Just one or two. Somebody says something to one of 'em, and—pow!—kid wastes him. Folks hear stories like that, they just stop trying to talk to these young cats out here. We start generalizing about 'em just like the white folks do. We see 'em hanging out, we head the other way. After a while, even the good kid starts realizing ain't nobody out here gonna look out for

him. So he figures he's gonna have to look after himself. Bottom line, you got twelve-year-olds making their own damn rules."

Though Johnnie admits that he is sometimes afraid of the boys, Obama doesn't react with the same fear:

Wandering through Altgeld or other tough neighborhoods, my fears were always internal: the old fears of not belonging. The idea of physical assault just never occurred to me. Same thing with the distinction Johnnie made between good kids and bad kids—the distinction didn't compute in my head. It seemed based on a premise that children could somehow set the terms of their own development.

The passage is remarkable for the clarity with which Obama presents his evasion of fear—flirting with danger by "wandering through" rough neighborhoods, the "idea of physical assault just never occurred to" him—although it occurred to him enough to set the scene with the vivid image of "blood spreading in a glistening, uneven pool." He denies or intellectualizes the threat that would otherwise induce fear—much as he intellectualized the threat to his sense of self that was caused by his father's departure, the rupture that set his fear of change into motion. Even more remarkable is the extent to which the image of the absent father—his and others'—resonates throughout the passage. The only fears that he does acknowledge are "the old fears of not belonging," a lifelong struggle closely identified both with his lack of a family role model whom he looked like to help him find where he belonged and with his having been abandoned at different times by both parents. But more explicit references to fathers and parenting abound. We read about the fathers absent due to incarceration, "whose prison records had been passed on from father to son for more than a generation." We see roughnecks symbolically attacking fatherhood by "idly snapping a row of young saplings that an older couple had just finished planting in front of their house." His friend Johnnie contrasts the old, better times, when "if an adult saw you getting loud or wild, they would say something," with the unsupervised youth of the moment. He wrote that kids soon realize that nobody will be there to help and that they have to fend for themselves. But Obama couldn't accept that those kids could "set the terms of their own development"—almost in direct denial of the fact that, as a twice-abandoned child, setting the terms of his own development was exactly what he had to do. Writing about his fearless response to a situation that is almost overdetermined with reasons to be frightened, Obama returned (likely unconsciously) to the image of the absent father frequently enough that it points toward the very link between being fearless and fatherless that he attempts consciously to disavow.

Obama's deep denial of his own fear of change, and the initial childhood trauma that caused it, raises a question: what does he feel about all those voters he inspired to embrace change as something to believe in? Candidate Obama appeared to present himself as a change agent, popularly defined in the business world as an individual whose presence can incite and inspire a different way of approaching problems. In the psychoanalytic literature, however, the "change agent" is not the analyst but the patient—for it is the patient who makes the changes, proposed by the analyst, a reality. Exhorting his followers to believe in the change he is advertising, Obama is embracing a definition of change agent far closer to the psychoanalytic take on the role. Echoing the dynamic of his days as a community organizer, facilitating others' efforts to change their circumstances without having to make those changes himself, he now encourages his followers—as well as his opponents—to take responsibility for bringing about the change they want, rather than creating the change for them. As he declared in a February 2008 campaign speech, "Change will not come if we wait for some other person or some other time. We are the ones we've been waiting for. We are the change that we seek." In so doing, he is unconsciously urging us to be what his mother urged him to be as a little boy, someone willing to grow and make the most use of his experiences and abilities—something that requires facing rather than denying the fear of change that stems from some of those experiences.

It seems that Obama wants the United States to repair itself the way he repaired himself and managed his own psychological and innately divided self. Obama is asking us to be change agents, to accompany him on his journey through our active participation into his suggested better world of change—a world not simply purple but red *and* blue, not red *or* blue. The common ground he envisions reconstitutes his broken family, as well as his once broken self. He persevered with the healing process over years, and now he thinks that we can persevere into the future by what we start to accomplish together now. If his parents could live with and accept their differences, they could remain linked by that "improbable" love he so movingly describes.

But he remains frightened of change. Unable to claim the fear, he projects it onto the very change agents that he invites and inspires us to be. In fact, he at times seems frightened by the change agents he recruited, repeatedly disappointing them, almost compulsively so. And if they want more change than he's ready to accept—regarding health insurance reform, ending the tax cuts on the wealthiest Americans, or economic advice from seasoned economists such as Paul Krugman and others who met with him in early 2011—he lashes out, most notably in his December 2010 press conference:

> *So this notion that somehow we are willing to compromise too much reminds me of the debate that we had during health care. This is the public option debate all over again. So I pass a signature piece of legislation where we finally get health care for all Americans, something that Democrats had been fighting for for a hundred years—but because there was a provision in there that they didn't get, that would have affected maybe a couple million people, even though we got health insurance for 30 million people, and the potential for lower premiums for a hundred million people, that somehow that was a sign of weakness and compromise.*
>
> *Now, if that's the standard by which we are measuring success or core principles, then let's face it, we will never get anything done. People will have the satisfaction of having a purist position and no victories for the American people. And we will be able to feel good about ourselves and sanctimonious about how pure our intentions are and how tough we are. And in the meantime the American people are still seeing themselves not able to get health insurance because of a preexisting condition or not being able to pay their bills because their unemployment insurance ran out. That can't be the measure of how*

we think about our public service. That can't be the measure of what it means to be a Democrat.

The image of Obama indirectly characterizing his liberal base as indulging in "the satisfaction of having a purist position . . . able to feel good about ourselves and sanctimonious about how pure our intentions are and how tough we are" is a long way from "change we can believe in." The change he takes credit for is better described as "change we can defend," while the alternative he outlines is a difference he clearly fears, or at least wants to avoid. But it's clear that the more liberal element of his party represents a force and yearning for change that frightens him—perhaps because of the damage he thinks they can do to his autonomy as a man—as if it were his mother forcing him to confront evil when he feels ill equipped to do so or because he can't control it, or simply because by embracing a more significant degree of change its members are flirting more perilously with the danger of the unknown that has unconsciously haunted him since childhood. It's clear that he identifies with the very people he is criticizing—he sounds as sanctimonious and self-satisfied about his (compromising) position as he accuses them of being.

Unconsciously his supporters become his secular humanist mother, who insisted on the triumph of reason and justice over greed and selfishness. And their once-invited support turns persecutory to him, something to be mocked and rejected, much the way he treated his mother when he was angry at her demands that he try harder in school.

The irony is that he is indeed the change he's been waiting for—he wants to be the father who makes change safe, the person he has waited for his entire life. But he also contains the little-Barry part of himself, a part that wanted more support and paternal input than he got. Obama ends up being both father and son, promising change and fearing it, and each acts out on the other as he seduces and abandons his most loyal supporters. When he seduces them, he is both reasoned and passionate. When he abandons them, he is unreasonably critical or disconnected. At times, when the Left functions as it should, pushing him to take bolder action the way it once pushed Franklin D. Roosevelt, he sees them as his mother demanding that he do things her way. He suddenly becomes the angry son push-ing back. He has repeated this process several times since becoming president, drawn to this particular conflict between asking others to be passionately involved and disparaging them when they show more passion than he does. He did this during the health care debate, drawing in supporters with Internet messages, only to attack them when they kept urging their congressmen to support a single-payer option. Sometimes he is his father, offering dreams; other times they are his father, offering their own dreams, which overwhelm him. At such times he shouts like an angry son, as if screaming "Don't push me to do things I'm neither prepared nor desiring to do!" At that point the players shift, and he imbues his followers with his internal dispirited little Barry waiting for Daddy to fulfill the promises his mother told him about. Their demands for more, for him actually to make good on his promises, turn them in his mind into a gang of unruly children who want total change now without understand-ing that change takes time. He gets irritable and testy with his most loyal supporters as he unconsciously personalizes their criticism. If he can get his hurt and angry younger self out of his head, even for a short time, he thinks he's in a better position to transform some of those promises into actual fact. The irony is that if he faced his own hurt, anger, and fear of change, he would not have to accommodate without genuine compromise when dealing with Republicans' rage.

Change is interactive and involves collaborative efforts. Obama's attempt at self-integration has taught him the necessity for societal integration, a drive further fed by his history of conflict avoidance. The problem of change for our society is that we have a depressive-position leader in charge of a paranoid-schizoid nation—that is, a leader who sees his own and his country's capacity for destructive-ness in charge of a nation that sees all threats as external. Though the change he talks about has ostensibly to do with open government, accountability, and transparency, the unconscious change he doesn't talk about is change from the paranoid-schizoid to the depressive position—toward a nation that takes responsibility for itself and its own, a reflection of his own internal struggle and his abiding belief that we are our brothers' keepers. Obama understands that a nation that turns its back on the uninsured and the poor is unconsciously doing violence to them. The United States can never be an organic whole without our living out that center of Obama's clear dream, making the sacrifices that dream entails (such as the rich and corporations both paying their fair share of taxes).

We live in a nation dominated by fear, some of it justified, which has long been present and has always been at least partially internal; for example, the whole system of checks and balances on which the government was formed was based on fear of power over the many being monopolized by the few. Nuance is the enemy of paranoid clarity and the perversely reassuring comfort it offers; the more Obama talks about change, the more nuanced he is in his opinions and worldview, the more defensive the paranoid become. But paranoia today is not limited to Obama's opponents, and he doesn't seem to understand that his supporters are motivated by the same process, for example, how so many of his 2008 supporters became so frightened of health care reform and paranoid about government intervention they voted the very congressmen whom they supported in 2008 out of office by the droves in the 2010 midterm elections. Most Americans—both left and right—are easy marks for the politics of fear. The source of danger is different, but whether it's economic or deterioration of education, infrastructure, worldwide respect, health care, or constitutional rights, the anxiety is paranoid, and the "Yes we can" chants are rallying cries to triumph over those evil negative forces.

While his supporters are looking outside themselves for things to change, Obama's goals are more in line with the depressive position: he wants us to change ourselves. And the change he wants unconsciously more than anything is for us to create a land of civility in which we all get along. He wants us all to see how much we have in common, just as his black and white selves have long struggled to do.

The historical record of leaders who push for internal change is not encouraging. The last to be so self-revealing was Jimmy Carter, who understood his own aggression, accepted that he could hate and care at the same time, and memorably spoke openly about having lust in his heart in a 1976 *Playboy* interview. Most Americans don't talk or think like that. It's easier to externalize, to feel danger as lurking outside rather than within, even if that doesn't make the anxiety go away but just keeps danger coming from outside rather than from the person next to you, let alone the person within.

Every time one of my patients has a major psychic breakthrough, there is a reaction against progress that also comes out. That reaction has to do with fear of change, unconscious hatred of having beliefs dislodged, fear of facing the unknown, and fear of being shamed or being attacked. Multiplying those fears exponentially will give an idea of the scale of our national anxiety about change. Societal resistance to change can be overcome only when our paranoid anxieties are effectively confronted and managed, since they can never be eliminated, and kept from destroying any march toward progress.

To manage that paranoid anxiety, Obama needs to find and use the paranoid parts of himself—the elements that are fundamental to life and do not have to be excluded from the depressive position. But when faced with the degree of hatred emanating from the right, he struggles to see it, to find "the killer inside" who can recognize the destructiveness of the fellow Americans who are also his opponents. He needs to see that their opposition is not simply political and ideological, something he continues to hope is not the case—as when he confided to friends in late 2010, according to Jonathan Alter, "All I want for Christmas is an opposition that I can negotiate with." Though he speaks aggressively from the podium at times, occasionally revealing a sudden awareness of being hated, he thinks he needs to deny his opponents' destructiveness in order to search for common ground. He'll be more effective helping those on the left discover the saving graces of those on the right, and vice versa, if he can model a healthy expression of the depressive position, one that both recognizes and faces the violent hatred of many of his fellow Americans. By modeling the change he needs in himself, he'll facilitate the change in others that he wants us all to achieve.

CHAPTER 6

The Achiever

> The tough mind is sharp and penetrating, breaking through the crust of legends and myths and sifting the true from the false. The tough-minded individual is astute and discerning. He has a strong austere quality that makes for firmness of purpose and solidness of commitment. Who doubts that this toughness is one of man's greatest needs? Rarely do we find men who willingly engage in hard, solid thinking. There is an almost universal quest for easy answers and half-baked solutions. Nothing pains some people more than having to think.
>
> —Martin Luther King, *Strength to Love*

Despite his various blind spots, Obama maintains a generally high level of mental health. In light of the challenges he has faced, his mental health can be considered among his finest and most significant accomplishments—the ultimate achievement, perhaps, of a very driven and successful achiever. We can see how certain elements of his mental health, sometimes developed in almost direct response to the challenges of his circumstances, can be linked directly to his success in other areas of his life, just as his success can be linked to the psychological functions that it sustains. Still, even his drive to achieve is not without its blind spots; indeed, his success and some of the attributes to which he owes it can be seen as holding back both his further psychological development and his presidency.

One of the limiting aspects of my profession is that there are far more definitions of mental illness—specific and agreed upon—than there are of mental health. One notable exception is the work of Dr. George Vaillant, who studied male psychological health by following the Harvard class of 1946 longitudinally—at five-year intervals from college age into their seventies—and concluded that its hallmarks are best measured by the levels of defenses used in times of crisis, such as humor, intellectualization, and self-reflection. Health is described not just as the absence of disorders but as the presence of key capacities, such as the ability to form long-term lasting relationships, work and be productive, love and be loved, and take care of oneself physically as well as emotionally. Vaillant believed that the healthier the defenses used in earlier life, the healthier the long-range lives were.

We've seen all of these traits in abundant supply in our young president. Most impressive to me as a psychoanalyst has been his capacity to bear psychic pain and to think in the face of anxiety. His intelligence functions as a regulator of his reactions, enabling him to think about things and modify his anxiety, using it as a source of information—recognizing it as a signal that there is something more he has to think about rather than something to run away from. We saw this in his response to the Fort Hood shootings in 2009, when he used his and the nation's anxiety over the tragedy and threat of terrorism forces dividing it to fuel his call for unity, just one of countless examples from his life and presidency: "In an era of divisions [the fallen soldiers] call upon us to come together. In a time of cynicism, they remind us of who we are as Americans." This constructive approach to facing anxiety feeds Obama's capacity for self-examination, which in turn enables him to take responsibility for mistakes rather than blame others, a clarity that empowers him to face the limits of reality and to differentiate it from the fantasies and wishes that can prove to be a perilous distraction to the unexamined self.

Obama has long been driven to test the bounds of material or external reality, an impulse required for the level of ambition necessary to run for president. But his ambition is leavened with some measure of humility, as he articulated in his 2006 interview with Charlie Rose (albeit when he was still only a U.S. senator). He told Rose, "[I am] mindful of the sense that, you know, when you decide to run for president, unlike any other office, I think, in the country, you are saying to the American people, I am giving my life to you, that my problems, my issues, my fears, my doubts, my quirks, my idiosyncrasies are not relevant. And what is relevant is whether or not I'm making the country safe and making you—giving you more opportunity and making sure your children have a better shot at life. And that's not a decision that I think you can—can or should make solely on the basis of ambition. It transcends ambition."

Despite his humility, he appreciates the effectiveness of using himself as an example, never more effectively than in the speech about race that he delivered in 2008 in the wake of the revelation— played in taped loops on all TV channels for a week—of inflammatory remarks pulled from sermons delivered by his pastor Reverend Jeremiah Wright. Describing his own shock at discovering that his beloved grandmother Toot, who was so central in his upbringing, also revealed some racist feelings after feeling threatened by a black panhandler while waiting for the bus, he engaged the nation—at least those who listened—in complexity, in the depressive position of loving and being angry at the same person. The profound effectiveness of his approach was immediately apparent in the number of Americans, pundits and citizens alike, who started talking about their own mixed feelings toward people close to them who were racist. By sharing freely about his own experience, he made it safe for others to identify and relate without guilt or shame. From my perspective, he seemed at that point like a master psychologist, as if he had raised the nation's psychological awareness a few levels higher.

The race speech also demonstrated another important element of his mental health—a reparative drive that motivates him to use his intelligence to heal splits that he perceives. The reparative drive traditionally originates in the individual's awareness of his own destructiveness or in the need to evade recognizing (which leads to false repair, absent true contrition or individual responsibility). In Obama's case, the drive to repair has familiar circumstantial origins in his biracial heritage and twice-broken home, splits not of his own making that he wants to heal. He uses himself as a reparative example in a variety of ways. On an unconscious level, he projects the damaged parts of his own personality into the nation's less fortunate citizens—the "folks I got into politics for, the reason I'm here," he told a 2011 Milwaukee audience to which he acknowledged that "there's still a lot of pain out there." But he also consciously presents himself as a emblem of reparation, telling House Democrats during the 2008 campaign that "it has become increasingly clear in my travel, the campaign, that the crowds, the enthusiasm, 200,000 people in Berlin, is not about me at all. It's about America. I have just become a symbol of the possibility of America returning to our best traditions."

In such instances, Obama not only uses himself as an example but sees how others use him as an example as well, inviting their projections, offering himself as a container for their hopes and dreams. To be sure, he does so imperfectly, often unconsciously failing to recognize in his supporters the needy, damaged child parts of himself he has projected onto them—and in turn resisting the impulse to serve them as the father figure that he once yearned for. But on a conscious level he is blessed with an ability to connect with their aspirations, a result of a keen thirst for knowledge about the hearts and minds of those different from him that can be traced back to another key component of his mental development, the powerful curiosity that dates from childhood and continues to this day. We see young Barry's healthy curiosity in action repeatedly in *Dreams from My Father* as he tries to apply the *Origins* myths to his own experience, for example, or attempts to figure out the stories behind the photos in *Life* magazine. His curiosity later led him to read black writers in an attempt to clarify his own racial identity, which in turn led to his years in New York living, as he describes it, "like a monk," to focus on reading and study while a student at Columbia University.

His curiosity also contributes to another central element of his mental health that helped him face his unique challenges: his enormous capacity to listen with both empathy and intelligent skepticism. He was able to listen to his mother but keep his own mind; rather than just believe everything he heard, he read and looked things up to challenge or validate his mother's stories about his father. He also listened to stories from men in his life, particularly his grandfather and stepfather. In high school, he listened to his friends who broadened his horizons as well as to the old poet Frank, who had great perspective on living as a black man in a white world; indeed, it was this struggle, to find his mixed-race place in a black-and-white world, that likely compelled him to sharpen his listening skills and deepen his curiosity for what he heard.

Working in concert with his ability to listen was the skill he developed at holding his tongue. This is most evident in the Indonesia passages of *Dreams from My Father*; on his first day there, he had a powerful experience in which he witnessed the beheading of a chicken that his family ate silently that evening—unable to speak together about the violence they had just witnessed. I'm reminded of the saying, "The tongue is the enemy of the neck"—that is, it's best to keep your mouth shut because someone might slit your throat. I think Obama learned this at a young age, most explicitly from Lolo. He wrote that he "could hardly believe [his] luck" to be there, conveying the child's strong attraction to the very violent acts that cause him great fear and anxiety. Lolo thus set a tone that hung over the family in one form or another for the next four years and taught young Barry the value of not revealing his feelings, a thread that continues to run through his presidency, except in prepared remarks.

This lesson, I think, dictates his judicious approach to Fox News and the dangers of right-wing attacks. He said in an interview in October 2010 with *Rolling Stone* that he considered Fox News part of an old American tradition typified by William Randolph Hearst in the first half of the twentieth century. He saw that what looks like cruelty from one perspective is survival from another. And for Obama, there is room for both perspectives.

At a basic level, his success stems from his ability to learn from his experiences as he did during his formative years in Indonesia. His unflappability on the campaign trail was legend, which made the rare moments in which he did misspeak—telling Hillary Clinton she was likable enough or lamenting the bitterness of God-fearing, gun-toting Pennsylvania voters, for example—all the more glaring, particularly in contrast to his gaffe-plagued ticket mate, Joe Biden. Obama typically avoids such gaffes because his intelligence empowers him to access his defenses more easily than most; he also understands, processes, and internalizes what others are saying more quickly, so he has more time to decide how to respond.

But even though he often plays the role of the patient intellectual, he's still able to mix it up, something he was apparently comfortable doing on the basketball court: He can mix it up where the rules all but expect that kind of aggressive physicality. And he applies the free-speech rules of the Constitution to everyone equally, Fox News included, without seeming to see that some of his critics don't care what the rules are and will do anything to slit his political throat. For them it may also be about survival, but from a psychoanalytic perspective it appears also to be about pure hatred and murderousness. As president, he continues to maintain his rhetorical restraint, put on vivid display during his February 2011 interview with Bill O'Reilly. Its berth on the schedule just before the Super Bowl clearly sent the message that the meeting of Obama and the Fox News team was designed to be more contest than conversation and that Obama hoped to capture a large but politically knee-jerk audience of intense football fans. O'Reilly certainly tried to get a rise out of the president by declaring that the health care reform bill would definitely be overturned and sounding hysterical about the threat posed by the Muslim Brotherhood. But Obama was calm in the face of O'Reilly's aggression, toning it down as O'Reilly kept ramping it up. As telling as his resisting O'Reilly's claim that he was "hated" rather than just "disliked" (discussed in an earlier chapter) was the way he handled the Fox host's goading him in disbelief about his gridiron savvy about a quintessentially American game:

> O'Reilly: But are you going to watch the game? Are you going to—
> Obama: Of course. I'll watch the game.
> O'Reilly: Are you going to sit, and you're going to watch?
> Obama: I'm not going to—
> O'Reilly: You know, like, football, you know, like, blitzes and coverage and all that?
> Obama: Oh, I know football, man.
> O'Reilly: You do?
> Obama: Absolutely.
> O'Reilly: I know you're a basketball guy.
> Obama: I know football, man.

By adding "man" at the end, Obama was able to demonstrate that he could hold his temper, talk tough, and still try to connect, even in the face of O'Reilly's attempts to rattle him. Forced all his life to connect with people who were visibly different from him and who also had preconceived notions about him based on race—from his white family to the culture and people of Indonesia to his prep school classmates in Hawaii and into adulthood—Obama learned that holding his tongue and looking for common ground, rather than asserting difference, was essential to his success in his life, education, and work.

Anyone who has read *Dreams from My Father* knows that Obama's success as a writer is about more than his way with words. His vivid portrayals of relationships and moments of deep introspection are illuminated by a richness of associations that draws upon an essential part of the skills and intelligence he developed to transcend the challenges he has faced. As carefully wrought as each page no doubt was, what brings his writing to life is his powerful observational capacities. To find his place in his family and his world, Obama had to look outside as well as inside, a skill we see him deploy as a writer to great effect.

One of the best examples of that mix of intelligence with experience is his description of life in New York after transferring from Occidental to Columbia. He spent most of his time walking the streets and observing—and what he observed was a land of extremes, a land without a middle. Seeing the decay of Harlem and the wealth of black professionals who shared only race with their less fortunate neighbors, he realized that the poles between rich and poor were not dissimilar to those between black and white. He stopped drinking and cavorting and became a "bore," according to his roommate and old friend. The temptations of New York were manifold and limitless; yet in the midst of all that stimulation he started to study, ran three miles a day, and stopped barhopping. He wrote that he didn't know why he changed but then looks inside to see how the process unfolded. "Uncertain of my ability to steer a course of moderation," he wrote, "fearful of falling into old habits, I took on the temperament if not the convictions of a street corner preacher, prepared to see temptation everywhere, ready to overrun a fragile will."

The acceptance of his fragile will and his admission to himself that he was seducible are both important discoveries of his intro-spection. But he added that his reaction of a total shift in focus was also due to other observations about the city he had hoped would answer some questions and provide the community he'd longed for.

> *Beneath the hum, the motion, I was seeing the steady fracturing of the world taking place. . . . I began to grasp the almost mathematical precision with which America's race and class problems joined; the depth, the ferocity, of resulting tribal wars; the bile that flowed freely not just out on the streets but in the stalls of Columbia's bathrooms as well, where, no matter how many times the administration tried to paint them over, the walls remained scratched with blunt correspondence between niggers and kikes. It was as if all middle ground had collapsed, utterly.*

Here he describes one source of his drive to find the middle, to rediscover a lost and collapsing middle ground that should exist among Americans regardless of color. He sees the crumbling around and inside the halls of Columbia, and at some level he is more able than others to see and feel that crumbling because it resonates with his own internal broken family, his lost father, and his brief but pow-erful experience with Lolo and in Indonesia—all of which height-ened his perceptual capacities. The ability to look both outside and in enriches his writing, no doubt, but also clearly informs the pro-cess of his personal growth. His poignant speech after the shootings in Tucson described the important ways he links introspection to growth: he urged Americans

> *to reflect on the present and the future, on the manner in which we live our lives and nurture our relationships with those who are still with us. We may ask ourselves if we've shown enough kindness and generosity and compassion to the people in our lives. Perhaps we question whether we are doing right by our children or our community and whether our priorities are in order. We recognize our own mortality and are reminded that in the fleeting time we have on this earth, what matters is not wealth, or status, or power, or fame— but rather, how well we have loved, and what small part we have*

played in bettering the lives of others. That process of reflection, of making sure we align our values with our actions—that, I believe, is what a tragedy like this requires.

Other techniques deployed so skillfully in his memoir also reveal coping mechanisms he has developed to handle anxiety. The passage that follows the first night in Jakarta—the night that concluded with the formerly fatherless young Barry falling asleep thinking, "I could barely believe my good fortune"—begins with Lolo telling him, "The first thing to remember is how to protect yourself," as he teaches young Barry how to box. We soon learn that two years have passed—a not uncommon compression of narrative time in the memoir form. But the segue from one event to the next means that Obama learned the proper lesson from that first night—that he must learn how to protect himself. Clearly, his new father figure has in those two years taken it upon himself to teach his stepson how to manage challenges. The way the story moves associatively also reveals to the reader a technique Obama uses to manage anxiety, by shifting gears and focus. When something bothers him, Obama moves quickly to something else. And he does it brilliantly: just a page later he offers the fundamental observation "The world was violent, I was learning, unpredictable and often cruel." But when he turns the page, it is not to deny the past; it is simply not to dwell on it. He doesn't have the obsessional's ruminative nature of self-dissection. Rather, he is introspective without agonizing over whatever his self-examination might uncover.

As a result, he can turn the page and stay in the same book—in life as well as in *Dreams from My Father*. It is as if he were his own doubles partner in tennis, playing at net and baseline simultaneously. Living by turning the page means that when a deed is done, it's done, and hopefully something is learned from it—but positive or negative, it's time to move ahead. For Obama, turning the page is more complex than it is for most people who live this way, because his telling the Left to turn the page means to them to forget what Bush, bankers, and Wall Street CEOs did. Though Obama is not forgetting anything, many on the left want them prosecuted for their various crimes and brought to justice. Ironically, by declaring in his announcement about bin Laden that "Justice has been done," President Obama gave the word new meaning—that an execution can be just even without a courtroom procedure. And though he's not opposed to saying Bush and Wall Street are culpable, he wants to move ahead and assign neither the Department of Justice nor the Navy SEALs to make sure justice is done. His ability to do this deftly enriches our understanding of his quip to Senator McCain when he told him, "The election is over." When he took issue during the campaign with McCain talking about turning the page, Obama felt that McCain was evading responsibility for the economic disaster rather than simply urging us to move forward.

Another way to manage anxiety is to put oneself in another person's shoes, thereby defending against being surprised by what the other person says or does while also getting the chance to be outside oneself for a moment. For a person who grew up feeling he didn't belong, in search of a community where he could fit in, the ability to shift into another's perspective and find the missing commonality he craved was an essential technique for bringing himself closer to his albeit elusive goal. When he's put on the spot, this tactic allows Obama to manage anxiety and deflect whatever question might have challenged him. We see this in the scene in *Dreams from My Father,* discussed earlier, when his college friend Marcus questions why he is reading the "racist tract" *Heart of Darkness*—embarrassing him in front of his friend Regina. In this scene Obama makes a fast recovery by quickly and sequentially assuming two other perspectives. First, he agrees with Marcus that it is a racist book, but then he goes even further, identifying with the perspective of the author, telling Regina that "the book's about the man who wrote it. The European. The American. A particular way of looking at the world. If you can keep your distance, it's all there, in what's said and what's left unsaid."

When examining Obama's memoir writing from a psychoanalytic perspective, it's hard to overlook a statement as rich as "If you can keep your distance, it's all there, in what's said and what's left unsaid." If ever there were any doubt, this particular moment in Obama's impressively articulate exegesis of Conrad, presented as a verbatim quote remembered decades later, is of course about much more than *Heart of Darkness*. Here we see Obama's coping mechanism writ large—distancing himself, assuming the other's perspective, studying the said and unsaid—as a vital and powerful technique deployed so he can understand what may be the biggest question of his life: what makes the white in his family and in himself so afraid of, detached from, and even hateful toward the black—perhaps even his own blackness. Though he has evaded the self-hatred that he observed in many of the black authors he read, he may be afraid of himself, of letting his own powerful black self see the full light of day. Thus he somehow has to keep both white and black selves in check, though it is the furious and frustrated black self that he must also keep from public view. He fears that if he fully felt his power he would risk both destructive outbursts and even greater retaliation from detractors. Nevertheless he remains willing to use that extraordinary power selectively and in a focused way, as in the elimination of Osama bin Laden. This disconnect was most dramatic when he cracked jokes at the 2011 White House Correspondents' Association dinner while knowing full well that his orders to kill bin Laden were already in motion. He was not only shifting perspectives—between being entertainer in chief and commander in chief—he also did so with dramatic completeness: just compare photographs of Obama in his tuxedo with the man in the Situation Room photo the following day. At the dinner he was in complete command of the audience and at his ease; in the Situation Room he looked tense and jittery, the youngest person there, sitting on the edge of his seat—not the center of attention.

Whereas the *Heart of Darkness* exchange depicts Obama shifting perspectives within the action of the narrative, *Dreams from My Father* also shows Obama shifting perspectives within his role as narrator. Never is this more audacious than in the scene when the point of view jumps from young Barry in the yard with the wisdom-dispensing Lolo ("If you can't be strong, be clever and make peace with someone who's strong. But always better to be strong yourself. Always") to the perspective of his mother watching her husband and son through the window. The passage imagines Ann reflecting on several years of her life, from before she left Hawaii through her gradual and growing disappointment with her life in Indonesia and the man who had brought her there, concluding with the troubling realization that "power was taking her son."

Another way to manage anxiety is to use projection, and that's part of what we see at work when he describes his mother watching him from the window: he imagines that his mother is sad watching him grow, because it's safer to project the sadness into his mother than to feel the pain that comes from the recognition that growing up means losing her—and safer still to ascribe the loss to the vague cultural force referred to simply as "power." I think it has to do with his sense that she will lose him when he becomes a man—perhaps like she has lost her other men.

It's hardly a stretch to assume that Obama must have at some point interviewed his mother to learn the intimate and difficult truths he depicts her considering, all beyond the ken of the young boy she's watching. And the seamless leap to her perspective certainly makes for a smoother, more cinematic and engaging experience for the reader than presenting his mother's experience as recalled in an interview or in some other format outside the context of the narrative. But again the perspective-shifting device serves a psychological function for the author/narrator; coming as it does shortly before his mother's decision to send him back to Hawaii, the passage brings to life his struggle to make sense of why he was uprooted once again—if not "to understand how people learn to hate," then to understand why his mother chose to become the second parent to abandon him, a decision that was scarcely explained to him at the time. There's a poignancy to the force of his need to get inside the head of his mother—the mysterious, different-looking, abandoning other (mother without the "m") who likely inspired him to develop the skill of shifting perspectives that has served him so well.

As effectively as Obama assumes his mother's perspective to engage in secondhand self-reflection, he is even more convincing in his own flights of self-analysis. His self-analysis in *Dreams from My Father* is of course retrospective, as all written analyses must be. Still, he successfully re-creates his mood at the various stages of his growth that he describes in the book, making the reader feel very present in his life as he tells it. Exposing various painful episodes that most people would never write about, he does the analysis by narrative and not by stepping back from events (though he does also write from his current level of understanding) to intellectualize or theorize. He is a both/and, rather than either/or, writer. Tellingly, his most vivid self-reflection is in the presence of a variety of maternal swaddling—the musical swaddling of Billie Holiday, for example—that allows him to remember and revisit the past, particularly past conflicts and crises. His mother's voice must have been musical to him when he was a baby, as he clearly establishes an atmosphere conducive to reverie. He uses Billie in the space of several pages in different ways—always for mood but often to reveal his own different perspectives on the world and thus on himself. She was his companion whose voice—to the refrain "I'm a fool to want you"—reached out to him "like a lover"; who taught him the trick of forgetting and of "not caring that it hurts"; who could laugh at life with a "ragged laughter"; and who was willing and able to "endure." That's a lot for one person. And when the songs ended, her absence also had an effect—it sharpened his perception of everything around him, as well as oppressing him with silence.

His states of reverie are not unlike those described by some psychoanalysts writing about the mother's use of reverie to better know her baby, to know his needs and fears and hungers and love. At such moments Obama seems unconsciously to live inside his mother's mind as well as in his own. Did he unconsciously assign Billie Holiday the role of the black mother he never had? Regardless, her presence in song as a catalyst to his flights of honest introspection supply further evidence that the powerful tool of self-analysis that had served him so well is tied up with his lifelong attempt to understand his mother.

Whatever her shortcomings as a parent, Obama's mother played a central role in his transforming himself into the superachiever he has become. Beyond the now-famous 4 A.M. tutoring sessions to supplement the education he was getting in Indonesia, the scene recounted earlier in this book, in which she confronts the high school senior Barry for being a "good-time Charlie," was likely a turning point for him. Though "instead of shouting, [he] laughed," he was bitter about the confrontation and accused her of being scared he'd end up like her father, a likable man full of dreams that bore little relation to reality. He "tried to explain . . . the role of luck in the world, the spin of the wheel," a glimpse of his ongoing struggle with parents who clearly prized reason, education, and the committed pursuit of achievement and credentials. At the time of the confrontation, he was still harboring an unstated, bitter self-assessment as his mother's "experiment [that] had failed." But at some point afterward he revised his position and committed himself to the pursuit of achievement—in spite of, or perhaps due to, his resentment toward his mother's pushing him.

In normal development, rage is often sublimated into achievement and curiosity. Though the drive to achieve has many sources, sublimated rage is certainly one of its essential components, which can also include the sublimation of sexual drives—particularly the Oedipal drive to possess the mother—as well as exhibition fantasies, such as being the forever-special family favorite. It's easy to see how both could come into play for young Barry, driven unconsciously to hold on to his mother and his special place in the family constellation over the course of her two failed marriages and the addition of a half sister to the family. But lacking the presence of a father both to model the healthy expression of rage and to receive his natural share of it, Obama's need to control or deny unexpressed rage at both parents—the absent father and the hard-driving mother—is an obvious explanation of how vigorously he pursued achievement once he made the commitment to pursue it. Interestingly, it wasn't until he was far from his family, first at Columbia and then at Harvard, that his ambition came fully into flower, as if the destructive impulses into which it was sublimated had been too strong to handle when his family was any closer.

Of course, there's love as well as rage present when a son sublimates hostility toward his mother, and Obama has been quite vocal in his appreciation of his mother's contribution to his life. *Dreams from My Father* was written shortly before his mother was diagnosed with the cancer that claimed her life less than a year later, just a few months after the book's publication. His updated afterword to the 2004 reissue acknowledged that he might have written a different book had he known she had so little time to live; one can imagine that he would certainly acknowledge that her "experiment" with him had succeeded, well enough to get him elected president of the *Harvard Law Review.* And he repeatedly cited his mother's values as inspiring his own during his meteoric rise in politics.

Perhaps his most poignant and revealing tribute to his mother wasn't even consciously about her. In a memorable moment in his Nobel Peace Prize acceptance speech he proclaimed, "Somewhere today, a mother facing punishing poverty still takes the time to teach her child, scrapes together what few coins she has to send that child to school—because she believes that a cruel world still has a place for that child's dreams." The statement is at some level autobiographical, revealing an unconscious recognition of how much his mother had to struggle in order to manage, particularly in the years between Barack Sr. and Lolo. In light of his family history, it's not surprising that he sees the mother as the primary protector of the child, the defense against the cruel world, the guardian of the child's dreams. Obama's mother fulfilled all of these roles, encouraging and protecting his dreams, and like the mother in the speech she certainly taught him and sent him to school—going so far as to send him from Indonesia back to Hawaii. In that moment in Oslo, Obama revealed that teaching a child, sending a child to school, is the ultimate expression of motherhood, the most powerful act of maternal love—or at least of the love he received from his mother. Hence, to live up to his education, to pursue the goal of achievement that his mother set for him, is an attempt to maintain a connection with his lost mother, despite his impulse to push her away, and to realize the message she unconsciously passed along that pursuing education and accruing achievements and acclaim can help ward off the self-hatred she worked so hard to defend her mixed-race son against.

Obama's intelligence and powerful drive to achieve are more than the building blocks of his material success: they have their own complex psychological roles, equipping him to face the challenges of his early circumstances and maintaining a path to both connecting himself with and distancing himself from the memory of his parents. His drive and intelligence have served him so well enough materially, professionally, and psychologically that it's predictable and understandable that he would hold on to them, as well he should.

However, his almost magical faith in his abilities and ambition has at times also undermined his effectiveness as president, blinding him to the limitations of his powers of mind and persuasion in a society that does not always place the same premium on intelligence and rationality as he does.

Some critics have linked Obama's intelligence to what they consider his emotional disconnect with the American people; the Republican pundit and *Wall Street Journal* columnist Peggy Noonan went so far in 2010 as to differentiate between multiple varieties of alienation, describing "the president's rhetorical disconnect . . . [in which] he is not emotional enough when he speaks, he doesn't wear his heart on his sleeve, he is aloof, like a lab technician observing the movements within a Petri dish called America" and the "iconic disconnect . . . [in which] the president refuses to or is unable to act as a paternal figure." Both observations have their validity, though probably not as much as his Republican critics would like to believe.

But even members of the Obama team have lamented the downside of the value he places on intelligence. In *Obama's Wars,* Bob Woodward offered a quote from Obama's aide John Podesta, who said that he "was not sure that Obama felt anything, especially in his gut. He intellectualized and then charted the path forward, essentially picking up the emotions of others and translating them into ideas." But this was a weakness, in Podesta's opinion, "an Achilles' heel."

Obama's extreme intelligence can be obstructive in a variety of ways. First, he tends to assume that others are enough like him that they pick up on things quickly and follow his thought patterns. During his time in office, he has had ample opportunity to learn that this is not the case. He admitted as much in the period of introspection that followed one of his first term's darkest moments, Scott Brown's victory in the Massachusetts Senate race, telling George Stephanopoulos:

> Obama: And, you know, if there's one thing that I regret this year, it's that we were so busy just getting stuff done and dealing with the immediate crises that were in front of us, that I think we lost some of that sense of speaking directly to the American people about what their core values are and why we have to make sure those institutions are matching up with those values. And that I do think

is a mistake of mine. I think the assumption was, if I just focus on policy, if I just focus on the, you know, this provision or that law or are we making a good, rational decision here—

Stephanopoulos: That people would get it.

Obama: That people will get it. And I think that, you know, what they've ended up seeing is this feeling of remoteness and detachment where, you know, there's these technocrats up here, these folks who are making decisions. Maybe some of them are good, maybe some aren't, but do they really get us and what we're going through? And I think that I can do a better job of that and partly because I do believe that we're in a stronger position now than we were in a year ago.

It was revealing for Obama at such a moment to acknowledge the possibility that he presents himself as remote and detached—acknowledged, albeit, at arm's length, in the jumbled syntax of others "seeing" a "feeling" of remoteness and detachment, a testament to the difficulty he still has making such an acknowledgment. But his response to this is equally telling: he both gives himself an assignment and lays claim to it being within his capabilities—"I can do a better job"—even as he can't resist taking credit for being in the "stronger position" that will enable him to do so. In other words, he will be able to convince people that he is more than the sum total of his achievements because convincing them is something he thinks he can achieve—and is more likely to do it because of what he has achieved already.

Obama's conviction that he "can do a better job" explaining his programs and priorities leads to a second blind spot obscured by his faith in his abilities: he places such a premium on being able to bring people together and explain complex issues that he forgets that some people cannot be persuaded—some actively refuse to be affected at all—even if his arguments are brilliant and correct. In a sense, he developed his powers of persuasion as an alternative to the opposite route to getting one's way—anger and aggression, which he evaded growing up in the wake of his father's disappearance. His difficulty acknowledging hatred in himself makes it hard for him to see it in others, leading him to retreat from the depressive position. When he can't acknowledge hatred in himself, he precludes ambivalence and replaces it with trying to be evenhanded with everyone. This is not a genuine depressive-position attitude but an evasion. Sometimes one needs to use intelligence to recognize the paranoid-schizoid position, taking into account the power of black-and-white thinking and the fear of the Other. It is not only that he wants to get everyone inside the "tent," as he calls it; he is able everywhere to see bits of a little Barry needing something from him and thus can empathize with his most rabid critics. That is why he listens so well, because everyone has some kind of trouble, and that informs his patience with so many people.

His blindness to the rage and hatred of the Republican opposition is magnified by the belief that everyone has hidden needs, as well as his supreme confidence that he can get through to people who are simply closed down to him. This harkens back to the naive, magical faith he had in his words even before his public speaking debut. Wolffe describes his very intellectual approach to the often unintellectual task of connecting with voters, in this instance dating back to the primary season when he was third in the polls as late as fall 2007. "'I have to figure out how to connect with them,' Obama had told his senior aides. 'I'm not connecting with them. It's a safe, and I've almost got the combination of how to get it open.'"

Of course, he eventually found that particular combination, connecting with enough voters to win the nomination and the White House with a breathtakingly slim record of executive experience or government service. This historic feat fuels a level of self-confidence that can easily tip into arrogance, a favorite label of his critics. Yet the singular nature of his success can also cause great anxiety, because he has little access to models of great, seasoned world leadership—other than perhaps former President Clinton or Nelson Mandela—whom he can turn to for help filling the gaps in his experience. He needs identification figures on a practical level, a signal-savvy catcher to his pitcher. He has searched far and wide for them both inside and outside the self, but his search is complicated by his need to shun anyone, especially on the left, who would remind him of his mother's political passions. The resulting isolation can fuel his anxiety, which triggers a compensatory response that further exposes him to charges of arrogance. But the anxiety does break through in sometimes conflicting ways—when he assumes the role of the scold, for example, or reveals his uncertainty by mentioning the guiding hand that he prayed for in his June 2010 speech on BP.

Most people, when facing a problem they can't solve or understand, either withdraw from the problem or immediately take action to avoid the anxiety of uncertainty. Obama is uniquely able to push through the anxiety of not understanding and learn more about the problem. Unfortunately, his ability to live with that anxiety can inhibit his ability to shift perspective to the point of view of those of us who can't. As intimated by Noonan's categories of disconnection, there are times when we unconsciously need a parental figure—not simply a thinking president but a reassuring president who conveys that he understands our anxiety.

As a result, while his psychological maturity has enabled him to solve problems by thinking about them and not jumping to conclusions—something he did in his response to the Libyan crisis in March 2011, as well as his extensive behind-the-scenes planning to kill bin Laden—his ability to think about different sides of issues interferes with his satisfying the needs of the child parts that each of us has within us. To return to Libya, some of the pressure for intervening that doesn't have to do with oil (and that's the source of most of the pressure he's getting) has to do with wanting a good daddy to protect the Libyans from a bad, murderous one. In these times of economic crisis and international instability, the anxiety of the general public increases, and it is up to the president to reassure without being patronizing, to demonstrate genuine empathy and optimism. Instead, Obama rests too squarely on his record of achievement, for which he struggles to receive the credit he thinks he deserves. Thus we get the list of accomplishments and promises kept that he was rattling off everywhere during the fall 2010 campaign season, from *Rolling Stone* to *The View.*

Compiling an impressive list of achievements isn't the same as healing the pain that those actions sought to address, however. For example, the profits posted by General Motors in early 2011 erased any doubt that the president's bailout of the automobile maker was a major achievement that saved a job and an industry. Yet several of my friends from Detroit, perhaps the most economically devastated and racially tense place in the United States outside Louisiana, confided that the Eminem ad in the 2011 Super Bowl did for that city's hopes and dreams what Obama did in his 2008 campaign but has utterly failed to do since. As the black columnist Melissa Harris-Perry put it in *The Nation,* "The solidarity and creativity of the Obama campaign was quickly replaced by the sober predictability and insularity of the Obama administration." Such lack of creative energy leaves hopeless people still hopeless. That remains the case, with the dramatic exception of the Navy SEAL operation against bin Laden.

Further contributing to his difficulty sustaining the hope of his discouraged supporters is the speed with which he processes emotions—so quickly that he underestimates their power over others who are genuinely suffering and yearning for something to ease their anxieties. Even adult voters have child parts that, like all children, need authority figures to explain exactly what they're doing and why. Obama seems so unwilling to do this that one suspects that his intelligence makes it hard to see this need without patronizing or talking down to people.

Finally, Obama's challenges connecting with people less intelligent than he is might have been ameliorated had he surrounded himself with people more adept at it. Instead, he has tapped advisers and cabinet members who embody his own blind belief in the primacy of achievement. This is hardly news to Obama observers; in his review of Jonathan Alter's *The Promise* in *The New York Review of Books,* Frank Rich zeroed in on this trait and added his own two cents: "Alter's chronicle confirms that the biggest flaw in Obama's leadership has to do with his own team, not his opponents, and it's a flaw that's been visible from the start. He is simply too infatuated with the virtues of the American meritocracy that helped facilitate his own rise. 'Obama's faith lay in cream rising to the top,' Alter wrote. 'Because he himself was a product of the great American postwar meritocracy, he could never fully escape seeing the world from the status ladder he had ascended.'" As we'll see in the next chapter, we can all benefit from taking a long look at what motivates his decisions regarding the company he keeps.

CHAPTER 7

The Company He Keeps

People need each other far more than most of us can bear to
know.

—C. Fred Alford

He must have felt that he had lost the old warm world, paid
a high price for living too long with a single dream. He must
have looked up at an unfamiliar sky through frightening leaves
and shivered as he found what a grotesque thing a rose is and
how raw the sunlight was upon the scarcely created grass. A
new world, material without being real, where poor ghosts,
breathing dreams like air, drifted fortuitously about.

—F. Scott Fitzgerald, *The Great Gatsby*

By the time he wrote *The Audacity of Hope,* a decade after his
mother's passing, Obama could describe both parents' influence on
his life with elegance and clarity:

*It is only in retrospect, of course, that I fully understand how deeply
this spirit of hers influenced me—how it sustained me despite the
absence of a father in the house, how it buoyed me through the rocky
shoals of my adolescence, and how it invisibly guided the path I
would ultimately take. My fierce ambitions might have been fueled
by my father—by my knowledge of his achievements and failures, by
my unspoken desire to somehow earn his love, and by my resentments
and anger toward him. But it was my mother's fundamental faith—in
the goodness of people and in the ultimate value of this brief life we've
each been given—that channeled those ambitions. It was in search of*

confirmation of her values that I studied political philosophy, looking for both a language and systems of action that could help build community and make justice real.

Inevitably, Obama's fond memories are colored by the myth-making he engages in when presenting his family history, especially regarding the particulars of his parents' separation. All children make myths of their own about their parents, usually to escape troubling realities of their existence and become part of a better or different life, and one way of looking at *Dreams from My Father* is as part of that process, particularly in light of young Barry's fondness for myth. Freud wrote about the ubiquity of something he called "family romance," fantasies by which children invent new families for themselves. In one respect, the family Obama describes in his memoir—the mother and son left by the father—is a fantasy, as her living in Seattle at the time of Barack Sr.'s departure at the very least complicates the dynamic of who left whom to an extent that is not addressed in his memoirs (although he does use the conspicuously circumspect statement "a separation occurred" to describe the event). His myth is a protective one; I think that if he had begun to examine what role his mother had in their separation, he might have found himself angrier at her than he'd ever imagined—or was willing to risk.

Obama's myth of his family also includes his version of the best qualities of both parents that he still emulates today. They clearly shared the capacity to dream, even on a global scale of cultural cooperation and world peace. Both parents politically and socially believed that they were their brother's keeper. His mother insisted on academic excellence, even though she expressed resentment at his father's being "stubborn," putting his own education ahead of his family. Both had personal dignity that they were willing to defend: the legends about his father often involve him teaching someone a lesson about some form of trespass, and when his mother overheard his prep school friends commenting on "the lack of food in the fridge or the less-than-perfect housekeeping," she informed him that as "a single mother going to school again and raising two kids," she wouldn't put up "with any snotty attitudes" from him or his friends—the only instance in the book of her even acknowledging the burdens of her circumstances.

Though he espouses his own version of his parents' beliefs in his speeches, he has also revealed a skepticism about their naiveté—dismissing his mother's "needlepoint virtues" as reliant on "a faith that rational, thoughtful people could shape their own destiny" that he didn't share—that reveals that his attitude about their more noble attributes has at least an element of ambivalence. And one is left to wonder about their not-so-good qualities. His father was violent and drank too much, and his mother was virtually blinded to her abandoning husband's serious faults, driven by a need to see goodness in everyone that she in turn impressed on her young son. These and other qualities have to be considered among the influences on Obama in both his early years and adulthood, and we will see how they continue to resonate in the relationships he maintains with the people around him today.

For a coming-of-age memoir of a boy who essentially lost two fathers growing up, *Dreams from My Father* is noticeably absent relationships with any surrogate father figures that fatherless boys and young men often find or cultivate. Obama is so dismissive of any early childhood contact with Barack Sr. that he refers to his father's 1971 visit to Hawaii, when Barry was ten, as "the first and only time we'd met." There were two real father figures in his life—his stepfather and grandfather—but by age ten he had been taken away from Lolo and was coming to see his grandfather as the ineffectual dreamer he would one day antagonize his mother by comparing himself to. He grew progressively disappointed with both: the former had compromised his idealism right in front of his stepson Barry, and the latter was sad that he had given up so much in life and that he couldn't protect his grandson from his grandmother's racism. "These men had become object lessons for me," Obama wrote, "men I might love but never emulate, white and brown men whose fates didn't speak to my own."

It's hard to imagine that young Barry didn't project any of his inevitable father hunger onto a coach, a teacher, or some other paternal stand-in, but the male authority figures in this stage of his life are only sketchily drawn or mentioned in passing. Instead, he wrote, "It was into my father's image, the black man, the son of Africa, that I'd packed all the attributes I sought in myself, the attributes of Martin and Malcolm, DuBois and Mandela." It was an image forged out of fantasy and nourished by his need to compensate for feeling any pain or anger at having been abandoned. Of course, his father died in November 1982, before he could test the fantasy against reality, before he went to Africa to find his father through finding his half siblings and others touched by the "old man." He wrote poignantly of the moment of discovery about the truth of his father—how he felt "giddy" that "the king [was] overthrown" when he learned that his father was an abusive and bitter drunk, a ghost he had been trying to capture for himself, into which he could breathe his own life. He realized soon, however, that "the fantasy of my father had at least kept me from despair. Now he was dead, truly. He could no longer tell me how to live." With a living father one can move from despair to repair; the despair in Obama's case can better be called a break or even a rupture. Despair implies total loss of any anchoring belief—in oneself or another. Most important, however, despair is the opposite of hope. His father's reality was by far too disappointing, so he adapted his father's dreams and looked elsewhere for reminders of the man he had once thought his father was.

In adulthood, Obama has displaced his father hunger onto other men with characteristics he is unconsciously drawn to—aggressive, successful men who are seemingly unafraid to speak their minds and unworried about what others think of them. Narcissistic and self-confident to a fault, they embody qualities of both his father—or at least his fantasy father—and to a lesser extent Lolo. They represent fantasies from his past, when his mind was filled by his mother's version of his father's dreams. A hero-worshipping romantic with stars in her eyes, she fell for men unlike her own father in virtually every way, strong dark men with ambition and passion, until she got to know them and saw that they were also stubborn dreamers who liked to drink. They proved to be disappointments to both mother and son; since his father's death, however, Obama has made room in his personal and professional life for a series of narcissists who can fill his father's shoes and who offer an unconscious identification with his mother by mirroring her own attraction to men like this.

With this in mind, we can see a connection between the strong, willful, and confident men who have played roles in his adult life, from Chicago Mayor Harold Washington—who played a largely fantasy role, because he died two years after Obama moved to Chicago—to Trinity Church pastor Jeremiah Wright up to such current, high-powered, accomplished advisers as Treasury Secretary Timothy Geithner. Whereas Washington and Wright ultimately abandoned him, repeating the pattern—Washington was like the father he never knew, while Wright was a palpable person to whom Obama related and who betrayed him—the draw is not to repeat tragedy but to find sources of strength. He so completely internalizes the characteristics of such strong men and incorporates them into his daily affairs, regardless of their race or age, that he unconsciously gains help by having a father figure nearby instead of one buried in an obscure Kenyan cemetery.

Harold Washington, the first black mayor of Chicago, was the first such father figure, albeit at a distance. During Obama's initial interview for the community organizer job in Chicago, his soon-to-be boss, Jerry Kellman (called Marty Kauffman in Obama's memoir), asked what Obama knew about the city.

> *"America's most segregated city," I said. "A black man, Harold Washington, was just elected mayor, and white people don't like it."*
>
> *"So you've been following Harold's career," Marty said. "I'm surprised you haven't gone to work for him."*
>
> *"I tried. His office didn't write back."*

Obama introduces Washington as a remote, unreachable and controversial black authority figure who rejects him. The father parallels are even clearer the next time Washington comes up; shortly after Obama's move to Chicago, the new mayor is already seen like young Barry's absent father—as mythical and larger than life:

> *His picture was everywhere: on the walls of shoe repair shops and beauty parlors; still glued to lampposts from the last campaign; even in the windows of the Korean dry cleaners and Arab grocery stores, displayed prominently, like some protective totem. From the*

barbershop wall, that portrait looked down on me now: the handsome,
grizzled face, the bushy eyebrows and mustache, the twinkle in the
eyes.

The new mayor became a symbol for others to project their hopes
onto. "Like my idea of organizing, he held out an offer of collective
redemption," Obama wrote. "People weren't just proud of Harold.
They were proud of themselves." But Washington proved to be the
effective realist that Obama Sr. wasn't, alienating blacks and activists, among others, by his closeness to the white and business communities. Perhaps angry at the parts of himself he sees in supporters
who fell for a father figure, Obama's sympathies are with the mayor
in his account, rather than with "people who preferred the dream to
the reality, impotence to compromise." Obama's dismissing people
who hold too tightly to their dreams as clinging to impotence is a
glimpse of how he was working through his anger at himself for letting himself be let down by his dreamer father. Washington was able
to get reelected by a huge margin even though various factions were
not happy with him, with a formula for political success that likely
provides a model for Obama, whose description of Washington's
reelection campaign resonates with Obama's own postelection first-
term strategy: "a cautious campaign . . . a campaign of consolida-
tion, of balanced budgets and public works. . . . He saw no reason to
take any big risks, no reason to hurry."

Washington died within a year of his reelection, which may be
why he reminds Obama of his mythologized and severed connection
with his own abandoning father enough to evoke anger at Washington's followers. His next father figure would abandon him too,
but not until long after he wrote about him in two books. Obama
first heard about Jeremiah Wright when the Trinity Church pastor
expressed interest in bringing fifty disparate churches together to
forge a common goal. This wish, part of community organizing, was
congruent with how he understood his father's drive to unify Kenya
as well as to unify peoples who have all kinds of different cultures
and values. We all have unconscious templates from the past onto
which the present is sometimes written—often incorrectly. Perhaps
an unconscious template of Obama's was activated in his first meet-

ing with Reverend Wright, who was late. He was funny and charming about it, much like the story Barry had heard and romanticized about how his father had been very late for the first date with his mother—and how his father's charm had won the day. He too had been full of excuses.

But as Barack was getting to know Wright, he felt accompanied on paths he was already on, appreciating Wright's capacity to tolerate and even maintain close contact with groups whose views differed greatly from his. Obama had already realized this capacity in himself as president of *Harvard Law Review* when he befriended and worked with conservative law students as much as—or more than—he did with the more liberal students. The way Reverend Wright described his church must have been music to Obama's ears and reminded him of things his father had said years earlier: "Some of my fellow clergy don't appreciate what we're about. They feel like we're too radical. Others, we ain't radical enough. Too emotional. Not emotional enough. . . . Half of 'em think that the former gangbanger or the former Muslim got no business in a Christian church. Other half think any black man with an education or a job, or any church that respects scholarship, is somehow suspect."

Obama saw in Wright an effective father figure who genuinely practiced what he preached—something not all that common in any walk of life, certainly not in a field plagued with hypocrisy and scandal. His identification with Wright happened fast, cemented by an item in the 1979 Trinity Church brochure that cautioned parishioners against intense pursuit of "middleclassness," which "hypnotizes the successful brother or sister into believing they are better than the rest and teaches them to think in terms of 'we' and 'they' instead of 'US.'" For someone who had been healing divisions all his life, this sounded like the music of home.

Wright was also a realist, mincing no words when he cut through Obama's wish to see social conditions in Chicago as being about class and economics more than about race: "Life's not safe for a black man in this country, Barack. Never has been. Probably never will be."

Like Washington, Wright provided a stark contrast to his father's idealism; by helping him contain conflicting views, he provided a vital and supportive structure he was missing from his childhood, a psychic scaffolding that freed Obama to develop his own ideas. Obama was thus able to ask of Wright a variation of the key question he never had a chance to ask his father, about the true cost of preserving unity, an issue Obama's followers have asked about his presidency: "Would the interest in maintaining such unity allow Reverend Wright to take a forceful stand on the latest proposals to reform public housing? And if men like Reverend Wright failed to take a stand, if churches like Trinity refused to engage with real power and risk genuine conflict, then what chance would there be of holding the larger community intact?" He was prescient about his own trouble as president standing up to power.

There is one other essential element in Obama's decision to join Trinity Church, and that is Wright's insistence that the problems facing his parishioners were about race more than about class. Though Obama argued about this, Wright was steadfast. Moreover, Wright's church was black—only marginally integrated—and his politics were born out of the civil rights struggles of the 1960s. By that time Obama had clearly devoted himself to being black, not biracial. He had been tending in that direction and, though he continued to be comfortable with whites, had found a mostly black community in South Side Chicago, where he remains, when not in Washington, through the present day. Reverend Wright was an important figure solidifying his decision to self-identify as black. It was imperative, once he decided to be black, that he join a black church, because otherwise he would have been pulled back into internal conflicts about his racial identity, since he was raised—with the exception of Lolo—entirely by white people before leaving home for college.

His father hunger made Wright the one figure who could substitute—at least for a time—for his actual father. Obama took the title of his second book, *The Audacity of Hope* (2006), from one of Jeremiah Wright's sermons and adapted some of Wright's homily rhythm in his own speaking style. I think it was in fact his father hunger that unconsciously drove Obama to identify himself as black—just as much as his comfort around kids of similar skin color that contrasted with whites' dis-ease around him. It was the dream from his father that he become black—a dream promoted actively by his mother. But it was his father hunger—and his need to belong—that make his choice of church so psychologically congruent. As the sociological researcher Shelby Steele wrote in *A Bound Man: Why We Are Excited About Obama and Why He Can't Win*, "Too much of the Obama who grew up in Hawaii and Indonesia is lost to the Obama who joins a South Side black church with a 'Black Value System' focused on 'Black freedom,' the 'black community,' and the 'black family.' In this church, the adjective 'black' is a more consistent theme than any of the nouns it modifies. It is invoked as an atavism, a God-given specialness that is thought meaningful in itself. It is a claim not just of racial difference but of racial difference to the point of an essential superiority." The irony is that Obama could remain internally white without having to dye his skin and keep his whiteness secret from others, something he decided to do by the time he was thirteen. Many of his most lasting friendships evolved from meeting members of that church.

Of course, Wright ultimately caused his own share of conflict in Obama's life; after presiding over his wedding to Michelle and contributing the title of his second book, Wright became a problem for then-candidate Obama. When given the chance to restore unity on the national stage, Wright only made things worse, blaming Jews and then Zionists for keeping him from Obama. In that respect Wright fulfilled his father figure role even more completely, becoming one more charismatic figure who turned out to be a disappointment.

Now Obama is aligning with less apparent or compelling father figures: Timothy Geithner, Ben Bernanke, and others on his economic team who share his father's confidence and narcissism, though not his charisma. It's not clear who seduced whom, but, dazzled by the glamour of the Clinton financial advisers who brought the United States such prosperity in the 1990s, Obama appeared to lionize and idealize the economic team members he assembled. Among them were educated men who, in the years after their initial public service, had amassed enormous wealth working for the same industries they had once and now again regulated. In Obama's defense, he wanted experienced people who knew how to protect wealth—and hopefully protect the United States' wealth as well—and didn't want to risk giving the assignment to unproven economists in a time of national crisis. Still, evoking another of Obama's father figures, it's as if he chose people who ended up like his stepfather, Lolo, working for the oil companies rather than for the people he had once championed.

Obama searched for a father, for someone to relate to who could help him—a strong man who knew what to do. When he seemed to be at his wits' end, speaking in New Orleans weeks too late after the BP oil gusher, Obama made another plea for a strong man, this time at the end of his speech. He spoke of the fishermen's prayer that they offered even after this incomprehensible disaster:

> *The ceremony goes on in good times and in bad. It took place after Katrina, and it took place a few weeks ago—at the beginning of the most difficult season these fishermen have ever faced.*
>
> *And still they came and they prayed. For as a priest and a former fisherman said of the tradition, "The blessing is not that God has promised to remove all obstacles and dangers. The blessing is that He is with us always," a blessing that's granted ". . . even in the midst of the storm."*
>
> *What sees us through—what has always seen us through—is our strength, our resilience, and our unyielding faith that something better awaits us if we summon the courage to reach for it. Tonight, we pray for that courage. We pray for the people of the Gulf. And we pray that a hand may guide us through the storm towards a brighter day. Thank you, God bless you, and may God bless the United States of America.*

One can cynically summarize the thinking behind the speech as "when all else fails, pray." But it is the specifics of his prayer that strike a deep chord: he is praying for his father's hand, the hand that was never there to guide him. His father told his mother and grandparents, during that emotion-laden visit with ten-year-old Barry in Hawaii, that his son "needed a firm hand." He has hungered for that hand throughout his life, at times looking to Lolo, then to his friend Ray, to Gramps, later to Frank, the old poet, and then to black literature by Ralph Ellison, W. E. B. DuBois, and Richard Wright, to Martin Luther King, Jr., and Malcolm X, later still later to Mayor Washington and to a fantasy of Michelle's father, Fraser Robinson, who was devoted to his family and continued to work for years without complaining about his multiple sclerosis, and then to Reverend Wright. Now, as president, he looks to various disappointing people: from Joe Biden to Rahm Emanuel to Larry Summers to Tim Geithner. But they all disappoint—by being human, like Lolo and Gramps; by betraying him, like Reverend Wright; by revealing what young Obama saw as their own unmetabolized self-hatred, like most of the black authors he studied; or by hating whites, like Malcolm. Then there are fantasy figures, potentially reliable fathers he barely knew who died before he could fully connect with them, such as Washington and Robinson.

All of us are unconsciously drawn to revisit our core conflicts throughout our lives. The reasons for these attractions are many: we may be hoping to rewrite and resolve our life's story, to relive familiar pain as a way of staying connected to our earliest attachments, or to prove to our parents that they were wrong about us. Obama's draw to men who look promising but ultimately disappoint him recurs with enough force and frequency to suggest a connection to a core conflict—namely, his unexpressed rage about his father's departure. What has changed, however, is that Obama now believes he is in control of what is and isn't repeated: in his new position as president, he is himself essentially the father he has been waiting for. He unconsciously said as much when he declared during the 2008 campaign, "We are the ones we have been waiting for." He is living out his father's dreams. The problem with being the father is that someone else is cast in the role of the abandoned son—namely, his most ardent followers, who have been disappointed by his compromises and reversals. Still trapped in his forgotten inner struggle between turning away from his father and hoping for his return, he has abandoned his base the way his own father abandoned him: turning his back on the heart and soul of his support, the kind of love only hero worshippers and three-year-olds have to give, and disappointing them the way he was disappointed, preventing them from getting the father they want since he wasn't able to get that father himself. This was perhaps never clearer than when he cut heating-oil budgets for the poor to pay for tax cuts for the richest of the rich.

Obama carried around the last letter received from his father, unopened, for years. And he wrote bitterly about the man to whom he would eventually address a response:

I had gone through several drafts, crossing out lines, struggling for the appropriate tone, resisting the impulse to explain too much. "Dear Father." "Dear Dad." "Dear Dr. Obama." And now he had answered me, cheerful and calm. Know where you belong, he advised. He made it sound simple, like calling directory assistance. "Information—what city, please?" "Uh . . . I'm not sure. I was hoping you could tell me. The name's Obama. Where do I belong?"

The passage offers perhaps the sharpest glimpse at his smoldering rage toward his father and the confusion that his yearning for him left in its wake. Obama's memories of his naive yearnings for a father and a family are painful enough that he resents their power over him; he blocks out these memories by housing them in his adoring supporters. Turning his back on them allows him to become his father or at least identify with the elements of his personality that hurt him—further blocking out the discomfort caused by painful memories. This is but a part of a self-perpetuating psychological feedback loop. Denying the pain allows him to deny his father's destructiveness; his blindness to his anger toward that destructiveness makes it possible to deny the very real destructiveness he faces today, as presented by a Republican Party determined to make him a one-term president. And by failing to see this real threat to his presidency, he is able to direct his antipathy toward his supporters, disappointing his base as he looks to see what he has in common with his opponents, unconsciously making nice to his father in the hope that he isn't really destructive after all.

In persistently trying to reach out to such obviously uncooperative naysayers, such as Eric Cantor and John Boehner, Obama unconsciously identifies with his mother, upholding her myopic myths about his father. But at the same time he resents the naiveté that allowed her to adore his father and projects that naive idealism onto his base. In this unconscious alignment of the Left with his mother, he equates their support with his mother's suffocating emphasis on his need to excel and to pursue social justice. And in his pursuit of ultraconservatives he almost mocks his mother's consistently lionizing her polygamous African prince. He resents the Left as he sees himself as their experiment the way he felt he was his mother's, the young black man they elected president like the young mixed-race boy his mother bore to become a new kind of American. And despite her fierceness and her insistence on personal integrity, Obama put his mother down, albeit gently, at several junctures of *Dreams from My Father*—as when he called her "a lonely witness for secular humanism, a soldier for New Deal, Peace Corps, position-paper liberalism." He was writing about his mother in 1994, but he might just as well have been discussing the progressive faithful whom he electrified as a candidate and abandoned as president, the very people whom his spokesman later referred to as the "professional Left." Obama feels so much contempt toward his mother and so much guilt over this contempt that he must diminish her causes as unrealistic while he continuously distances himself from New Deal politics. At a September 16, 2010, fund-raiser in Greenwich, Connecticut, Obama went on a mocking binge:

> *Democrats, just congenitally, tend to get—to see the glass as half empty. (Laughter.) If we get an historic health care bill passed—oh, well, the public option wasn't there. If you get the financial reform bill passed—then, well, I don't know about this particular derivatives rule, I'm not sure that I'm satisfied with that. And gosh, we haven't yet brought about world peace and—(Laughter.) I thought that was going to happen quicker. (Laughter.) You know who you are. (Laughter.)*

Though he disappoints his supporters, however, Obama has a counteridentification with father where his own family is concerned—that is, he clearly makes every effort not to abandon or disappoint his daughters. In *The Audacity of Hope,* he wrote candidly about how much he missed his family after starting his Senate duties—limiting his D.C. time to three nights a week and calling Michelle and his daughters often. Compounding this was the familiar source of discomfort deriving from his feeling like an outsider; observing that he couldn't really talk to other colleagues living apart from their families since the average age of new senators was almost twenty years more than his own. By that point, he had already found a community back in Chicago in Trinity Church, led by the father figure who hadn't yet embarrassed him, and his distance from this sense of community likely contributed to his sense of isolation. And his experience of being an "other" on the outside was probably further underscored by the nature of the U.S. Senate itself, where Obama had far fewer African-American colleagues than he'd grown accustomed to in the Illinois State Senate. All three environments— state senate, church, and family—provided Obama with opportunities to heal many of the dynamics that had long challenged him, but none was more important to this process than the family.

He also had a close circle of friends, one of whom was a basketball-playing classmate from Harvard Law School, the others people he'd met at Trinity Church. They all lived nearby, were well educated, and held the compatible values of the first post–civil rights generation. He remains friends with those men and women to this day, and has tried to stay close to them as best he can during his presidency. The company he keeps is yet another sign of his strong psychological health. The late Dr. Elizabeth Zetzel of Harvard, a psychoanalyst who influenced the research of George Vaillant mentioned earlier, looked at whether her patients had made lasting friendships as a sign of genuine ego strength, a sign that they were not dominated by narcissism. And Obama's friendships remain lasting and strong.

Obama's fierce protectiveness of his family is evident and admirable. But in addition to safeguarding his wife and kids, he's also protecting himself. There are two strains of self-protection at play: he protects himself from being destructive as his father was, and he also protects himself from confronting how destructive his father was. He has knit together a family, something he's always yearned for, and unconsciously made it into a magical protection against the pain and danger of not belonging to a larger community. At the same time as his lovingly established personal family serves as a healthy repair of his childhood family, painful conflicts from that original family get magically denied and replayed on the political canvas. Placating the Republicans with positive statements about their patriotism serves a psychological function similar to placating a frightening abusive father with love, telling him that he's really a good daddy; the bad fathers are outside his family, and thus there is only a good father on the inside.

The most visible difference between the father's and son's choices regarding their family lives involves the women they married. The selection of a spouse falls under the category of what psychoanalysts refer to as "object choice." We call people who do the choosing "subjects" and the people chosen "objects." The relationships between people, especially the emotionally freighted relationships that exist within the mind, we call "object relations." In selecting a partner, there are both complementary and concordant elements at play: complementary when choosing someone who is like one's childhood image of a parent; concordant when choosing someone who is like one's childhood image of himself. People who make complementary relationships have the capacity to see their partner as "Other" and appreciate the differences between them; people whose relationships are primarily concordant choose someone like themselves who share the same characteristics. In any event, all kinds of unconscious factors and forces come into play once a marriage starts. I once wrote a paper (in 1980) based on that dramatic marital change, which I called, "Who Are You and What Have You Done with My Wife?" Ironically, I could have titled this book "Who Are You and What Have You Done with My President?"

Object choice depends on many factors, such as the conscious need to get away from home while unconsciously choosing a part-ner who reminds them of that very home, or the need to have the kind of family one felt one didn't have as a child; people who do so marry for family. In Obama's case, he needed to find someone unlike his mother—to avoid the risk of both incestuous danger and Oedipal triumph over his father and to neutralize her constant psy-chic presence in his mind. The most obvious person would have been someone nonwhite, which also serves to help him evade or deny similarities with his father—as well as a woman who loved her father and therefore wouldn't get angry at that father and take it out on him (as he perceived his mother doing). Barack Jr. was choosing not to follow in his father's footsteps by leading a white woman to the altar (his father had two white wives). The accounts of Barack and Michelle's courtship make it clear that he was drawn to marrying someone who came from a strong family that, unlike his, was consistent and stayed together under one roof. That this strong family was African-American offered him another arena in which to repair his childhood family, while creating a familial space in which he wouldn't have to be self-conscious about his skin color. (It's revealing that he ended things with the one white woman he seriously dated before Michelle in large part because he felt he could never feel comfortable with her and would end up living in her white world, according to his description of the relationship in *Dreams from My Father.*)

Obama said as much in a 1996 interview for *The New Yorker* that was published in 2009: "All my life, I have been stitching together a family, through stories or memories or friends or ideas. Michelle has had a very different background—very stable, two-parent family, mother at home, brother and dog, living in the same house all their lives. We represent two strands of family life in this country—the strand that is very stable and solid, and then the strand that is breaking out of the constraints of traditional families, traveling, separated, mobile. I think there was that strand in me of imagining what it would be like to have a stable, solid, secure family life." His further comments about their bond revealed both concordant and complementary elements of his attraction, as well as the important sense of belonging their union offers, as "she is at once completely familiar to me, so that I can be myself and she knows me very well and I trust her completely, but at the same time she is also a complete mystery to me in some ways. . . . It's that tension between familiarity and mystery that makes for something strong, because, even as you build a life of trust and comfort and mutual support, you retain some sense of surprise or wonder about the other person."

Obama's yearning for family is linked to his long-held desire to find and belong to a larger community. When he heard Regina, his black friend at Occidental who also had a single mother, describe her extended family and neighbors in South Side Chicago, he responded with envy and longing for her "vision of black life in all its possibility." With little firsthand knowledge of black community life, he set out to fulfill that yearning through his work, first as a community organizer, then as a politician. As president he finds himself within and leading the ultimate community, but there are signs that the concept of community remains so distant and abstract that he fails to understand the power of true community. In the February 2011 press conference to present his budget he said that he would protect certain elements of the community, refusing to cut funds to food stamps, the elderly, and veterans suffering from post-traumatic stress disorder. But his focus on individuals and families does not convey that he sees and appreciates their being part of a larger community; he sees specific constituents rather than the community as a whole, a surprising blind spot for someone who—somewhat longingly—speaks about how much more we have in common than we realize.

He talks about one America but doesn't treat that America as the organic whole he says it is. He doesn't say, for instance, that the rich need to take some responsibility for the poor, that we are one nation. Instead he cuts needed domestic programs in order to spare the rich more taxes, communicating to them that he doesn't really believe we are one nation with responsibilities that embrace the whole. He grew up in a fragmented world—internally and externally—and has the idea of a United States without the experience of solidarity, with the possible exception of being part of a basketball team. Otherwise he has remained outside—an organizer or leader, not a member. This is true of most presidents, but many have a long tradition of working hard to elect other candidates from their party, for instance. Obama does not. He is a post–civil rights black American growing up outside a tradition of solidarity.

At times he was even at odds with that previous generation, as in 2000, when he decided to try for the congressional seat held by the popular Bobby Rush, a man who was once an officer in the Illinois Black Panther Party, who handily beat Obama and returned to office. (Rush later told Obama's biographer David Remnick that Obama was too close to Hyde Park "elites" to be connected viscerally to Chicago's black community and that it was "amazing how [Obama] formed a black identity.") Obama's ambivalence toward community was not entirely new. Even as he lamented it, the young Obama, years earlier, had perpetuated his outsider state by not telling his black friends about his white family, creating a secret that made him feel more alone than necessary, even though he ironically was doing it in order to fit in. As an organizer, his work certainly exposed him to communities, but he entered, served, and left them as an outsider. That work filled a psychological gap that evoked Obama's anger at some of Mayor Washington's discontented supporters but proved to be fertile ground for creating a fantasy of making a difference—the difference of creating a community where it wasn't there before. This fantasy is still at play in his presidency: we are the largest community imaginable, and he wants to organize it. Except we are not a community, and unconsciously he wants to do what can't be done. He sees commonality where there isn't any, much as his parents did. He confuses trench buddies fighting a common enemy for community—as when the announcement of the death of bin Laden included an evocation of the immediate aftermath of 9/11. "On that day," he said almost ten years later, "no matter where we came from, what God we prayed to, or what race or ethnicity we were, we were united as one American family." And as we've seen, his parents' philosophies can elicit from him responses that range from conflicted to contemptuous, though as a candidate he trumpeted many of their ideals.

What may be further undermining his position on community involves his complex, conflicted, and ultimately terminated dynamic with the man who finally helped him find a place where he felt he belonged. Reverend Jeremiah Wright's Trinity Church offered a previously unknown sense of a community shared by people with the same skin color as his own, where he could be himself and work with others like him to help cultivate their connection to the outside world. As described in *Dreams from My Father,* his epiphany took place during the sermon titled "The Audacity of Hope," whose message would have more direct and touching impact on Obama than the stories he had witnessed and been involved with during his previous three years as a community organizer. Wright begins by citing a sermon he heard years ago, from a pastor inspired by a painting of a bruised and bloodied harpist whose instrument has a single frayed string, sitting on a mountaintop surrounded by a valley ravaged by famine and strife:

> *"It is this world, a world where cruise ships throw away more food in a day than most residents of Port-au-Prince see in a year, where white folks' greed runs a world in need, apartheid in one hemisphere, apathy in another hemisphere. That's the world! On which hope sits!"*
>
> *And so it went, a meditation on a fallen world. While the boys next to me doodled on their church bulletin, Reverend Wright spoke of Sharpsville and Hiroshima, the callousness of policy makers in the White House and in the State House. As the sermon unfolded, though, the stories of strife became more prosaic, the pain more immediate. The reverend spoke of the hardship that the congregation would face tomorrow, the pain of those far from the mountaintop, worrying about paying the light bill.*

But as Reverend Wright leads his congregation to identify with the suffering and despair of the fallen world in the painting, he also encourages them to identify with the painting's harpist, "looking upwards towards the heavens. She dares to hope. . . . She has the audacity . . . to make music . . . and praise God . . . on the one string . . . she has left!" Soon Obama's fellow worshippers are on their feet, clapping and crying out, and he "began to hear all the notes from the past three years swirl about me. . . . The desire to let go, the desire to escape, the desire to give oneself up to a God that could somehow put a floor on despair." The sermon is constructed to shift focus from the inspirational to the specific, steadily deepening Wright's connection with his congregation. But as soon as Obama identifies with "the desire to give oneself up" to God, he expands his connection beyond the walls of Trinity Church and across centuries of black experience. Here is a community that can export its connectedness on a global scale, at once defined and limitless, which appealed to the ambitious young politician.

> *And in that single note—hope!—I heard something else; at the foot of that cross, inside the thousands of churches across the city, I imagined the stories of ordinary black people merging with the stories of David*

and Goliath, Moses and Pharaoh, the Christians in the lion's den, Ezekiel's field of dry bones. Those stories—of survival, and freedom, and hope—became our story, my story; the blood that had spilled was our blood, the tears our tears; until this black church, on this bright day, seemed once more a vessel carrying the story of a people into future generations and into a larger world. Our trials and triumphs became at once unique and universal, black and more than black; in chronicling our journey, the stories and songs gave us a means to reclaim memories that we didn't need to feel shamed about, memories more accessible than those of ancient Egypt, memories that all people might study and cherish—with which we could start to rebuild. And if a part of me continued to feel that this Sunday communion sometimes simplified our condition, that it could sometimes disguise or suppress the very real conflicts among us and would fulfill its promise only through action, I also felt for the first time how that spirit carried within it, nascent, incomplete, the possibility of moving beyond our narrow dreams.

Caught up in the commotion surrounding him—Wright repeating the sermon's title like a mantra, the choir lifting their voices in song, the congregation applauding its members who joined Wright at the altar in response to his call, Obama notices "a light touch on the top of my hand. I looked down to see the older of the two boys sitting beside me, his face slightly apprehensive as he handed me a pocket tissue." The scene ends with the boy's mother giving Obama a faint smile before returning her attention to the front of the church. "It was only as I thanked the boy that I felt the tears running down my cheeks."

With its frame within a frame within a frame, the episode is classic Obama in form—he's recounting Wright's memory of someone else's sermon, analyzing the story implied by a painting that no one sees. And he once again sees personal suffering in terms of societal and political conditions, an intellectual perspective he shares with Wright. But the layers of narrative nesting within one another, typically a distancing device, make Obama's emotional response to the sermon that much more powerful. Though he couches it in terms of Christian faith, Obama gleans from Wright's sermon a profound understanding of the importance of community spirit.

The sermon certainly echoes the kinds of speeches given by both his parents and his grandparents, just more elegant and coming from a man who had successfully converted ephemeral dreams into quotidian reality. Despite his intellectual barriers against recognizing the strength of his emotional response, the sermon brought from Obama the tears of an outsider who had finally found a community, with the promise of ties to larger communities across other places and times. Obama stops short of directly admitting the deep feelings the sermon elicits, portraying himself as unaware of his reaction until called to his attention by the child sitting next to him. Perhaps it really happened this way, but the symbolism is almost too good to be true—the fatherless young boy helping the grown man accept and celebrate the fulfillment of a boyhood dream to belong. Wright clearly invited Obama into the community he had been seeking since he was a fatherless black boy in a white family and world. Seen in this light, the scene underscores the psychological importance of both Wright and the community he offered, thus giving an unintended preview of the stakes that Wright's betrayal would ultimately represent.

Obama's rendering of the scene gets readers to cry along with him, just as he lifted the spirits of millions of Americans echoing the sermon's sentiments in the 2008 campaign. But at the same time, Obama is also letting the reader know that at times he is unaware of his deep feelings, and that he needs to have his sadness pointed out to him. Like Obama finding his spiritual place at Trinity, many of his followers felt as though they had found a home and community in Obama's vision of America. They were connected, validating years of struggle for civil rights, celebrating the triumph of hope over fear. But that sense was short-lived; though Obama certainly hasn't inflicted upon his supporters a betrayal that rivals Wright's, one must ask if the memory of his bitter disappointment with the man Wright turned out to be makes it a little easier, unconsciously, for Obama to let down the community he built. The question of just what Obama means to his supporters—on all points of the disaffected spectrum—is vital to our understanding of what the future holds for his ability to work with them. The next chapters will expand our psychoanalytic frame to consider the attitudes expressed toward Obama by opponents and supporters alike.

Chapter 8

"Their" Obama:
Obama in the Minds of His Critics

I imagine one of the reasons people cling to their hates so stubbornly is because they sense, once hate is gone, they will be forced to deal with pain.

—James Baldwin, *The Fire Next Time*

There were those who argued that because I had spoken of a need for unity in this country, that our nation was somehow entering into a period of postpartisanship. That didn't work out so well.

—Barack Obama, January 2010

The second reason that the charge of racism is leveled at patriotic Americans so often is that people making the charge actually believe it. They think America—at least America as it currently exists—is a fundamentally unjust and unequal country. Barack Obama seems to believe this, too. Certainly, his wife expressed this view when she said during the 2008 campaign that she had never felt proud of her country until her husband started winning elections. In retrospect, I guess this shouldn't surprise us, since both of them spent almost two decades in the pews of the Reverend Jeremiah Wright's church listening to his rants against America and white people.

—Sarah Palin, March 22, 2011

People who could not spell the word vote or say it in English put a committed socialist ideologue in the White House—name is Barack Hussein Obama. . . . The revolution has come. It was led by the cult of multiculturalism aided by leftist liberals all over who don't have the same ideas about America as we do.

—Tom Tancredo, February 5, 2010

It is perhaps the nature of U.S. partisan politics that the party out of power will attempt to demonize the opposition, and just as likely that animosities between camps will escalate with the passage of time. But the vitriol directed toward Obama, fueled by the right-wing media, goes beyond what has passed for normal and has found expression in terms and tone that politics alone can't explain. By applying some of the concepts already introduced—positions, splitting, projection, and more—we can better understand the psychology of the anti-Obama mentality and examine the unconscious forces that underlie the right-wing media's rhetoric.

In addition, no use of applied psychoanalysis to understand the current political landscape would be complete without considering the Tea Party phenomenon from a psychoanalytical perspective. We will see how its vehement antigovernment stances embody the most profound dangers posed by individuals who see destructiveness solely as a force outside themselves. Tea Party members have become so invested in the fantasy that Obama is some form of evil that to think otherwise—to suggest that he might have something positive to offer along with the negative—would risk a paralyzing onslaught of cognitive dissonance and discredit their steadfast belief systems. By naming the dynamics at play here, we increase our chances of understanding their positions and identifying ways to confront them effectively—especially important as we near the 2012 presidential election.

Our attempt to understand the tendencies in some Republican circles to regard Obama as a menace personified must begin with the universal fear of the "Other," learned in childhood, that finds adult expression in such attitudes as envy, racism, and fear—all of which we see in the anti-Obama rhetoric. Children need clarity and predictability to provide scaffolding for their developing psyches. In addition to manifold loving impulses, very young children are bombarded by envious fantasies and destructive desires, some of which are so frightening that they prefer to project them into the environment around them in order to protect themselves from fears of internal implosion. This is a normal part of development, dividing the perceived world into simple and manageable elements. There are good guys and bad guys, cowboys and Indians, cops and robbers, humans and space aliens. The possibility that one can be a good Indian, when the dominant culture says "the only good Indian is a dead Indian," causes anxiety and feelings of insecurity.

The innate fear of the Other begins with the infant recognizing that his mother is a separate person from him. Compounding this is the awareness that the same person is both mother and other—a figure who is good and bad, loved and feared, depended upon and resented. This confusion can lead to moments of anxiety; internal hatred risks self-destruction, as a conflict between internally held good and bad mothers can lead to mental chaos, adult versions of which we see in acute schizophrenic confused states. In order to get things straight, the infant tries to see his mother yet again as the good mother and displaces the scary feelings of anger and frustration and otherness onto an actual material other, a person who really is not the mother; this is the root of early-childhood "stranger anxiety," which is later replaced by fear of the unknown in general.

This dynamic of trying to manage fear and hate expresses itself in several familiar developmental stages, such as when young children insist that their food groups be kept separate. The danger that a speck of parsley poses to a delicious dish of macaroni and cheese can threaten to overwhelm the entire meal. Many parents remember this phase of life as amusing, but to the child the sight of green on white is terrifying, a vivid illustration that the bad can get inside the good and spoil it.

To some of his opponents, Obama is the parsley in their macaroni and cheese. His otherness is evident on many levels—from his name to his exotic and varied biography to his mixed-race heritage, which makes him Other to both black and white people. Because of this, the response he elicits from many people can best be understood as a deep-seated, almost reflexive reactivation of this primitive childhood coping mechanism, which has at its root the basic emotion of fear, which in turn is largely composed of projected hatred.

We can clearly see the Other mentality in the attitudes of the contingent that questions Obama's citizenship. Xenophobia is an adult variation on childhood stranger anxiety; by denying the facts of Obama's U.S. birth, the so-called Birthers give expression to a common, primitive, and virtually lifelong coping mechanism that enables them to make him the repository of their fears and insecurities. He becomes an imposter and a menace at whom any label can be directed—terrorist, Communist, socialist, all terms that have been leveled at Obama that have more to do with his difference than his decisions.

Obama's middle name no doubt reactivates that primitive anxiety as well, confirming his status as an un-American, un-Christian, dangerous Other. These attitudes are familiar to people locked in a paranoid-schizoid position of mistrust. Like a child's need for an ordered dinner plate, their worldview is threatened by change and driven by a need to preserve the illusion of predictability and simplicity that is exemplified in certain notions of what it means to be an American—notions that include the fantasy of American exceptionalism that Obama challenged by acknowledging that the citizens of other countries consider their nations exceptional as well. Such fears are not unique to those on the right—many liberals have a deep distrust of him that they can readily displace onto Islam in general, despite knowing that Hussein is simply his middle name.

Exceptionalism has its roots in a fantasy at once grandiose and insecure: to the exceptionalist, the Other is both inferior and threatening, consistent with the paranoid-schizoid externalization of destructiveness. The American exceptionalist expands the notion of the self as a virtuous victim to a national level, which intensifies the sense that the threat is located outside its borders—or was at least born there.

People who think in a paranoid-schizoid way need an enemy in order to evade seeing their own destructiveness to themselves and others and to preserve the illusion of victimhood. Once the Other becomes the enemy, a victim mentality takes over that makes escaping the yoke of the victimizer a higher priority than thinking things through. Adults latch on to slogans and simple phrases such as "death panels" without giving serious attention to thinking through what they mean. Consider a two-year-old who wants to have a bowel movement whenever he wants, rather than follow his mother's rules: he just says no and doesn't think through the reasons she might want him to use the bathroom or the consequences of going in his pants. The danger of self-appointed victimhood in adults is that the victim doesn't try to see things from the perceived oppressor's perspective; victims are already too self-righteous to care and have dehumanized the oppressor. Victims don't have to take responsibility for injuring others but instead can justify their actions in the name of survival and self-protection. Psychologically, this impedes the possibility of growth, locking would-be victims in a paranoid stance that prevents their developing compassion for those they feel are wronging them.

The paranoid-schizoid position keeps the good and bad far apart—the "bad" Other is only bad, and the good is idealized—to help preserve the illusion of certainty. Part of the national celebration after the death of Osama bin Laden was an expression of our self-idealized exceptionalism, as well as a feeling of absolute good having triumphed over an absolute evil that was located outside ourselves. A common unconscious anxiety management technique, an attitude of certainty, helps defend against the chaos of the unknown. This is expressed in the self-righteousness with which the victimized paranoid denies any claim or evidence of goodness in the demonized Other. The possibility that the Other is anything but bad is a potential source of internal conflict, a threat that must be evaded. Thus we see Rush Limbaugh equating Obama with Hitler and filling the airwaves with discussions of "similarities between the Democrat party of today and the Nazi party in Germany"—a bandwagon joined by once rational people who should know better, such as Newt Gingrich—and Glenn Beck accusing him of being a racist with a "deep-seated hatred of white people." It is not possible for such people to see good in Obama because it would cause too much internal anxiety and threats of disordered mental states, and it has distorted the popular discourse into terms that externalize the anxieties of the fearful at the expense of reason and fact—especially since facts threaten their internal worldviews and peace of mind.

The separation of good from bad is also an essential element of unconscious envy, another major force we see among Obama's Republican opponents. One of the central hallmarks of envy is that it attacks the good, trying to spoil the positive; we see it in action, for example, when Obama repeats or supports points or policies suggested by Republicans, who then turn around and attack him for adopting the position they previously took. Thus we see Republicans rejecting Obama's support for policies they had originally proposed, such as the research and development tax credit that they requested in early 2010, then rejected once Obama came on board in the fall. Envy requires that one keeps good separate from bad, so Obama must be enviously attacked and his goodness spoiled if he is even remotely seen as good. The compulsion by Karl Rove and others to credit Bush's policies for finding Osama bin Laden is a case in point: they need to spoil what Obama accomplished, as they cannot bear their envy for having failed so obviously and completely. Interestingly, Obama himself, in his announcement to the nation, gave credit to the Bush administration for having gotten the ball rolling and putting people in place who could complete the mission. It's unlikely that the opposition could be so thoughtful, as being locked in a paranoid-schizoid stance precludes it.

Envy leads us to attack attributes that we perceive as positive in the Other—typically not the whole person but only a capacity that the envied person possesses, most likely a quality that is lacking in ourselves. Envy of Obama's effectiveness has become so pervasive among Republicans, for example, that John Boehner, on May 10, 2011, indirectly (and somewhat inarticulately) criticized Obama's articulate manner of speech by hyping the presidential prospects of Indiana Governor Mitch Daniels because Daniels "speaks English . . . English like in plain talk." Envy is a primitive emotion, based on hatred of the helplessness of having to ask for what we can't provide in and for ourselves. It finds expression in destructive feelings and urges, directed at something we regard as unattainable for ourselves. Obama is more intelligent and more articulate than many of his critics and remains civil and respectful even in the face of criticism. This angers envious people who are insecure about their own intelligence and who cannot stand kindness in people they hate. Thus Sarah Palin declared in fall 2010, "I think ordinary Americans are tired of Obama's global apology tour." The famously unsophisticated and untraveled Palin is clearly (if unconsciously) the one apologizing here—for her own ignorance of foreign policy and international realities. Instead she lashes out against Obama for apologizing to foreigners at the expense of patriotic values. She cannot face her own ignorance—hence her recent world "tour," which indicates an unhappiness with the mounting evidence that the American people are more tired of her than of Obama.

One of the first manifestations of envy is confusion, an inability to appreciate the good about the person who is envied or what he is offering. This is true of attacks on health care reform, for example. Many of the people who stood to benefit from the proposed changes in health care were too confused by the hatred the Republicans—from Kentucky Senator Mitch McConnell to Minnesota Congresswoman Michele Bachmann—directed against Obama to appreciate clearly the positive benefits they might receive and feared having to experience or express gratitude if they were to acknowledge these benefits. That is not acceptable in a scenario in which good and bad are completely separated, even if only unconsciously. Instead, the good is experienced as an imposition—triggering a primitive anxiety that dates back to infancy, when the baby enviously attacks the nurturing mother, who can do for the baby what it absolutely cannot do for itself, and then fears that its mother will force something into it in response. Thus many Republicans respond to anything good that Obama offers or enacts by making it seem as though they've been force-fed. The Glenn Beck faction's denunciations of a socialist takeover of the automobile industry, for example, are adult expressions of the infant's fears of the invasive retaliation it will experience in response to the envy it projects into its mother.

The mantra of Emersonian self-reliance repeated by some of Obama's critics as a justification for shrinking the government to get it out of their lives can also be traced to the infant's envious response to its helplessness. The government these critics want to shrink is in fact a huge breast on which they don't want to admit they depend. The wealthy conservatives funding the Tea Party's fixation on the size of the government rely on the government for more than tax exemptions; the existence of a social safety net prevents them from having to face the prospect of having concern for others and confronting their own greed and destructiveness. Thus they project their greed into the recipients of government aid, rather than seeing how they themselves are getting government welfare in the form of massive tax advantages that allow them greedily to hold on to their own wealth and resources, while they enviously attack Obama and others on the left for the generosity they lack.

There are also racist overtones to the Birthers' hatred, and they are thinly disguised. Once Obama showed his "long-form" birth certificate, the Birthers were among those who started to attack Michelle Obama for inviting the rap artist Common to read his poetry at the White House. Common's work is fundamentally anti-inflammatory; he identifies as a Christian and a "conscious" artist, meaning he delivers an inspiring and affirmative message to his listeners. But he is black, and his words were pulled out of context to indict him with a vigor one can't imagine the same critics turning against a white artist.

Projection is at the heart of the unspoken racism that we also see underlying much of the opposition to Obama. The psychological roots of racism involve the projection of devalued parts of the self into the Other, whose differences in appearance and background facilitate such projection. What is typically projected is a disavowed trait: the racist doesn't want to admit his own indolence, for example, so he projects his denied sloth into the black community, which he then stereotypes as lazy. Once the projected trait is disavowed, the racist can hate it in others without feeling any guilt—he sees the trait as evil and disgusting, meriting his contempt for the Other and protecting himself against recognition and self-hatred.

White racists have long projected unwanted parts of themselves into black people, whom they then degrade for having the very same unwanted characteristics. This helps them deny the envy they might feel toward blacks who display qualities the racists wish they had. The oft-repeated story of a black first-grader reading aloud to an all-white class is a case in point: the teacher accuses the little girl of cheating because no black child could read that well, when in fact the teacher unconsciously couldn't bear the child's ability—especially compared to her less accomplished white students—and had to discredit it out of envy.

This dynamic is writ large in some factions' inability to accept Obama as the first black president. Obama demonstrates a level of intelligence and success that surpasses what most white racists can see in themselves, let alone in a degraded black Other. Rather than envy Obama for his positive qualities, the racist opposition clings to the fantasy that a black man simply couldn't be elected president, which is the psychological motivation behind the Birthers' discrediting of his citizenship (and thus his election). And cling they must—racists hold on to their prejudices because letting go of the position risks internal chaos and the psychic disintegration that would result from having to question the certainty of their convictions and confront the denied, unwanted aspects of themselves. Their reactions to Obama bring to mind the fired television sports announcer who got into trouble a few years back when he declared that though blacks may be good football players in general, they are not intelligent enough to play quarterback.

Some of the most insidious racism is unspoken or hidden in code. In November 2010, Bill O'Reilly said on his Fox News show to his guest Juan Williams, "I'm starting to get even more worried—that's the word, worried—for the country because I don't know who Barack Obama is." After Williams replied, "I don't think there's any question that he loves America," O'Reilly countered, "But I don't know what America he loves, whether it's his vision of America he loves or the tradition that we have. I just don't know." The tradition favored by the "we" whom O'Reilly mentions is likely a tradition of dominance by skin color that started receding in the late twentieth century, a trend that Obama personifies. O'Reilly's vision of America is one that is lost in the changing demographics of contemporary society. In that timeworn vision, Obama is an Other far more than he is in the America of today; but today's ever-changing America is so confounding to O'Reilly that he's the one, not Obama, whose America is unknown to him. This is a classic example of unconscious projection in defense against confronting an unwanted truth. It's interesting that O'Reilly felt comfortable making the remark to Williams, one of the rare African-American regulars on Fox News, just a few weeks after Williams was fired from NPR in the wake of anti-Muslim comments on *The O'Reilly Factor* the previous month. At the time, Williams prefaced his remarks about how Muslims on airplanes make him nervous by declaring, "I am not a bigot"—a statement which, of course, means anything but. Williams's presence likely made O'Reilly more comfortable indulging in his own racism—which neither of them, of course, would acknowledge.

Racism, envy, the demonization of the Other, and other dynamics we've been discussing all come together in the Tea Party, a group of people who feel the government, personified by the president, has robbed them of what they once had: a lost, white America where they had the freedom to do what they wanted, even if they accepted that they couldn't own slaves anymore. The fantasy of being robbed of the freedom we once had and think we still deserve is familiar to all of us because we once were children and felt and lost such freedom. In the first stage of life the infant cannot distinguish between reality and fantasy or between what is inside and what is outside—he is what he thinks and what he sees, a mental attitude that reverberates throughout the life cycle. When the persecution fantasy returns or is continued in adulthood, the self-proclaimed victim—of the government, of his neighbor, of whomever or whatever—will project all personal aggression onto that particular threatening person or organization. This prolongs his primitive state of understanding the world, because anyone who aims to help him see a different point of view is experienced as aggressive and destructive, which ultimately affirms his original position or worldview. The problem with confronting delusions is that fixed ideas remain fixed in the face of reason or argument. Questions are perceived as attacks, so confronting people who have paranoid delusions results only in anger. No one can help the victim see his situation differently, because he, like a very young child, doesn't have enough self-awareness to see how he is seen, let alone to recognize his own hatred as being anything other than reactive.

Members of the Tea Party are stuck at this level of emotional development, obsessed with the unchallenged fantasy of frustrated, stolen freedom. They are aware enough that governments make laws, some of which, such as having to stop at red lights, are necessary, but they still think that government's main intention in creating laws is to control or take things away from citizens. They are in fact afraid of government in general and Obama in particular, driven by a fear of the internal chaos that would result if they had to accept that President Obama and the Democratic Party were not all bad, a realization that could shatter their rigidly organized worldview. Maintaining that split between all-good and all-bad requires a truly irrational and unnatural level of fear and hostility—as heard from the Utah Tea Party Congressman Jason Chaffetz the morning after the 2011 State of the Union address. "I was so scared to death I was going to have to sit next to [New York Democratic representative Anthony] Weiner, and I thank goodness that didn't happen," Chaffetz told Fox News, months before Weiner was disgraced. "This is the morning hour. I know people are eating oatmeal right now, I didn't mean to prepare people to hurl by thinking about that scene."

A comprehensive 2010 CBS News survey of Tea Party supporters revealed much about how the dynamics we've been discussing play out in the group's attitudes and demographics. According to CBS's findings, the Tea Party is 89 percent white and 1 percent African-American, a composition that at least suggests an atmosphere conducive to racism without confirming its presence. The poll found that supporters "tend to skew older: Three in four are 45 years old or older, including 29 percent who are 65 plus"—which leaves ample room for the group that is holding on to a fantasy of the America of their earlier years. In fact, almost 60 percent told the survey that "America's best years are behind us," at least when it comes to jobs for American workers. To a Kleinian psychoanalyst, these findings support the view that the Tea Party is allied with destructiveness out of hatred toward the reality of modern life and resentment that they feel like strangers in their own land and can't see themselves in their president.

We have already explored some of the attitudes the survey found—ideas that Tea Party supporters are more likely than average Americans to embrace, such as the belief that Obama was not born in the United States. Other findings are fairly simple and obvious in terms of their connection to psychological principles: their favorable view of George W. Bush, despite his responsibility for TARP and other policies they say they oppose, for example, is a simple case of splitting, where all things Bush are good and all things Obama are bad. But other feelings and misconceptions identified by the survey reward closer inspection in light of the concepts we've been discussing, and further analysis can help clarify the psychodynamics of the

Tea Party movement and of the broader opposition to Obama. The following explores the major attitudes that the survey reported that Tea Partiers are more likely to hold:

They are angry about the way things are going in Washington—particularly feeling that the government does not represent the people.

Adult anxiety about being ignored by authority figures or institutions can be traced back to childhood defenses against parental neglect. Almost all children have experience with parents who at times don't listen to them. The child retreats into various forms of solitude and fantasy life to manage the feeling of being ignored—it's easier to go on the computer or play a video game than to keep making demands that one feels will never be met. The world of the child is largely defined by defense mechanisms, attempts to cope with and manage inner fears, through which experience is filtered far more in youth than adulthood. But these feelings never disappear, and in adulthood they can become repressed filters through which they perceive the world around them—filters that are unconscious but that often determine our emotional reactions to what feels like neglect. Obama's calm, unemotional demeanor may mirror for some their self-involved or otherwise disinterested parents. Thus the feeling of being ignored in adulthood by a parental or authority figure can trigger the familiar defensive retreat into fantasy.

We all have these feelings to some degree, but as we aggregate into large groups such feelings form a common substratum among group members and can increasingly dominate how reality is experienced. People will do things in groups that they would rarely do as individuals—participating in mob violence, irrational nationalism, religious fervor, Woodstock love-ins, and sporting-event boisterous behavior—because shared passions and fears can overwhelm the restrictions that our conscience, or superego, typically imposes on us. Hence, adolescents are braver in groups than as individuals because of these shared emotions, which find more easy expression. This strength in numbers can extend to individuals who are laboring under feelings—or delusions—of being ignored by their government; together their individual estrangement can be emboldened into group anger.

They say they "just don't like" Obama.

Antipathy that is based on a belief that cannot be articulated, other than in generalities of likes and dislikes, may be prejudice or simple discomfort with an Other too different to identify with. It would be interesting to find out whether the overwhelmingly white Tea Party dislikes blacks in general or whether there are specific qualities about this particular articulate, educated, successful black person that they dislike—elements they label as elitism, arrogance, expertise, or class incongruities. Either way, what we see here is envy, and Obama forms a convenient receptacle for the alien or uncomfortable parts of the self that are projected in envy or prejudice. If the qualities the Tea Party members wish they possessed are never articulated, the envy is unconscious—and is therefore pathological and prejudiced. Awareness of the pain of not having those qualities—having thought about those feelings enough to make them conscious—would be less pathological. Self-awareness of their own envious feelings wouldn't mean that they would suddenly like Obama, but they might gain enough perspective not to automatically jump to conclusions about his every policy decision. For example, if they faced their envy of his capacity to think clearly when bombarded by different opinions, they might accept his deliberate style without having to deride him for being indecisive—even if they disagreed with some of his decisions.

The respondents' inability or unwillingness to cite a reason, however, leads one to suspect that what's really going on here is unexpressed racism—which, as we've seen, is its own form of unconscious envy. Most people are too embarrassed to say they are racist, so they can't say anything specific for fear that something impolite or politically incorrect will come out. Of course, they may be able to articulate plenty of reasons in the privacy of their home. In that case, their resentment of being called a racist creates another negative attribute to project onto Obama, compounding the envy and hatred that they can't admit to the interviewer.

They say that Obama's policies favor the poor.

Animosity toward the poor derives from mistrust of the Other: immigrants, people of color, and alleged abusers of the system accused of taking advantage of its generosity. Family psychology often plays a role as well: resentments from the unconscious past directed toward younger siblings who forever changed their family constellations. Obama's compassion for the poor is thus a point of envy for the Tea Party supporters—a quality missing in them, incompatible with their views that government is the problem and that the poor could better themselves if they were simply treated with tough love. They also envy his ability to think about the poor in the first place, which leaves less room for him thinking about Tea Party members. There is sibling rivalry here, accompanied by splitting—a wish to deny that the poor are in fact psychic siblings and therefore part of our society as a whole. Poor people also represent disavowed needy parts of the self-reliant self, giving rise to defensive contempt. Seeing the poor as Other helps Tea Party members perpetuate the split and avoid feeling guilt, at least the guilt that might come from shirking their biblical responsibility—one explicitly espoused by President Obama—of being their brothers' keepers.

They believe that Obama has increased taxes, despite their receiving a tax cut.

Taxes arouse paranoid anxieties in which people project bits of their own greed onto the government. We see this in wealthy people who resent the government, especially if they have a conscious sense that they are overpaid or that they amassed their wealth on the backs of their employees. Rather than see themselves as greedy, they see the government as taking away their freedom, their belongings, and their wealth—even if, like most Tea Party supporters, they're not wealthy and have bought into a delusional overestimation of their prospects of building wealth on a playing field that is becoming less level all the time.

One consequence of delusional beliefs—such as insisting that Obama has raised taxes or that the United States is not the land of equal opportunity that it once was—is that the distortion of external reality becomes fixed and etched as fact in the minds of the deluded. This false belief system is the outgrowth of projection, denial, splitting, and specifically of envy and devaluation. It is also the result of lies peddled by envious media figures and politicians. The psychoanalyst Roger Money-Kyrle wrote that a particular kind of delusional system can develop over time, well after the most intense projections are toned down, but becomes so entrenched that to dispute it would lead to terrible confusion and anxiety. As John Kerry learned the hard way after the Swift Boat smear, false beliefs that slip into daily speech can, through repetition, solidify paranoid thought into a widespread delusional system that is hard to correct.

Psychic coherence eventually rests on believing and treating as fact whatever it is that keeps a person feeling calm and organized. Otherwise anxiety threatens to disrupt the entire psychic system—something we see, for instance, in children of abusive parents, who need to make up false belief systems in order to function. The belief that Obama raised taxes is a good example, because to question that belief would risk having to reassess everything the Tea Partiers were taught to believe about Obama. It's easier to maintain their ill-founded beliefs, even in the face of evidence to the contrary, than to tolerate confusion.

They feel that Obama doesn't understand their needs and problems.
Feeling not understood stems from prejudice as well, from a sense that Obama is so different that he can't possibly understand. This is coupled with a fear of dependency on an Other, of needing this person who is so much "not me." How I can rely on him to understand me, the thinking goes, when he's so very different from me?

Bush and his folksy talk and manner made it easy for a wide range of Americans to see themselves in him; the fact that he was rich and privileged was lost because he spoke their language, shared their anger and black-and-white thinking, and even misspoke in familiar and recognizable ways. Obama presents qualities that make him an Other beyond his color and inhibit many Americans' attempts at narcissistic projection: educated and cultured, knowing arugula and Kierkegaard as well as football and basketball and rock and roll. On top of all that, he is so different-looking that people cannot see themselves in him the way they can in other presidents. He is the least narcissistically gratifying of all presidents—with the possible exception of Carter—since the famously and catastrophically detached and wooden Herbert Hoover.

They believe that Obama doesn't share American values.

The respondents to this survey did not identify the "values" that they think Obama doesn't share, but in the past few decades the term has functioned as a code for white values, a subtly racist appeal to white voters commonly attributed to Nixon and later exploited by Reagan. In 1988, family values became a clear reference to race, as in Lee Atwater's successful campaign to destroy Governor Michael Dukakis because he had a weekend furlough program for certain approved Massachusetts prisoners in which one such prisoner, the convicted felon Willie Horton, didn't return to prison at the end of his furlough but committed robbery and rape. Those who lack proper family values—as Dukakis apparently did—evoke fear in white voters.

But they were not talking about genuine family values. If the values they're referring to are really about family, there is no better example than Obama—he is a loyal and loving husband and father and even has his mother-in-law living in his house! Likewise he personifies the values of honesty, hard work, and leading a balanced life—not bad for a president. We're left to conclude that what they're saying is that they can't see the values they share because of his black skin, his otherness. This disconnect also speaks to the trouble that people have seeing themselves in him. One way I work in psychoanalysis is to find myself lost in the patient, seeing aspects of myself—often uncomfortable ones—and thinking them through. This happened to me with Obama only after months of intensively getting to know him, albeit from afar, through deep analysis of his writings, speeches, and public appearances. I was often startled by his responses to stressful events in his life, at first admiring his self-control. It was only later that I saw that control as a defense against his fear of being excluded and becoming a pariah, as a way to get along and avoid controversial situations.

They believe it is justified to take violent action against the government.

Violence is, of course, an expression of helpless, murderous rage, a natural reaction when one is feeling under attack. Facing painful cultural changes beyond their control, the Tea Party members adapt a victim mentality that experiences change as attack that justifies an angry and even violent response. This behavior is consistent with that of the NRA, which also sees itself as a victim, despite its numerous legislative victories over gun control. The dehumanization that results from constructing Obama as a remote, alien Other further facilitates the justification of violence—as does Sarah Palin, tweeting after the passage of health care reform, "Commonsense Conservatives and lovers of America: Don't Retreat, Instead—RELOAD!" amid the threats of violence toward supporters of the bill, thereby excusing her followers in advance from having to feel guilt over their violent fantasies.

They believe the Tea Party reflects the views of most Americans.
Narcissistic people see themselves in others wherever they go, and the Tea Party is no exception. People love to belong to a group of others who agree with them, which offers validation of their point of view. And when charges of guilt and bigotry are a possibility, the association with like-minded others can help manage those superego concerns, sending the message that if so many people are members of a group, they must be good people or at least right.

They believe that Obama is pushing the nation toward socialism, defined as government ownership or control.
The sense that Obama is pushing us toward something foreign, and that because of this we are going to lose control, is an example of paranoid thinking and involves massive splitting, with his opponents projecting all of their unwanted aspects of themselves onto him. That anxiety is yet another example of childhood fears that parents will take our things from us and even give some of them to our siblings. This is one source of the Tea Party's feeling of victimization. The distorted equation of any government participation with socialism also provides a vivid example of the intolerance of complexity that is central to how they preserve their certainty in their positions.

Whatever ultimately happens with the Tea Party, whose relevance has outlived many predictions, looking closely at the psychology of the Republican opposition in general and at the Tea Party in particular can create the impression that Obama has his work cut out for him. Indeed he does; the depth and extent of the murderousness that his opposition feels still escapes him, due to his inability to confront his own rage and destructive impulses. As Money-Kyrle wrote, "We are unable to imagine any passion or sentiment in another unless it has been in some degree, either consciously or unconsciously, experienced by us."

By ordering and overseeing the successful raid on Osama bin Laden in May 2011, Obama gained invaluable and unprecedented experience in confronting and expressing his murderous impulses. In that respect, bin Laden served a valuable function for the president seeking to balance his depressive and paranoid-schizoid positions, by providing him an enemy so universally opposed that his defeat could bring the nation together, thereby giving him a chance to simultaneously destroy a threatening enemy and bring together the nation he loves.

On a lesser scale, the Republican opposition may also ultimately serve as a long-needed catalyst for Obama's full recognition of himself and his destructiveness. If its genuine and relentless attacks can break through his defenses and he experiences how brutal some of his opposition truly is, he will be better equipped to acknowledge and handle the full force of the anger and resentment directed at him. For all of their delusions and prejudice, the Republicans and the Tea Party may in fact assume the role of his best therapists, pushing him to a position where he must face his denied fears, become less dissociated, and get more in touch with the relentless opposition to whatever he proposes.

As we'll see in the next chapter, however, instruction need not come only from the opposing side. Obama's supporters have much to teach him—and all of us—about the psychodynamics of his appeal. By looking closely at what drives some of the unique and powerful attraction to him, we'll see how he has lost some of the support he originally had—and how he can regain it.

Chapter 9

"Our" Obama,
or My President, My Selves

Violence is a dead end. It is a sign of neither courage nor power
to shoot rockets at sleeping children or to blow up old women
on a bus. That is not how moral authority is claimed; that is
how it is surrendered.

—Barack Obama, Cairo, June 4, 2009

Ethical thought consists of the systematic examination of
the relations of human beings to each other, the conceptions,
interests, and ideals from which human ways of treating one
another spring, and the systems of value on which such ends
of life are based. These beliefs about how life should be lived,
what men and women should be and do, are objects of moral
enquiry; and when applied to groups and nations, and indeed,
mankind as a whole, are called political philosophy, which is
but ethics applied to society.

—Isaiah Berlin, *The Proper Study of Mankind*

I first heard of Barack Obama when my son Abe called me early
in 2002 after hearing a totally unknown politician (whose name
my son couldn't even remember at the time) talk about projection,
about putting oneself in another's shoes, which my son said sounded
just like me, his psychoanalytic dad. I was later able to put together
that Obama had been a last-minute substitute speaker for Cornel
West on Martin Luther King Day at Rockefeller Cathedral at the
University of Chicago, where he spoke at length about empathy.

At one point he said that the 9/11 hijackers couldn't have carried through their attacks—which at that point were less than six months in the past—if they had looked into the eyes of a child on the plane and "recognized" their own child there. Projective identification, the ability to recognize an aspect of oneself inside another, is a major root of empathy. Obama told his audience that day that our nation was lacking in that capacity as well, going so far as to say that we suffer from an "empathy deficit" that is worse than the federal deficit! My son was so impressed that he spoke about it in vivid detail, over several conversations.

I was reminded of this when Obama spoke about race in April 2008; I found him so perceptive about human psychology that I thought that as president he would effectively act as psychoanalyst in chief and raise our consciousness about seeing ourselves in others as a path toward narrowing the deep chasms between red and blue Americans. But then I was talking with a lawyer friend who was impressed by Obama's approach to things who said that an Obama victory would amount to our electing a lawyer in chief. Ditto with a writer-friend who said that Obama, whose appeal as candidate relied so heavily on the poetry of his speeches, would serve in the White House as the writer in chief, building on the extraordinary success of his two best-selling books about himself.

To some extent this process is replayed with each sitting president—he represents parts of us that we split off and project onto him, a process that ultimately influences how we perceive and experience him. But Obama's not being known allowed observers to project parts of themselves onto him with more ease than any other presidential candidate. All of the 2008 Democratic candidates were better known than Obama, who often joked about being unknown—a skinny dark-skinned man with a funny-sounding name. Candidate Obama offered an element of the unknown that invited narcissistic identification, perhaps as a means to fill in the blanks and assuage our anxiety. Projections are best made on blank screens; this is why psychoanalysts try not to reveal much about themselves while working with a patient, who can in turn put more of himself—his past and present fantasies driven by unconscious energy—into the clinical setting. Obama took great pleasure in people having different fantasies about him and said so on the campaign trail, as he painted himself with broad brushstrokes.

Those who listened carefully, however, could hear him saying more about exactly who he was. He wanted change and transparency and thought Iraq was a stupid war, which his supporters on the left were glad to hear. He also talked about wanting health care insurance for everyone and how he intended to prosecute the war in Afghanistan, to which the Left paid less attention, along with reversing his antisurveillance stand by voting for the Foreign Intelligence Surveillance Act that July. After he was elected, however, more liberals started taking notice through a different lens. His choice of the anti–gay marriage minister Rick Warren to give the inaugural convocation was the first shock, and soon his supporters had to confront the difference between universal health insurance (which he embraced) and universal health care (which he didn't) and acknowledge that his positions on Afghanistan were hardly those of an anti-war president.

Three years later, he still remains unknown to many of us who initially supported him. Frank Rich wrote about the puzzling, "enigmatic Obama" in April 2010; after the 2010 midterm elections, *The New York Times* headlined an editorial "Waiting for the President"; a year after the Rich "enigmatic" piece, the columnist Paul Krugman declared, "The President Is Missing," and asked, "What have they done with President Obama? What happened to the inspirational figure his supporters thought they elected? Who is this bland, timid guy who doesn't seem to stand for anything in particular?"

Krugman's questions, which predated the following month's successful bin Laden mission that showed President Obama in an entirely different light, echo much of the inquiry embarked upon in this book. The transition from inspirational to timid brings to mind his stepfather, Lolo, who was as close to a father figure as Obama ever had. As described in *Dreams from My Father,* Lolo changed from a fun-loving, worldly, outgoing athletic man who played nightly with little Barry in Hawaii when he was four and five into the taciturn husband and father who was determined to provide material comforts for his new family after Ann and Barry moved to

Jakarta. Though still very attentive to young Barry, teaching him how to defend himself, behave like a strong man, and make friends with strong people if he couldn't be strong himself, in Jakarta Lolo became silent and joyless. Lolo was ultimately so thoroughly devalued by Stanley Ann that she removed Barry from the home when he was ten and deposited him back with her parents in Hawaii. One explanation for the transition to the man we saw in the months leading up to the bin Laden mission, residing inside our once fiery and inspirational president-elect, is a "melancholic identification" with this once charismatic, almost revolutionary man who receded into himself as he acquired more power and responsibility.

Whatever the cause, there has clearly been enough of a transformation that we must look at three time periods to define "our Obama": before his election, in his first years as president, and finally as the commander in chief who ordered the raid on bin Laden (which will be addressed in full in the next chapter). Much of the promise that Candidate Obama offered us was conveyed through his speeches. He also listened better than any world leader in memory, thinking about what people said and asked and responding without judgment in a way that indicated how closely he listened. He seemed to understand and appreciate everyone's point of view, no matter how disparate, somehow leading many supporters to think he was speaking directly to them and taking their wishes and feelings into consideration. He exuded perspicacity, a quality that some mistake for virtue and others for a liberal perspective. His keen discernment of subtlety, penetrating and patient curiosity, and ability to present an ample worldview, in total contrast to the simple and narrow perspective of George W. Bush, was seductive to a public grown tired of American parochialism. Obama fit into the mold of our wise and perceptive parents, who inspired a sense of wonder when, as children, we still thought they knew everything. But his perspicacity turned out to be politically neutral, seductive without a particular point of view. Observers who decided that he must be liberal because he is so sensitive to the needs and thoughts of others were jumping to a conclusion that proved to be false.

This isn't to say that everyone distorted what they saw all the time or that all the feelings we had about Obama were simply naive wishes. Obama's language invited real confidence, and his voting record was meager enough to allow that confidence not to be eroded by signs like his Senate vote in favor of the Foreign Intelligence Surveillance Act, which didn't occur until his presidential nomination was virtually certain. He also demonstrated a considerable ability to accept differences in a nonjudgmental way, his perspicacity again being easily confused for a more liberal philosophy than he truly embraces.

In the course of writing this book I've learned that each of Obama's supporters has his or her own Obama. Most of their feelings are clearly based on projections, distorted or not: when Obama gives a speech, each member of the viewing, listening, and reading audience notices different things about him. But there are some qualities that are broadly, if not universally, admired. Candidate Obama inspired many people because instead of immediately reacting he would take time to think in the face of pressure, a sign of true strength of character. This unconsciously positioned him as the antiparanoid president who didn't believe in knee-jerk retaliation the way his predecessor did. He was a breath of fresh air as someone without any history linking him to Bush or even to old Democratic politics the way Hillary Clinton and John Edwards were linked. In the same vein, his deliberate, thoughtful style made it likely that his decisions as president would result in fewer unintended consequences than had those of President Bush.

Candidate Obama elevated our psychological levels of thinking: he could admit to hating someone's bigoted belief while still loving the actual person (as he did with his grandmother), a level of thinking and introspection that struck many as revolutionary coming from a politician after eight years of Bush. Further, because he was a black man, Americans of all colors could project onto him the living symbolism of how far we had come as a nation and our pride in that accomplishment.

He appealed to my psychoanalytic colleagues, especially for saying in September 2008 that "we can't steer ourselves out of this crisis if we're heading in the same disastrous direction. We can't steer ourselves out of this crisis using the same old map; we can't steer ourselves out of the crisis if the new driver is getting directions from the old driver, and that's what this election is all about." This is, in essence, what psychoanalysis is all about—at least from one perspective. We are all the time getting directions from old, unconscious drivers, and our work is to get to know those old drivers so we can have more choices, go in new directions. Lurching onto a new path may work in the short run, as in government bailouts, but in analysis we look for long-term understanding in order to make substantial changes. This, I think, is the intersection between psychoanalysis and politics. We can't throw away the rearview mirror, as it were; but we shouldn't stare at it or we'll crash. To me, Obama understood this better than any presidential candidate in many a campaign.

Elevating our level of thinking is not easy and requires helping people entertain competing thoughts and feelings. When Obama did it in his race speech, for instance, he was doing what Wilfred Bion urged psychoanalysts to try to do in the consulting room—that is, to be open to un-understanding. Bion wrote about the capacity to tolerate negative capability, not to lurch after answers or jump to conclusions simply in order to manage anxiety, a quality Obama seemed to possess. Obama wanted to transform old ideas into new ones— wanted to help us to do that by acknowledging the reality of the old ideas, such as the nation's legacy of racism, and the capability for transforming the nation that we've seen over the past few decades.

This approach is against compartmentalization, and too often we are out of touch with our own political experiences, as beautifully described by Thomas Frank in his book *What's the Matter with Kansas: How Conservatives Won the Heart of America*. Frank introduced unemployed, economically suffering voters who supported the same politicians who caused their problem in the first place. Though compartmentalization is necessary for growth and development—we have to forget fights at home in order to think in the workplace, for instance, or we have to push out of our minds that we just ordered the Navy SEALs to go into Pakistan in order to be the jocular guest of honor at the White House Correspondents' Dinner—it can also impede development. When the whole self remains fragmented, it is easy to be politically manipulated and even end up voting against our own interests. In a sense, despite our recent discovery of how well he can compartmentalize, Obama's approach to political life was holistic, taking into account the whole person as a member of society, as well as of the United States as part of the world.

The cracks were there, however, in the unified "our" group. By the time of Obama's moving speech at Notre Dame, for example, questions arose not so much about his brilliance or eloquence but about whether he was just putting off having to take a stand on abortion. The speech was artful and managed to embrace all points of view, especially acknowledging that people with passionate views don't have to hate the other side, as their views are just as sincerely held. He seemed to try to separate the views held from the people holding them. He felt an urgent need to make sure that we learn to live with differences without killing off one side—not only must we live with knowledge of different viewpoints, we also need to understand that those with opposing views are equally passionate. Though the speech was given early in his presidency, he gave the impression that he was already postponing having to make a decision himself. Fast-forward to April 2011, and we see that he did offer federal protection to Planned Parenthood from Republican attacks, despite numerous other compromises, although he allowed the states to continue their attacks on Planned Parenthood without comment. So he stands up but then holds back, a back-and-forth that has happened with enough frequency to turn some of his supporters into critics.

Even as president, a characteristically strong speech could win back his straying supporters. On Memorial Day of 2009, Obama said in a speech at Arlington, "This cemetery is in and of itself a testament to the price our nation has paid for freedom. A quarter of a million marble headstones dot these rolling hills in perfect military order, worthy of the dignity of those who rest here. It can seem overwhelming. But for the families of the fallen, just one stone stands out—one stone that requires no map to find." That speech was Shakespearean in scope, combining the broad sweep of crosses covering the cemetery hills with the pain of individual loss, making us proud again to be American, able to see our own sacrifices and hold our heads up high. He again reminded us of what we have in common as Americans and helped us face our losses. We live in a world dominated by denial, where everything feels immediate, from video games to voting on *American Idol,* and the past gets pushed aside. In that speech he demonstrated that he understood sorrow and spoke directly to it, recognizing that the sorrow of our losses continues to be present in our lives and helps us become stronger. Through reactivating the mourning process, he helped us internalize the people who died to sustain our nation—those we loved as well as those we never knew.

Many of us measure Obama's presidency by speeches, such as those at ASU, Notre Dame, West Point, Cairo, Tucson, etc. As noted earlier, however, Obama has a tendency to fade from view between appearances, either neglected by the media or simply choosing to remain offstage. Whatever the cause, when he does this he seems to eschew the power of the presidency in more than one way. But most significantly, when he loves and leaves, connects and disconnects, walks onstage and then off, our Obama fails to recognize that he *is* our Obama. For all the talk of continuity, his presidency is segmental, leaving many of us like Obama's Portuguese water dog, Bo— wagging our tails when he comes into the room and then resting quietly until the next time. He takes our Bo-like transferences to him for granted and doesn't fully understand or accept the actual power he has. He seems blind to our transference to him and instead acts out his transference to us, repeating defense mechanisms learned in childhood. He felt such love from adults who cared about him and left him, but their absences were dealt with by his withdrawing into his fertile mind, seemingly without protest, as witnessed in his reading of classic black writers to better understand himself. He behaved like some highly intelligent only children who use their precocious understanding of external reality as something that must be accepted without question, making them seem autonomous, very well adjusted, and without hurt or rage. My sense is that he never said, "Mom, what's more important—your son or an Indonesian village?"

Now that he is president, when he withdraws from view it makes it hard for us to maintain the sense that our Obama is still ours, giving new and ironic meaning to his being the Obama we are waiting for. In those moments between speeches, or in the absence of any clear belief system other than bipartisanship, we become little Barry waiting for his mother to come back from her travels. He is letting us know what it's like to have absent parents, to feel what it means to be the kind of orphan he called himself years ago. Just when things look good and we believe we have a new leader who will take charge, he leaves, thereby avoiding and denying the very transference he so powerfully excited during his campaign.

At the same time, he's also still trying to come to terms with dual identifications with his two fathers—his birth father, whom he barely knew, and his stepfather, who was like the earth to him. In *Dreams from My Father* he wrote, "I raised my arms, throwing soft jabs at Lolo's palm, glancing up at him every so often and realizing how familiar his face had become after our two years together, as familiar as the earth on which we stood." We are that familiar with our Obama, and the love that he obviously showed in that passage is the kind of love many of his supporters still hold for him. So many people have told me how much they love him and that even though he is at times disappointing, he is special and someone always to be cherished. I think Obama himself captures that feeling when describing those boxing lessons with Lolo so long ago. Lolo paid attention to Barry's needs and noticed him in ways that his mother could not.

For the first months of his campaign we looked at Obama with the same sense of wonder with which he looked at Lolo—the genuine feeling of being with a special, knowledgeable, steady person who was calm and able to think while also being eloquent and able to persuade. Identification with the president is natural; those who admire qualities they perceive in Obama are able to project their ideal selves into him and then, through identification, become more like their view of the president. As a strong leader, the president gives unconscious permission to his admirers to be more ambitious, more competitive, and more successful in their lives. All presidents serve unconsciously to make people feel more comfortable with who they are; sadly, President George W. Bush made many people more comfortable being mean to one another, especially in Congress and on Fox News. Obama makes many of his followers feel more comfortable getting along with those who have different politics or who come from different cultural backgrounds. He also makes people feel good about choosing family over work.

But numerous voters have written about their disappointment, thinking they had voted for someone other than the man who now occupies the Oval Office. Disaffection with Obama on the left stems in part from the projection of wishes that he be completely different from George W. Bush. In writing or saying this it means that we are still unconsciously influenced—if not dominated by—Bush's basic psychopolitical stance: "You are either with us or against us." Obama was seen as the anti-Bush candidate, or at least as the not-Bush candidate. He had none of Bush's characteristics, so it seemed, and his rhetoric was complex and forceful and clearly challenged the direction in which our country was headed. But we have yet to shake the "us/them" psychology of the Bush era—something that forever resonates with our inner ten-year-old—so when Obama inevitably disappointed, he became one of "them" to many critics on the left. Some friends remarked to me that they had started to call Obama "Bush lite." Once in a while his critics rightfully see him as the complicated man he is, but for the most part they adopt the poison paranoid-schizoid position so exploited by Bush.

Disappointment with any leader is inevitable. It is greater with U.S. presidents because they are set up structurally to be both parental figures and officials elected to do a particular executive-level job. Transferences become confused this way. I wrote about this process at the end of *Bush on the Couch*, warning of the dangers of seeing Obama as the rescuer, the anti-Bush candidate who would close Guantánamo, restore the Constitution, stop wars, and repair our economy. Obviously he hasn't been able to do all of that, but the danger lies less in what remains undone than in how we respond to things not going our way on our schedule.

When the Left feels betrayed, it risks doing what is called projective counteridentification to Obama. Instead of accepting Obama's projections onto us—that the Left is demanding, whining, as it unconsciously represents unwanted and discarded aspects of little Barry—we may feel the urge to counterproject, to experience President Obama as being the same as George W. Bush: we then see him as prosecuting wars, neglecting the poor, and in the pocket of Wall Street. This counterprojection represents the part of us that remains monolithic and still in the paranoid-schizoid position. That part sees the world in all-or-none images reminiscent of how Bush himself saw it. Attacking Obama in this way, from this viewpoint, does no good, as we debilitate ourselves in the process, becoming less and less able to think rationally about the president and the massive obstacles he faces. Instead, if we could face and reclaim our projections we would become stronger and thereby better able to both criticize and help our president—just as he would surely get stronger if he faced his own.

It's normal for children to be disappointed when they discover that their parents don't know everything and can't always live up to their expectations. Obama played a role in creating the expectations that he hasn't always lived up to: they were fed by his rhetoric, rather than simply arising from a needy populace. Many people blame their disappointment on him, because that's easier than seeing themselves as naive or stupid or that they ignored all kinds of clear warning signs about who he is and what he believes. *Tikkun* editor Rabbi Michael Lerner saw it early in Obama's presidency when he wrote that pragmatism is dangerous without clear ideology, a sign that he recognized something that was lacking in this man. But self-blame is really hard, and it's easier to feel betrayed by the container of our projected aspirations than by our blindness to our own either-or needs. Still, the betrayal is all the more painful to those of us who have projected the better aspects of ourselves into him, an unconscious connection that makes it harder to tolerate his separateness and otherness.

When he doesn't follow through on his promises that had fired up our own hopes and dreams and yearnings, we turn on him for being independent and not doing things our way. We can feel that he's a treasure to be protected, feel more parental toward him than toward any president in memory, and then have trouble accepting his reliance on the Beltway and Wall Street insider Larry Summers after promising change in Washington, for example. It's not just that Obama doesn't do what he promised; those promises and our projection of ourselves onto those promises—and onto Obama himself—make his independent judgments even more painful than they would be in a president to whom we felt less connected.

More vocal disaffected supporters have been emerging, among

them African-American Princeton professor Cornel West, who on May 16, 2011, called President Obama "a black mascot of Wall Street oligarchs and a black puppet of corporate plutocrats. And now he has become head of the American killing machine and is proud of it." West's is a particularly vitriolic attack that is consistent with a somewhat common theme of betrayal in liberal circles, the sense that Obama has turned his back on supporters he feels are enough outside the mainstream that allying with them would interfere with his getting elected.

Regardless of the source of the betrayal—and it's likely attributable in part both to us and to him—what ultimately matters most is what we do to reverse the process or prevent it from happening again. We have seen that it is our imperative as a nation to shine whatever helpful light possible on Obama's blind spots as well as our own. As we see more clearly who he is and how he got to be that way, we expand our behavior options in much the same way that patients do at the end of their analytic treatment. Even now, however, calling them Obama's blind spots may be blind in and of itself; he is honest and devoted to changing America but is probably not very liberal. The process is inevitably dynamic; the president is changing, as are we. And as I'll discuss in the next chapter, when President Obama told the world on May 1, 2011, that Osama bin Laden had been found and killed, events can suddenly cast a new light on much of what we thought we knew about our president— events that, when examined in detail, can help us see Obama even more clearly.

Chapter 10

Mission Accomplished

If one just knows how to surprise, one always wins the game.
—Søren Kierkegaard

Good evening. Tonight, I can report to the American people and to the world that the United States has conducted an operation that killed Osama bin Laden, the leader of al Qaeda and a terrorist who's responsible for the murder of thousands of innocent men, women, and children.
—Barack Obama, May 1, 2011

Making surprise discoveries is a compelling, unsettling, and rewarding element of my psychoanalytic practice. Just when I put the picture together of a patient I thought I knew well, I am thrown off track by a shocking disclosure, an unexpected behavior, or a blazing new insight. Such was the case across the board with Obama's May 1 announcement that a Navy SEAL team under his orders had killed Osama bin Laden. The disclosure that he had been planning it a long time and had known it was imminent even as he had been convincingly playing the "entertainer in chief" the night before was shocking—even though I knew he could compartmentalize and that part of his strength is not to reveal his feelings, something we've seen that he learned as a child. The act itself was also unexpected; most people hadn't been thinking much about bin Laden, and the Navy SEALs carried out the operation with a deft precision as surprising as his Sunday-night announcement.

The fact remains, however, that Obama had never hidden his desire to "get" Osama. He made a point of reminding Steve Kroft in the postraid *60 Minutes* interview that he had campaigned on a pledge to take him down in Pakistan, if necessary. But his stance even predates his run for the U.S. Senate: in October 2002, while still a state senator, Obama challenged President Bush. "You want a fight, President Bush?" he asked. "Let's finish the fight with Bin Laden and al-Qaeda through effective, coordinated intelligence and a shutting down of the financial networks that support terrorism and a homeland security program that involves more than color-coded warnings." Color-coded warnings, as well as bin Laden himself, are now things of the past. But the Bush-driven deficit and two long wars are not.

Nevertheless, the insight that Obama himself is decisive, phallic, and able to kill—all while being detached about it in public—cast a new light on the analysis in these pages. Negative capability in the consulting room means that the analyst is open to what the patient brings. I have been genuinely surprised over the years, as when a patient almost parenthetically told me after four years of intense therapy that he had a sibling who had died or when another patient told me that the right side of his mother's face was paralyzed by polio. And not all surprises have been from the past, such as when a patient casually said her six-year-old son had slept in her bed since his birth, a revelation that certainly occasioned a reexamination of what we had discussed.

Preconceptions are always subject to revision, and the process of transforming them into new understanding is also an essential part of analytic work. When a patient does something unexpected and surprising—what we call "out of character"—it is essential not to try to force the new information to fit into a familiar conception. In fact, what was thought to be a concept about the patient is modified by the experience; what was a conception was in fact a preconception. In that sense, all our ideas about people have elements of preconceptions. Just think how many friends and spouses finish each other's sentences or say "I knew you were going to say that" as they put their friend neatly into a familiar mental slot or cubbyhole. Obama, as we have seen from this study, doesn't fit into any simple slot or category, and the bin Laden mission, which seemed at first blush like a stand-alone mission that changed who I thought Obama was, was an act that doesn't just add another slot, it enhances our understanding of what we've been examining already. The raid came well over a year into my deep analysis of this man, and though my surprise is real, it's also clear that the planning, execution, and presentation of the mission is still very much a part of who Obama is as a person. In this chapter, then, we'll see how this mission deepens our understanding of who President Obama is, as we look at it through the same lenses we've developed over the course of our inquiry. But we will also look at what surprised me most about his bold initiative, as well as at certain themes that persisted without much change. The responses to the mission by both opponents and supporters were more predictable but still bear at least brief mention.

The mission appeared at first blush to challenge one of the central tenets of this analysis—that is, that Obama is afraid to reveal the killer part of his personality to himself and to others, let alone act on it; in fact, rather than contradicting it, the exception actually clarifies the rule. Obama's aggressive instinct has been so difficult to see that at times I have questioned whether he was even aware that it existed, as when he has seemed so blind to the destructive Republican opposition. At other times I have surmised that he learned to bury it in order to get along in the white-dominated culture, particularly in light of his writing about his tight coil of inner rage after years of trying to find a good way to deal with the subtler and often unconscious white racism. This sustained internal conflict between the killer part of his personality—more overtly visible in the bin Laden raid than ever before—and his ever-present need to accommodate on the home front is at the core of his behavior. It raises an obvious question: what is it that made Obama unafraid to act against bin Laden in contrast to the accommodation and even paralysis he has so often demonstrated in response to domestic challenges?

We've seen how Obama's internal strife still causes inaction in the face of domestic opposition. In the case of bin Laden, the opposition was an external and universally reviled villain, suggesting that Obama can unleash his inner killer on an enemy that can clearly be externalized, against whom Obama can show himself to be the clear and decisive leader that he has failed to be at home. Bin Laden killed thousands of innocent men, women, and children, said the president, to be sure. But we're left to ask how many innocent men, women, and children are going to suffer due to the dismantling of the social safety net through drastic cuts and government inaction. When the enemy lurks within, Obama speaks up but does little else; as money is taken from programs to help the poor in order to let big oil avoid paying corporate taxes on massive oil profits, for example, he does little but recommend offshore drilling yet again with the excuse that this will help lower gas prices. He doesn't have to send in the Navy SEALs to stop big oil, but he could insist on proper regulation and force action.

I have linked his paralysis in taking domestic action with the inability to see the destructiveness of many in the Republican Party, but he sure saw it in his 2002 speech, quoted earlier, when he identified the nation's "empathy deficit." Speaking on Martin Luther King Day, he went on to say, "The spirit of empathy condemns not only the use of fire hoses and attack dogs to keep people down but also accountants and tax loopholes to keep people down. I'm not saying that what Enron executives did to their employees is the moral equivalent of what Bull Connor did to black folks, but I'll tell you what, the employees of Enron feel violated! When a company town sees its plant closing because some distant executives made some decision despite the wage concessions, despite the tax breaks, and they see their entire economy collapsing, they feel violence."

Obama echoed some of these sentiments only two weeks after the raid, when he spoke on May 16, 2011, at the all-black Booker T. Washington High School commencement in Memphis, Tennessee. The students were deeply moved to have the United States' first black president there to offer himself as a beacon of inspiration at a time when Memphis is one of the most depressed cities in the United States, with massive unemployment and terrible conditions for its large African-American population. His speech was predictably full of empathy and deep compassion. By empathy he means two fundamental and linked qualities: the ability to walk in another person's shoes and the ability to see aspects of oneself in the other person.

But as we've seen, his most uplifting speeches are often followed by periods of letdown. He flies in, inspires with a speech—and then flies out. I think he is trying not to be one-sided, when sometimes it's necessary for a president to take action. It is on this cusp that we again see Obama using the language of substitution—more subtly so when he's being so connected and empathic—instead of the Language of Achievement, by which walking in another person's shoes must result in taking action. The bin Laden mission was action taken, and it offered the bonus of distracting us from the violence of unemployment in a way not very different from his extremely moving and meaningful appearance at Booker T. Washington High School. In the latter case, however, empathy and understanding substituted for action. He named individual students and described their struggles to take two buses each way to get to school after their housing projects had been torn down. He applauded their grit and determination but somehow left it at that.

As president, Obama still exhibits great empathy, but until the mission to get bin Laden, he suffered from a decisiveness deficit; he's more comfortable taking decisive action against an external threat to Americans than on his empathy for the citizens and followers who face homegrown threats posed by legislators who protect the wealthy while slashing needed domestic programs. Instead of acting on his empathy, he outsources action to members of Congress. It is the difference at one level between his mother and father: his mother got up with him at 4 A.M. daily to help and push him with schoolwork; his father told him to turn off the television and then flew back to Kenya. Obama sometimes behaves too much like his father, flying into a place and then leaving without follow-through. And although the SEALs who took out Osama certainly flew in and out in short order, Obama's careful, decisive planning more clearly resembled his mother's methodical, focused approach. She gave her son the clear message that you can't just rush into things but that learning takes time and effort. What we see is the decisive result, when the specifics of the mission were hard-won—not based on either dreams or unbridled retaliatory fury.

At the same time, one can see that he was able to complete the mission almost in spite of his mother, from whom, he has said, he inherited an ability to see the good in everyone. The meticulous planning of the bin Laden operation was in part driven by Obama's need to keep his mother's worldview from stopping him from following through. The risk that bin Laden, the monster, would morph into a human being if Obama ever met him face-to-face was a risk that I think Obama refused to take. It could prove too great a risk, that Obama might see an element of himself inside bin Laden—especially that coil of rage. Not only is it essential that bin Laden is an agreed-upon monster and a completely alien Other; it is also essential that he remain that way in Obama's mind. The possibility that his bipartisan disorder could take over made bringing bin Laden back alive psychologically unacceptable. Political concerns about having to stave off American lynch-mob pressure also played a role, as did the potential problem of Obama's feeling he'd have to greet bin Laden with dignity—something already not accorded to Guantánamo inmates, who are nowhere near the monsters bin Laden was.

Obama's obsessive bipartisan disorder remains his primary defense. Even with the triumphant killing of bin Laden, he emphasized American unity more than anything else. After announcing that we had killed bin Laden, he said, "On September 11, 2001, in our time of grief, the American people came together. We offered our neighbors a hand, and we offered the wounded our blood. We reaffirmed our ties to each other and our love of community and country. On that day, no matter where we came from, what God we prayed to, or what race or ethnicity we were, we were united as one American family." Just before his speech ended he sounded the note of unity again: "And tonight, let us think back to the sense of unity that prevailed on 9/11. I know that it has, at times, frayed. Yet today's achievement is a testament to the greatness of our country and the determination of the American people." At such moments, when not taking direct credit for the mission, Obama is not simply invoking American determination but he is also disavowing his own individual murderousness.

Obama appears always to look for a chance to put unity into his speeches, and this time it served to distract others from what has become an open admission of his murderousness—all in the name of protecting our nation more than its laws. On closer inspection, however, he didn't hide his aggression in the *60 Minutes* interview with Steve Kroft. Toward the end of the interview he said flatly, "the fact of the matter is, is that we've been able to kill more terrorists on Pakistani soil than just about any place else," meaning that the United States is in the business of assassination abroad.

By killing bin Laden, Obama continued to push for healing the split in America, but he did so in what I feel is an unrealistic or manic, triumphant way, because he vaulted over having to look at the divisiveness caused by Republicans, much less at what the Republicans mean to him. They're not unrelated, because Obama has unconsciously linked the Republicans to terrorists. He said as much in December 2010 after the Republicans trounced the Democrats the previous month: "I have said before that the middle-class tax cuts were being held hostage to the high-end tax cuts. I think it is tempting not to negotiate with hostage takers unless the hostage gets harmed." But although he made the analogy of Republicans to hostage takers, he ended up making a deal with them not to reinstitute the former tax rates for the wealthy—so he must have thought the hostage, that is, the middle class, was not being harmed. He knows one thing and says another—unlike how he dealt with bin Laden. The contrast is important, given the clear understanding of the violence done against the middle and lower classes that his 2002 speech revealed. This contrast is the one new issue that is outlined in bold relief, giving us the new perspective that Obama has an easier time seeing the good in bad people than he does seeing the bad in good people. It's as if John Boehner's American tears blur Obama's vision of how adamant and violent Boehner is about never negotiating on taxes.

Killing bin Laden relates to Obama's drive to address his familial splits as well, but in this case he reacted against those splits with violence rather than healing with compromise. He was able to pursue his action against bin Laden in part because bin Laden offered a displacement figure for Obama's rage toward his own parents. On the unconscious level, bin Laden embodied a lifelong target for Obama's revenge—a combined parent completely dissociated and split off from any overt similarities to Obama's actual parents. But similarities to one or both are there: he was exotic—seductive and tall and once a friend and trusted ally; he made surprise, unexpected, but destructive visits; he was impossible to find, get hold of, or track down; he didn't listen; he didn't care whom he hurt because he's driven by inner demons and hatred that at some level is inexplicable. With the exceptions of abandonment and intrusiveness, bin Laden's hateful qualities match pretty well with how Obama viewed his parents. This displaced murder protects Obama's relationship to his internal parents, to the yearned-for original family of his imagination. He doesn't risk endangering his internal family, and instead of owning his rage at both parents he takes care of it in an anxiety-relieving fashion. By killing bin Laden, he killed the man who embodied some of his parents' most hateful attributes.

It's worth considering what bin Laden represented to the rest of us as well. The slips of the tongue confusing Obama and Osama, common since the former arrived on the national scene in 2004, certainly escalated in the days following the raid. They came from all corners of the political map—even though some of them, particularly by Fox News, may have been intentional—so one must be careful reading too precise a meaning into them. For the most part the slips have to do with the fact that Obama and Osama share an otherness in the minds of many. Inevitably this involves some unconscious racism; people have lumped them together and, in a subtle form of paranoid-schizoid thinking, don't want to do the work of delineating the two of them in their minds. But even their otherness is different: Osama was the agreed-upon Other, clearly alien and dangerous to all, while Obama's otherness is expressed in different ways to different people (he's black to whites, mixed to blacks, foreign to Birthers, and so on). By killing bin Laden, Obama asserted to us that he is in fact less "Other" than many had previously thought.

But old habits die hard, and Obama's otherness was simply too much for many on the right to acknowledge his role in the success of the mission. From the Bush administration veterans lobbying for credit in the days after the raid to Bush's refusal to join Obama at the World Trade Center site later that week, the Republicans' envy was in full display, revealing their hatred that Obama had been able to do what they couldn't. Here, too, there was likely racism at work: the blackness of Obama's otherness made their recognition of his success that much more difficult and painful. So pervasive was their envy that it extended to the soldiers themselves, as House Majority

Leader John Boehner refused to introduce legislation to salute the SEAL team that had carried out the mission in a transparent rebuff to Obama only three days after the raid. If the sense of unity Obama recalled from September 2001 returned at all in the aftermath of bin Laden's death, it didn't last long.

Epilogue:
O'Bama on the Couch

Without some self-pity, pity for others is likely impossible, for in pity we echo another's pain.

—C. Fred Alford

I had grown tired of trying to untangle a mess that wasn't of my own making.

—Barack Obama, 1995

We end our analysis by looking forward—epilogue as prologue, a proposition for the work that lies ahead. Observing and analyzing Obama is an open-ended enterprise, and the bin Laden mission reminds us of the risk of publishing an in-depth psychoanalysis before events offer it a conclusion. Far more than it did his predecessor, the presidency is changing Obama, and he will inevitably go through more changes in the period between the completion of these pages in the summer of 2011 and their publication in the fall. Bin Laden's death was reported on the eve of my returning the revised manuscript to my publisher, who agreed that the mission yielded insights into Obama's character, particularly regarding his approach to dealing with hatred and aggression, that had to be incorporated into the book. The mark that its revelations made on this analysis may turn out to be more enduring than its impact on the voting public, however, as the postraid surge in support for the president rapidly evaporated.

Three weeks after the raid, Obama launched his late May trip to Europe with a joyous pilgrimage to his ancestral home in Ireland.

In photos of the trip his smile was broader and his almost boyish delight more apparent than it had been in recent memory. Reveling in his Irish roots represented a fairly new approach to healing his black/white split, but the drive to search for a lost home was recognizable to the astute observer. "My name is Barack Obama, of the Moneygall Obamas," he joked to an adoring crowd of 25,000 Dubliners, "and I've come home to find the apostrophe we lost somewhere along the way." And by "retracing the steps of Presidents Kennedy, Reagan and Clinton," as *The New York Times* pointed out, he unconsciously attempted to mitigate his otherness by aligning himself with a heritage and tradition that came to light only a few years ago, when an enterprising villager traced his mother's lineage to the Irish hamlet. The fact that such new information brings new approaches to processing it—making public the white part of himself that is easily obscured by the simple fact of his skin color—is a sign that his mental health is both robust and evolving.

The underlying dynamics that were on display in Ireland are familiar to readers of this book—the drives to heal the lifelong splits, to find his place in the world, to align himself with his mother while still retaining his independence—and if the trip was in part consciously motivated to win votes back home, as some have suggested, we can recognize any such political objective as progress in Obama's attempt to heal the split between candidate and president that will likely be front of mind when this book is published. By indirectly introducing the world to Barack O'Bama—his less black, less other, apostrophied hypothetical alter ego around whom voters can perhaps more easily reunite—the president demonstrated that his drives to heal his divided self and his divided nation are unconsciously related and that he is willing to try new strategies to achieve his desired goals. He also reminds us that it is now up to the reader to keep the psychoanalytic portrait of the president up-to-date as he continues to present new and changing aspects of himself and his personality—with or without the lost apostrophe restored.

The change is there for us to see. Psychoanalytic inquiry should be considered a prologue to genuine change in the patient's life. In the case of applied psychoanalysis, the patient doesn't enjoy the benefits of analysis; but after becoming versed in its methods and terms, the educated observer can see the dynamics at work and notice change as it happens—an important addition to the process of observing Obama as we head into the election of 2012, when so many of his one-time supporters are deciding again whether he is in fact up to the job.

Of course, the unfiltered joy that he radiated so memorably in Ireland would never have been observed in a traditional clinical setting. Our exercise in applied psychoanalysis has afforded us the opportunity to examine and assess Obama's public persona—appropriate training for the reader to continue his or her assessment after finishing the book. Obama will continue to reveal himself in ways large and small, and will offer the close observer an experience that is more rewarding than conventional analysis would probably be. We can look at the unguarded juxtapositions and turns of phrase in his memoirs, particularly *Dreams from My Father,* as many initial months of sessions' worth of free association, but it's understandably unlikely that he will ever again speak or write at length with such revealing freedom. Thus, we owe it to ourselves to pay close attention to what we can see, to view his actions and hear his words in the context of the dynamics we have identified, if we hope to bring this still elusive and evolving man into sharper focus.

We have seen that our inquiry into what most deeply motivates President Obama ends up with his mother at center stage, especially his feelings about her and her intuitive efforts to heal his internal split. Not surprisingly, she plays a central role in his dynamic with his observers as well. So many women—and even some maternal men—have asked that I "be nice to our president" in this analysis that one has to acknowledge the power of the maternal transferences that he invites: for some supporters, watching him closely reveals the need for a mother that has persisted since Ann Dunham Obama unconsciously denied her son's helplessness by retreating to her studies and traveling the world. That maternal transference serves him well: by the spring of 2011, some of his most reliable supporters were college-educated white women, 56 percent of whom said they still strongly approved of his performance in an April 2011 Pew poll. To these women, he is the hope of the future—and perhaps a motherless son who needs protection from the dangerous men who resist his message of change.

We've also seen that his mother figures prominently in how he responds to his observers and supporters. His supporters on the left unconsciously reactivate early conflicts with his mother, eliciting from him hurt-little-boy feelings of resentment and betrayal; as a result, he experiences the Left's expectation that he'll live up to his promise and promises as maternal criticism. His ongoing attempt to relive and understand how and why his mother treated him the way she did contributes to his pattern of vanishing after he connects with his supporters: every time he disappears after a great speech it is as if, like his mother, he's off to a remote Indonesian village yet again.

Now, entering the period when he needs them most of all, he seems almost consistently detached from his supporters on the left. His parents' repeated abandonment contributed to a sense of insecurity that is manifested in the adult Obama as an overabundance of caution wrapped in a cool, calm, and collected package. The almost willful blindness that in the deepest layers of his mind protected him from facing both his hurt and rage at his mother now blinds him to his own effect on others—except for his rousing rhetoric, the predictable positive impact of which still calms and sustains him, as was evident in Ireland.

On one level, it is essential that any president remain detached; otherwise he could not make difficult decisions about life and death, or think in the face of the overwhelming economic deprivation experienced by so many Americans. On another level, he appears to be in touch with his empathy: the comfort he offered to tornado victims in Joplin, Missouri, in May 2011 seemed genuine, as one would expect from someone who knows what it's like to have his home torn away from him. But when it comes to the voters whose support he will need to be reelected, his lifelong chronic need to detach is taking its toll. Because he is walled off from his own yearning, he can neither recognize nor identify his supporters' feeling of yearning for him, impeding his ability to harness and direct that energy for his political gain when he needs it most.

Obama will need to acknowledge that yearning as he attempts to reassemble the coalition that put him in office. On a psychological level, Obama can assemble things almost too easily. Where analysis involves breaking down the mind into its component parts, the individual must then synthesize the disparate parts of his or her personality in new and more effective ways. Obama puts things together very well, and synthesizes new information smoothly into his well-functioning psyche. But sometimes he does it with such facility that the rough experiences of abandonment, resentment, and betrayal seem to have been mitigated rather than remaining as the indigestible bits they really are—and really will be until he faces them. The synthesis is incomplete because he is not internally aware of the pain that must be there.

In searching for his ancestry first in Africa then more recently in Ireland, Obama was attempting to synthesize his broken self. Now he must synthesize his broken nation—his psychological mission writ large, on a national level—and the blockage of emotions that inhibits his internal synthesis could threaten his externalization of that effort. The detachment that protects him from seeing the extent of the rage, fears, and vulnerabilities in himself prevents him from seeing it in others. Without fully appreciating the hatred in his opponents and the frightened yearning for security of his supporters who are becoming increasingly dissatisfied, Obama runs the risk of falling short in bringing together his divided nation. His own unconscious resentment toward his mother, and his detachment, have at times prevented him from making the links of psychosynthesis that would lead to bold action as president. This could profoundly fail him as a candidate for reelection, when victory will depend on his reestablishing connections with his followers and fostering their sense of connection between themselves.

What has become strikingly clear after nearly three years in office is that President Obama wants to repair America and himself at the same time. All of us are in some ways broken, and America as a nation has been fractured since John Adams crossed the street to avoid having to tip his hat to Thomas Jefferson. Our current fractures, however, are as deep as before the Civil War—and Obama both sees and denies the fractures in the nation he strives to lead and unite, just as he fails to confront the fracture inside himself and his broken family of origin. Where his inability to put his family back together resulted in a personal struggle, however, his failure to put his country back together would amount to a national tragedy.

How do we repair this deepening national fracture, especially since our current president seems detached from his own fractures? Our president insists that we must, as our brothers' keepers, restore our common humanity. But that message overlooks the negative commonality—our shared self-hatred, so evident in the viciousness of the opposition—that must be faced before our positive commonality can be truly strengthened. Our president's denial of his own capacity for hatred enables the nation to ignore its own, which prevents our divisions from truly healing. Only when he faces his own hatred will he again be able to talk about hating someone's beliefs without hating the person himself, as he did in his landmark speech about race in 2008. Unless Obama faces his own hatred, he will continue blindly to pursue the fantasy that a golf game with Boehner will detoxify a situation he thinks is based on divergent beliefs. This is psychologically untenable. Only after clearly looking inside will Obama be able to see what's in front of him: the destructiveness of people who play Cain to his Abel, who wholly reject America's social compact.

Even if Obama does claim his own hatred, he has his work cut out for him, because repair requires two parties to talk together. For reasons that date back to early infancy, groups—like people—are more comfortable preserving an internal sense of goodness while keeping the bad outside. The us-or-them mind-set is simply easier to manage psychically than a more subtle appreciation for the connections that we share. But after being stuck for years in an us-or-them world, our healing is only going to happen piecemeal, and will require regular attention and acknowledgment from President Obama.

Without denying our own hates and prejudices, we need as a people to look back, at least to the days when we weren't so badly fractured. In the 1950s many Americans were actually happy to pay more taxes because it meant that their income had increased and their public schools, infrastructure, and other services would continue to improve. Those days are long gone, and after years of finger-pointing and accusations it is absolutely necessary to restart the healing process once more; we need the president to look again at his own fractures, including those that we have seen he denies. As he tries to heal our fractures along with his own in the name of change—to civility, respect, and empathy—he continues to deny the fractures caused by his rage at his mother for abandoning him. He cannot empathize with our fear of being abandoned by him in the same way that his mother couldn't empathize with him: young Barry's needs scared her because she was herself still a child, and now we have a young and inexperienced president, almost as inexperienced as Stanley Ann was when she was a single mother raising little Barry.

Until he sees the United States of America as it is, rather than as he desires it to be, we will continue to drift with our fractures undiagnosed and make healing an increasingly unlikely possibility. I think President Obama needs to find a way to describe what's really there as effectively as he describes what he wishes were there. In 2004 he said he didn't see red states and blue states but the United States, inspiring many who were sick of polarization. But the polarization has only gotten worse, exacerbated by a relentlessly expanding election cycle that intensifies the period of finger-pointing and vilifying, and now he needs to name our specific fractures and clarify how serious and threatening they are to our nation.

If he could face the long-forgotten pain of that little child who was afraid to ask his mother if he was truly less important to her than the remote Indonesian villages for which she abandoned him, he would be able to get in touch with the pains and yearnings of a vast majority of Americans—pains and yearnings all too comfortably converted into paranoid hatred. In the long run, it was too dangerous for Barry to confront his mother directly; in the present, it is too dangerous for him not to meet his opponents in direct confrontation. When and if he faces the truth of his own needs and inner aggression, he will be able to transform them into meaningful and effective action.

This is the sort of leadership the nation craves and will gladly follow. With Obama as our guide, we can also try to take the first steps toward healing, by facing our own truths and resisting the trap of non-thought, which seduces us to remain detached and avoid confronting the unacceptable depth of our divisions and our role in perpetuating them. Once we break out of our patterns of blame and detachment, we can stop accepting the unacceptable and help this analysis become what was intended—a prologue to action and a blueprint for healing our president and our people.

Epilogue, Part Two

If I sound biased, that's because I am. Biased toward the actual record, not the spin; biased toward a president who has conducted himself with grace and calm under incredible pressure, who has had to manage crises not seen since the Second World War and the Depression, and who as yet has not had a single significant scandal to his name. . . . And I feel confident that sooner rather than later, the American people will come to see his first term from the same calm, sane perspective. And decide to finish what they started.
—Andrew Sullivan, *The Daily Beast*, January 16, 2012

In the six months that have passed since this book went to press, President Obama has shown signs of moving from the paralysis of his obsessive bipartisan disorder, sounding tough pressing for the American Jobs Act (albeit unsuccessfully), and winning extension of payroll tax cuts for unemployment insurance (though only temporarily). As his golf games with House Majority Leader John Boehner failed to bear any legislative fruit, Obama appeared to recognize that the Republicans were simply never going to compromise with him. By choosing to deliver his December speech rejecting the Right's failed economic policies in Osawatomie, Kansas, home of Civil War antislavery hero John Brown, he unconsciously let it be known that he was not going to tolerate being enslaved to Republican tactics that blocked any efforts to help the suffering American populace.

It's as if the scales have dropped from his eyes and he sees clearly, no longer stuck in that bipartisan cloud. He was most direct at a mid-December press conference when he quickly responded to being told that some Republican candidates had called him an appeaser, saying that he's guilty of appeasement in foreign policy. Obama said, "Ask bin Laden and the 22 of 30 al-Qaeda operatives taken off the field if I'm an appeaser."

Some of this renewed aggression can be attributed to the first stages of his integrating Candidate Obama with President Obama, internalizing the tougher part of his personality that he exhibited on the 2008 campaign trail. At the same time, the aversion to conflict he has demonstrated since assuming the White House has become more widely noticed; Chris Hayes of *The Nation* said it best on MSNBC on December 9, observing that Obama's desire for "progress without conflict" is the "central paradox" of his presidency.

And he still remains driven by this way of viewing the world that inhibits his ability to see willful conflict, as evidenced in this lengthy metaphor he shared in a *60 Minutes* interview with Steve Kroft:

> *Sometimes when I'm talking to my team, I describe us . . . as . . . I'm the captain and they're the crew on a ship, going through really bad storms. And no matter how well we're steering the ship, if the boat's rocking back and forth and people are getting sick and . . . they're being buffeted by the winds and the rain and . . . at a certain point—if you're asking, "Are you enjoying the ride right now?" folks are going to say "no."*
>
> *And are they going to say, "Do you think the captain's good—doing a good job?" People are going to say, "You know what? A good captain would have had us in some smooth waters and sunny skies at this point." And I don't control the weather. What I can control are the policies we're putting in place to make a difference in people's lives.*

Of course President Obama can't control the weather. Nor is anyone asking him to. But to use the metaphor of the weather to describe the political conditions through which he drives the ship of state is to deny and evade the Republicans' responsibility for those conditions, by putting the blame equally on the Democrats and Republicans in Congress. It is part of his deep need to apologize for his parents' hurtful behavior, as if they couldn't help themselves. The side effect is that he leaves the Republicans free to blame him for being a bad ship's captain—as Republican National Chairman Reince Priebus actually did on January 30, 2012, by comparing Obama to the Italian captain who abandoned his ship in the Tuscan seas—encouraged to forget that Republican policies caused the rough seas in the first place.

Obama's behavior makes further emotional sense if we see it as a function of his fear—not just of his own rage, as detailed earlier in the book, but of the Republicans' rage. The second half of 2011 did indeed bring some recognition on Obama's part of how destructive his opponents truly are, but he continues to deny his fear of their destructiveness, even when fear is an appropriate response to an opposition that is willing to destroy him at the expense of the next generation.

Obama has begun to see that change and progress are not possible without confrontation. But he is held back by an unconscious fear of the depths of the animosity—both his and the Republicans'—that is only barely being held in check and of the brutal, intractable conflicts that would ensue if both sides gave free rein to their hostility.

Obama's fear of confrontation contributed significantly to the dynamic at the heart of much of the rhetoric the Republicans directed against him in their protracted lead-up to the first 2012 primaries: specifically, that the fact that the economy wasn't any better was exclusively Obama's fault. This highly selective assessment reflects a collective amnesia among Republicans, who disregard the economy that Obama inherited after eight years of Bush's destructive rule and seem incapable of measuring where we are now against far worse conditions that would have resulted if Obama hadn't reversed the economy's downward slide. They continue to deny Obama's foreign policy successes—in Libya, in ending the war in Iraq, and in killing Osama bin Laden. But their denial was initially facilitated by Obama's reluctance to investigate and prosecute the wrongdoing that led to the economic meltdown—ostensibly to avoid distracting the country from the crises at hand, but due ultimately to Obama's fear of the conflict that such investigations would engender.

The Republicans have their own psychological issues at play in their position on Obama and the economy. Their willful denial of their party's responsibility—of keeping all war spending off the books; of their hatred of regulations, which permitted financial ruin of so many businesses—reflects a child's eagerness to deny and redirect blame despite all evidence to the contrary. Some Republicans deftly deflect blame while trying to appear reasonable, but knowing full well they won't ever agree with Obama. John Boehner is a good example: astute Democrats like Senator Charles Schumer (see *Morning Joe,* 12/19/11) say Boehner is a good guy who just can't say no to the Tea Party.

The attacks on Obama launched by Republican candidates for the nomination reveal other elements of how the opposition thinks. One of the most obvious was Mitt Romney's notorious television ad that showed Obama talking about the economy during the 2008 campaign, without clarifying that he was actually quoting John McCain. This separation between words and authorship makes it easier to understand the facility with which Romney and others can radically change their positions, sometimes on a daily basis. Behind this is a degree of splitting so pronounced and profound as to render impossible the tolerance of cognitive dissonance, let alone nuance—an unconscious rejection of the complex, nuanced thinking that is accurately associated with Obama.

Newt Gingrich demonstrated his own version of extreme splitting on numerous occasions, most notably when he claimed that legislators who support Fannie Mae and Freddie Mac should be put in jail—knowing all along that he had received over $1.5 million consulting for those agencies. Gingrich seems to operate with a split between who he knows he is and who he thinks he can get away with presenting himself as. In political parlance this is labeled gross hypocrisy. In psychoanalytic terms, his call to jail legislators aligned with his clients is known as projection that borders on the delusional. The importance of looking for the opposite of stated meaning once more comes into play: Arguing for transparency is often posturing for obfuscation. What a candidate says he is not may be what he is.

The Republican candidates uniformly constructed Obama as an Other: someone they had to defeat, about whom they could say nothing positive. Instead, each attempted to outdo the others in their efforts to assert how different from Obama he or she is. Gingrich echoed his fellow candidates when he said that he wanted to emphasize "the basic ideas that distinguish us from Barack Obama."

Beyond the economy, the area of policy in which they tried to assert their difference was the president's health care plan—shorthanded, of course, as "Obamacare," which with every mention emphasized his otherness by asserting the exoticism of his name. At the heart of the opposition to Obamacare is the issue opponents take with its mandates. As with measures to fix the economy, and with "big government," regulations are anathema to the Republicans; from a psychoanalytic point of view, this stems from a hatred of being told what one can and can't do. Ultimately this hatred covers up a paranoid anxiety about being controlled; Jon Huntsman revealed the connection between fear and anti-regulation when he referred to "ending the EPA's regulatory reign of terror." Fear dominated Gingrich, too, as when he said, "this is a president so committed to class warfare and so committed to bureaucratic socialism that he can't possibly be effective in jobs." Ron Paul expressed similar fears when he screamed, "that's what government does: mandate, mandate, mandate." Fear-mongering Rick Santorum warned, at a town hall meeting in Texas, that progressives "are taking faith and crushing it . . . [and that] . . . what's left is a government that will tell you who you are, what you'll do and when you'll do it. What's left in France became the guillotine."

At this writing, Republicans have started voting in their primaries, and Mitt Romney has been winning over a shifting field of opponents, despite Gingrich's spectacular victory in South Carolina. The spectacle of the party's serial infatuation with one candidate after another speaks to the Republican mind-set in 2011–12: they don't know whom they want; they just know both that they don't want Obama and that more than 50 percent of them don't want Romney either. But the support for each successive non-Mitt alternative to Obama proves to be prohibitively soft, necessitating that he or she be replaced by the next non-Romney/Obama. This is simplified, binary thinking that resists nuance; rather than deal with the uncertainty that inevitably results from close inspection of one character, the voter rejects him or her for the temporary certainty of the next. This binary approach stems from the anxiety-driven fear that any candidate who favors complexity threatens the safety of total certainty.

When the selection process is finally over, the dynamic will inevitably change to reflect the identity of the nominee. Whomever that turns out to be, it's reasonable to expect that he or she will cater to elements of the Republican psychology that we observed in the candidates themselves—splitting, fear of control and of the Other, historical amnesia, and so forth. Fortunately, by that point Candidate Obama may have shed more of the fear of conflict that President Obama developed. He will need to shed as much as he can; the psychological forces driving the Republicans will likely lead to just the sort of brutal confrontation that he has spent much of his life trying to avoid.

Glossary

Neurosis is the inability to tolerate ambiguity.
—Sigmund Freud

Transference and countertransference are the terms most important to our thinking about the issues raised in *Obama on the Couch,* and thus bear more elaboration than the other terms in this glossary, which are presented more briefly and in alphabetical order.

Transference is the basic tool used by the analyst in psychoanalytic treatment, and consists of—as Freud wrote more than a hundred years ago—new "editions or facsimiles of the impulses and fantasies which are aroused during the course of analysis," which are directed toward the analyst, and which set up particular expectations and perceptions of the analyst as if he or she were in fact the person or persons in the patient's life who originally aroused these impulses and fantasies.

Through transference, the patient relives, as if occurring in the present, the primary internal relationships to his or her surroundings—to his or her parents, siblings, and other primary influences—that are constructed as early as infancy and build up over time. It is easiest to discover how these relationships are relived during psychotherapy because the role of the therapist is more neutral than the roles of other people in the patient's life.

Transference feelings influence how we experience every new relationship, including readers' feelings toward Obama before reading this book; the strength of the readers' transferences affects how they let themselves be influenced by what they read or whether they try to fit the book into their preconceptions of Obama or of psychoanalysis. What gets transferred are a myriad of feelings and defenses that influence how we perceive others, how we interpret our experiences, and how we influence other people by pushing them to interact with us in old, familiar ways.

Because Obama was unknown to many Americans before he ran for president, our perception of him was originally based in large part on transference of our own hopes, fears, and expectations. If the trauma of 9/11 aroused fears of Muslims in general, for example, we might be extremely distrustful of a candidate whose middle name was Hussein, or interpret his support for building an Islamic Center near Ground Zero as driven by Obama's secret Muslim sentiments rather than by his belief in free speech and a healthy pluralistic society. If we want to influence him by our behavior, and discover that his already calm demeanor becomes even calmer when he is under attack, we may be frustrated by his calm—and feel totally dismissed by him.

Transference feelings intensify during times of stress—individual or cultural—when people often resort to old solutions to new problems, applying the familiar to help modify their anxiety of confronting the unknown, as well as to solve problems in ways more tried-and-true, even if the resolution wasn't always the best one. Thus the more regressed a population, the greater the tendency for transference distortions of experience. In 2008, for example, when the loss of jobs and homes was eroding the nation's sense of hope, the electorate transferred old coping mechanisms and wishes for parental rescue onto the current situation, to counteract their despair and deny their own responsibility for the greed that led so many to take out housing loans they couldn't repay. Seeing Candidate Obama as coming to the rescue gratifies the infantile wish to blame others while keeping people from having to face disturbing realities about themselves.

Finally, we may also transfer denied or unremembered parts of ourselves as children onto another person and then react to that person as if we were the scolding parent who anticipated a particular reaction. I had a patient whom I felt I could never reach enough to make a difference in a particular problem of hers, and it was some time before I realized that my frustration was what she had felt as a little girl trying to get her distant father to react to her. She had transferred this little-girl aspect of herself into me and I unconsciously identified with it. This leads to discussing *countertransference*.

Countertransference, the transference feelings the therapist has toward his or her patient, comprises expectations from the therapist's own past experiences as well as feelings that are specific to a patient's particular transference. For example, I found myself doing extra tidying in my consulting room before the arrival of a particular patient—something that obviously had to do with my countertransference feelings that his transferences provoked in me. It was as if I expected to be yelled at for being messy. What was transferred from my past was an experience of having been disorganized as a child and being scolded because of it. I was transformed by my patient's transference into behaving like an old object. His expectation that I always be punctual and neat was a feeling he had when he was a child, since his own mother was invariably late picking him up from basketball practice. I felt self-conscious and almost tyrannically scrutinized by him lest I make a mistake. He could never have made such demands on his mother, but the enraged dominant part of him came out in our work together. So there is an interaction between transference and countertransference.

President Obama evokes transference feelings in all of us, and he has transferences directed at us also. As described earlier, his transference to the Left is one of annoyance and resentment, as if he feels put-upon by them.

Containment is an active process originally between mother and infant that is later mirrored within the broader family structure and later still in the greater community in the form of the social compact. Originally the mother feels the anxieties of the baby, which she then thinks about before transforming them into an emotional or physical response to her baby by providing emotional comfort, food, new diapers, etc. Thus if the baby were crying and anxious it would be up to the mother to take in that anxiety and contain it long enough to think about it—rather than impulsively react or have to act—and then make the appropriate response. The process is an outgrowth of the holding process which, simply put, is parental support that is the opposite of abandonment.

A containing leader is able to think about what comes his or her way and not immediately react to it—especially if what is presented is dominated by extreme anxiety. In several interviews, President Obama was asked why he didn't speak up sooner about one particular issue or another. He replied that he wanted to know more before he simply reacted—a clear example of containment.

Dissociation here means the capacity for self-observation, that one part of the self can look at another. Taken to extremes, dissociation can lead to detachment and disconnection—from both self and other. Dissociation is not a psychoanalytic term, and has been used only in recent years to describe different self-states that are not internally connected. For example, one could say, and not incorrectly, that in each clinical hour I am disconnected from other clinical hours, and am in a particular self-state dominated by the transference-counter-transference relationship I have with a particular patient.

Dissociation has also been linked to the idea of a *false self,* a kind of different self-state. This applies more to children—often those raised in orphanages or brought up without intense parenting—who are pseudosocial and gregarious but are generally more superficial than one would expect at first blush. They hide in the open, seemingly connected to friends and caretakers but fundamentally apart from them all. *Self-states* is a more recent concept, based on clinical observation far more than on genuine theory. It is not dissociation in the sense that one part of the self observes another. The concept is closer to different internal selves that (unlike those in multiple personality disorder) maintain the capacity to comingle, at least as in this analysis of Obama. As we have observed, Obama keeps different self-states alive and available to environmental changes, without having to face his internal conflict between the different states within. It's an individual version of resistance to forming a union of self-states, because there lurks a nameless dread, a fear of authority. In the case of Obama the childhood authority was his mother, who could turn on or abandon him after intensely connecting with him. He learned how to talk in different ways to different people—to his mother, to his schoolmates, to Frank, to Gramps—and he described all those self-states in his memoir. But he never allowed the self-states to form an internal union to stand up directly and scream "foul!" when his mother would make unreasonable demands on him to study or when she'd go off somewhere and leave him. Because of that fear, he cannot protect the American people from the violence within.

Envy is the wish consciously to possess a quality of another person, and though it is often used interchangeably with jealousy, they are profoundly different conditions. Jealousy is about frustrated and endangered love, expressed as hatred toward the rival of a loved object, or toward a loved object for loving (or being suspected of loving) someone else. Envy is based more on hate than on love, on spite and spoiling the good, and involves a particular quality of the other person, rather than the entire person. Obama evokes a great and destructive envy in the Right, who particularly envy his ability to be calm when under attack, something they are incapable of, and as a result want to spoil everything he does. When it is conscious, and not so destructive that it must be defended against by feelings of contempt, envy can be healthy and can even lead to admiration and identification.

Identification with the aggressor, at its simplest, is when an abused child abuses someone weaker. Often it is the source of bullying, as the bully had a bullying parent (or two) and treats weaker people as the contemptible disavowed weak self he has projected into them. More subtly, one can identify internally with the aggressor and turn that identification against oneself—as when Obama put himself down after that first speech at Occidental. He had been thinking of his father before the speech, and how great a speaker his father had been; in the period of letdown after the speech, his conscience identified with his father (the aggressor, at least internally) and then attacked his own competence. One need not kick the dog after being kicked, when one can kick oneself.

Language of Achievement is a concept originated by Wilfred R. Bion (who capitalized it in this peculiar way) in 1970 to make a distinction from what he called the **language of substitution.** The former involves the capacity to communicate feeling and tolerate uncertainty without having to jump to conclusions. Obama in many ways operates within the Language of Achievement because of his security and sense of calm in the face of hyperbolically critical words hurled at him like weapons (a clear example of the language of substitution, a specialty of Tea Party members). The Language of Achievement must also be a prelude to action rather than a substitute for it, but in that sphere Obama often conflates the two "languages," and thought soon becomes synonymous with action. When this happens, words become substitutes for genuine change, and moral responsibility for one's sentiments and ideals is compromised.

Object is a neutral term for a person whom one loves or hates, or may eventually love *and* hate. Objects are internal constructs we make of the people to whom we relate. Thus we have good objects, bad objects, and whole objects about which we have "mixed feelings." Internally we relate to these objects in a variety of ways, and those relationships can help or hinder how we experience getting along with the real (or "material") people in our lives. Thus we have our internal reality that interacts with material reality—and internal objects that interact with material ones.

Bad object is perceived as mean or hurtful—or even dangerous— because it is made up of the baby's denied and projected aggression. If the baby is hungry and not fed at all, it experiences the breast as bad and dangerous because it has projected all its hate and frustration into the breast. This is the root of paranoid anxiety; a bad part-object can never contain any good.

Good object is the outcome of a healing in the split between bad and ideal—so a whole object is predominantly a good object. It may be frustrating but it is also vulnerable to attacks, so one tries to preserve it at all costs from one's own anger and frustration should those situations arise. Out of enough good comes the whole object— a whole person toward whom the child can experience love, ambivalence, and guilt.

Ideal object: Better than good, the ideal object is perfect. It is the ever-present breast available on demand. It is unrealistically maintained out of necessity, out of the need to keep bad and ideal as far apart as possible. To many enthusiastic campaign workers in 2008, Obama resonated with long-forgotten feelings of having an ideal object, an ideal parent, a person who would never disappoint. The baby projects all of his or her happy feelings into the ideal object and ends up with the sense we still get at times as adults—that feeling of pure joy that Robert Browning described as "God's in his heaven / All's right with the world!" We have all seen babies experiencing pure joy—and many Americans had a taste of that feeling the night Obama was elected president.

Part-object: In contradistinction to whole object (generally good), the part-object predates whole objects, originating in a time when the world is too overwhelming not to split into good and bad bits, good and bad objects.

Positions—The term *position* is best understood as a kind of mental attitude, describing how the internal world is structured, with its objects, its anxieties, and its defenses. There are two positions, according to Kleinian theory, and they are different from developmental stages in that they recur throughout life. Each position also consists of impulses pushing for expression and requiring management.

Paranoid-schizoid position is the earliest phase of development, and is dominated by part-objects that are split into good and bad. "Schizoid" means "split," and in this position the mind is compartmentalized to keep bad from contaminating good. Paranoid describes both the anxiety that is as well as the anxiety defended against: the person projects its bad objects into the environment to keep them even further distant from inner good, so anxiety is experienced as paranoid, in that all bad feelings and threats originate externally. A case in point is the recent preoccupation of some Americans with "exceptionalism," the notion that all good comes from within the United States and all bad comes from hostile foreign powers or even immigrants who cross our borders to soil our population, suggesting that we are stuck as a nation in the paranoid-schizoid position. In this position, our capacity to perceive clearly becomes segmented rather than linked historically; for instance, the links between offshore oil drilling and pollution or global warming are not perceived. Americans in the paranoid-schizoid position experience events as segmental, like a digital watch that tells neither past nor future time.

Depressive position first occurs when the infant recognizes its mother as a whole object who can be both frustrating and loving, and toward whom the infant can have more than one feeling. The child no longer projects anger into the mother or the world outside; the child becomes less paranoid and more anxious about hurting that very good person she or he also loves. This is the root of both ambivalence and the capacity for empathy, as the child tries to think about how the other person feels and how those feelings may be dictating the other's behavior. New fears emerge, especially the fear of losing the good object—both internally and externally. This healthier adaptation to reality is also accompanied by pain, guilt, and a sense of loss. The kind of anxiety that dominates this position is called "depressive" because it includes feeling concerned about the welfare of others and feeling sad about possibly having caused them pain. Actions—past, present, and future—are linked, like the sweeping second hand of an analog watch (to maintain the watch-face analogy). This is in stark contrast to the paranoid-schizoid position, in which many national events are not connected in our consciousness, such as the failure to link the Tucson shooting with the hate talk coming from right-wing zealots and broadcasters. Paranoid attitudes are a natural part of our inner world, but the dominance of paranoid anxiety virtually eliminates the capacity for linking, for concern, and for empathy. As noted earlier, our president, as a depressive-position leader in charge of a paranoid-schizoid nation, thus truly has his work cut out for him.

Reaction formation describes behavior that is the opposite of a repressed wish, such as shyness as a defense against repressed exhibitionistic impulses. Everybody uses reaction formations to manage unacceptable feelings, but they become symptomatic when repeated compulsively, as in the case of Obama's obsessive bipartisan disorder as a reaction formation against murderous desires. Obama's obsessive bipartisanship causes him to unconsciously deny others' murderousness as well, leading to such dangerous results as his negotiating with himself before he even talks with the Republicans.

Repetition compulsion is an unconsciously driven compulsion to put oneself into stressful situations. Each time, one is repeating an old prototype, but experiencing it as something new that has to do only with current circumstances. The cycle of exciting and disappointing his supporters is for Obama something out of his conscious control, a function of the pattern of seduction and abandonment that started in his childhood—rather than a function of the people and problems currently in front of him.

Splitting describes the primitive psychological process of dividing our environment and ourselves into good and bad in early-childhood development. The split allows the infant to organize its experiences, partly because the baby is unable to perceive whole (entire) people and has experiences that are segmented. When the baby has good feelings of being held and loved, everything is good; when he or she has colic or rage, everything is bad. We split our experiences into good and bad to protect one from the other, as we have not had sufficient emotional growth to tolerate loving and hating the same object. Infants and young children cannot believe that the same object that caused a great experience can cause a hated experience. As good experiences with good objects build up, the bad experiences become more tolerable and eventually the baby feels strong enough internally so that good feelings outweigh bad ones. Over time we identify with our internal objects and they become part of ourselves as well as remaining internal objects. Some people, however, have too much resentment or envy to take in positive experiences, and thus reject them—something that in later life weakens their capacity to love or to feel good about themselves and the world in which they live.

Unconscious: The part of the mind of which we are consciously unaware, the unconscious is dominated by forgotten memories that are often indistinguishable from fantasies, feelings, or wishes. Aspects of guilt and healthy judgment can also be unconscious; intuition, then, is one form of unconscious knowledge. Our conscious memories are affected by unconscious fantasies and distorted memories as well. In the age of videotape it is interesting to see how many people deny things they had said on tape the day before. This is a form of unconscious forgetting called "repression." Dreams involve what we are thinking about when asleep, though disguised enough to help us remain asleep.

The unconscious is one's ally more often than most people think. After all, survival and growth are fundamental drives that our unconscious helps us realize in ways we can't always consciously recognize. When a good marriage is called a "match made in heaven," for example, it is a match based in part on unconscious knowledge of the other.

The unconscious can also be a cauldron of hurt. Obama faced his own hurts from paternal abandonment clearly enough to make sure not to visit those on his daughters. But evading the hurt part of the self keeps that part unconscious and risks its being played out on the world stage. Obama may project that injured self onto the Left and then see them as trying to retaliate against him, the way he would have done against his father—had he been old enough and strong enough.

Source Notes

INTRODUCTION

4 Even the satirical TV show *The Onion News Network* chimed in with a "story": *The Onion News Network*, March 5, 2011

8 At the end of the 2007 edition of *Bush on the Couch* I predicted that our nation might "search for someone completely different from Bush in the 2008 election, someone not male or white": Justin A. Frank, M.D., *Bush on the Couch: Inside the Mind of the President* (New York: Harper, 2007), p. 257

CHAPTER ONE

11 There is as much difference between us and ourselves as between us and others: Montaigne, *Essays* (1575), trans. Charles Cotton

11 now President Obama attempted to silence his former rival John McCain: health care reform summit, Jan. 25, 2010, transcripts.cnn.com

14 Obama's early biographer David Mendell wrote: David Mendell, *Obama: From Promise to Power* (New York: HarperCollins, 2007), p. 217

14 In describing his core responsibilities as commander in chief: Bob Woodward, *Obama's Wars* (New York: Simon & Schuster, 2010), p. 214

18 When reporters researched the story: David Remnick, *The Bridge: The Life and Rise of Barack Obama* (New York: Knopf, 2010), pp. 238–239

22 he came close to acknowledging in an interview: interview with Charlie Rose, *Charlie Rose Show*, Nov. 23, 2004

23 The BBC newswriter Guy DeLauney was impressed: BBC News, Nov. 10, 2010.

24 John Owens told the biographer David Remnick: Remnick, *The Bridge*, p. 140

24 Nevertheless, in his student days: Mendell, *Obama: From Promise to Power*, p. 560

24 "According to his math and science teacher, Pal Eldredge": Remnick, *The Bridge*, p. 78

27 he was quick to remind *60 Minutes'* Steve Kroft: interview with Steve Kroft, *60 Minutes*, May 8, 2011

30 Though his April 2011 speech in response: remarks by the president on fiscal policy, April 13, 2011, www.whitehouse.gov

31 "I said, 'You want to repeal health care?'": audio feed of DNC fund-raiser in Chicago, reported by CBS Radio News, April 15, 2011

31 "I have got to take direct responsibility": presidential press conference, Nov. 3, 2010

32 Ever the healer of splits, he also vowed that day: ibid.

32 "I can't spend all my time with my birth certificate": interview with Brian Williams, *NBC Nightly News*, Aug. 29, 2010

33 "Every day, families sacrifice to live": State of the Union address, Jan. 25, 2011

33 "We may have differences in policy": ibid.

34 "Now is the time for both sides and both houses of Congress": ibid.

34 "What comes of this moment will be determined": ibid.

CHAPTER TWO

38 "Well . . . I think it had a profound impact," he told CNN, "except, you know, more as an object lesson of what it's like growing up without a father in the house": interview with Suzanne Malveaux, CNN, July 2008

38 Anyone who loses his father at a young age grows up with what the Harvard psychoanalyst James Herzog identified in 2002 as "father hunger": James M. Herzog, *Father Hunger: Explorations with Adults and Children* (New York: Analytic Press, 2001), p. 22

38 Obama came close to revealing to his biographer David Mendell at least an unconscious role that yearning played in his life: Mendell, *Obama: From Promise to Power*, p. 40

41 Describing his mother's core beliefs to her biographer Janny Scott, he said, "It was a sense that beneath our surface differences, we're all the same": Janny Scott, *A Singular Woman* (New York, Riverhead, 2011), p. 357

42 (His half brother Mark Obama Ndesandjo was so traumatized by his father Barack Sr.): "Obama's Half-Brother Recasts Story of Their Father," Louisa Lim on *All Things Considered,* NPR, November 13, 2009

43 But Obama minimizes the extent of his father's destructiveness to himself and to others, dismissing his plight: "An Honest Government, A Hopeful Future," speech at University of Nairobi, Aug. 28, 2006

43 And he speaks of his father with conspicuous circumspection, as in the following remarks, made to a Kenyan audience in 2006: ibid.

44 One notable exception to this attitude, according to his biographer Mendell, is that Obama "often told close friends that he grew up feeling 'like an orphan'": Mendell, *Obama: From Promise to Power*, p. 19

45 Secretary of Defense Robert Gates gushed that his decision to go through with the raid on Osama bin Laden was "one of the most courageous": interview with Katie Couric, *60 Minutes,* May 15, 2011

46 In *Revival,* one of the most detailed explorations of exactly how Obama conducts the office of the presidency: Richard Wolffe, *Revival: The Struggle for Survival Inside the Obama White House* (New York: Crown, 2010), p. 5

46 Later in the book, Wolffe describes what appears to be a rare outburst from the president at the end of the eleventh-hour negotiations between House and Senate Democrats: ibid., p. 80

47 He is afraid to admit the nature of the Republican threat—describing it to

Wolffe, when reflecting on Republican efforts to derail his health care reform bill: ibid., p. 75

51 When Bill O'Reilly asked him in their pre–Super Bowl Fox interview in 2011 how it felt to be hated, Obama replied that many presidents—such as Bush and Bill Clinton—had been disliked: interview with Bill O'Reilly, Fox News, Feb. 2, 2011

53 In April 2009, speaking on the economy at Georgetown, he cited the sermon's parable of two men who built their houses on sand and rock, respectively, with predictable results: speech at Georgetown University, April 14, 2009

53 The previous summer, in a speech in June at a Chicago church, he recycled the same imagery: Apostolic Church of God, Chicago, June 15, 2008

54 He was in his second year in the White House when he told CNN, "Without hesitation, the most challenging, most fulfilling, most important job I will have during my time on this earth is to be Sasha and Malia's father": Town Hall Education Arts & Recreation Campus (THEARC), Anacostia, Washington, D.C., June 21, 2010

54 He even found a way to joke about it: in a high school commencement speech on May 16, 2011, he said the principal's daughter had gone to a different high school: Commencement speech, Booker T. Washington High School, Memphis, Tenn., May 16, 2011

54 A few months earlier, just weeks before Americans went to the polls in 2010 for the disastrous (at least for Obama) midterm elections, he cut short his appearance at a Rhode Island fund-raiser: Democratic Congressional Campaign Dinner, Providence, R.I., Oct. 24, 2010

54 In his book *Revival: The Struggle for Survival Inside the Obama White House,* Richard Wolffe wrote that Obama even interrupted the final health insurance reform negotiations to attend a flute recital at his daughters' school: Wolffe, p. 5

CHAPTER THREE

63 I wanted to nudge history forward in the way a child would when wishing to make a flower grow more quickly: by tugging at it: Vaclav Havel, address to Academy of Humanities and Political Science, Paris, 1992

63 I find his "I'll stand up for your rights soon, or next week, or in two years" to be tiring and unconvincing: Christopher Durang, *Huffington Post,* Nov. 2009

64 "Grappling for consensus, [Obama] noted the general agreement on the difficulty of defeating the Taliban and the importance of protecting Afghans": Woodward, *Obama's Wars,* p. 228

64 Obama himself tells Woodward that he felt he needed to "get everybody in a room and make sure that everybody is singing from the same hymnal": ibid., p. 184

64 And when they did finally strike a compromise, Woodward noted, "in an unusual move, [Obama] said, 'I want everybody to sign on to this'": ibid., p. 302

65 This was perhaps never clearer than in his spotlight-claiming 2004 Democratic National Convention keynote address: keynote address, Democratic National Convention, Boston, July 27, 2004

66 Critics who say that Obama has no strong belief system—typified by the syndicated columnist Richard Cohen writing in *The Washington Post*: Richard Cohen, "President Obama's Enigmatic Intellectualism," *Washington Post*, June 22, 2010

71 Friends she met in Jakarta "were floored that she'd bring a half-black child to Indonesia, knowing the disrespect they have for blacks," her acquaintance Elizabeth Bryant: Scott, *A Singular Woman*, p. 107

72 Maya later wrote that her mother might have left because she "really got a voice," acquired both a professional and feminist language, and started to "demand more of those who were near her": *Washington Post*, Aug. 24, 2008

72 David Remnick, in his book *The Bridge: The Life and Rise of Barack Obama*, observes that "Obama is not always easy on Ann Dunham": Remnick, p. 239

73 By contrast, Obama's father, who was a present absence and an angry self-indulgent phantom who interacted directly with Barry for only one month, was the "singular object of the narrator's imaginings, at the center of a young man's quest to claim a race and a history": ibid.

76 Dunham's biographer Janny Scott wrote that his mother, "for whom a letter in Jakarta from her son in the United States could raise her spirits for a full day": Scott, pp. 7–8

76 He was a little clearer about both his resentment toward her and his discomfort expressing it when speaking to Scott, who asked him about the "serial displacements" of his childhood: ibid., p. 134

78 Others have dismissed it simply as political weakness, branding him the "conciliator in chief": Charles Lemos, MyDD.com, Feb. 24, 2010; John Zogby, Forbes.com, Feb. 11, 2010

78 Accommodation is something we all learn in childhood, one of five problem-solving methods identified by the mediation expert Kenneth W. Thomas in *Handbook of Industrial and Organizational Psychology*: K. W. Thomas, "Conflict and Negotiation Processes in Organizations," M. D. Dunnette and L. M. Hough (eds.), *Handbook of Industrial and Organizational Psychology*, 2nd ed., vol.3 (Palo Alto, Calif.: Consulting Psychologists Press, 1992), pp. 652–717

78 Pathological accommodation is closely associated with the work of Dr. Bernard Brandschaft, who in 1985 identified the condition in children who deny their own beliefs and needs in an attempt to please their parents: Bernard Brandschaft, "Systems of Pathological Accommodation and Change in Analysis": *Journal of Psychoanalytic Psychology* 24 (2007), 667–687.

79 In the 1930s, the psychoanalyst Helene Deutsch coined the term "as-if personality" to describe people who seem to be genuine but are in fact putting on a false front of which they themselves are not fully aware: Helene Deutsch, "Some Forms of Emotional Disturbance and Their Relationship to Schizophrenia," *Psychoanalytic Quarterly* 11 (1942), 301–321

79 Subsequently, the psychoanalyst D. W. Winnicott described what he called the "false self," which he felt arose from the child's feeling a need to protect his mother from his own anger at her, thereby protecting himself from experiencing that anger by consigning it to his unconscious mental life: D.W. Winnicott, *The Maturational Processes and the Facilitating Environment* (London: Hogarth Press, 1965)

81 When asked by Ann's biographer Janny Scott to identify her "limitations as a mother," Obama first describes her as "a very strong person in her own way . . . resilient, able to bounce back from setbacks, persistent": Scott, *A Singular Woman*, p. 356

CHAPTER FOUR

96 We see both qualities in his March 24, 2009, press conference at the height of the financial-crisis panic, when he patiently explained how AIG was different from a bank and thus "more problematic" to regulate: White House press conference, March 24, 2009

107 telling the nation that "just after the rig sank [he] assembled a team of our nation's best scientists and engineers to tackle this challenge, a team led by Dr. Steven Chu, a Nobel Prize": White House address to the nation, June 15, 2010

108 He's aware of his effectiveness as a speaker; when Senator Harry Reid complimented him on it, as Reid reported in the 2009 edition of his memoir *The Good Fight,* Obama simply and quietly replied "I have a gift, Harry": Harry Reid, *The Good Fight* (New York: Berkley Trade, 2009)

108 Wolffe's account in *Revival* of the development of his 2008 campaign slogan and catchphrases, in which he describes the pollster Joel Benenson's observation: Wolffe, p. 115

108 in his Oval Office address in which he declared the end of combat missions in Iraq. After telling the American people that "Through this remarkable chapter in the history of the United States and Iraq, we have met our responsibility," he concluded, "Now it's time to turn the page": White House, Aug. 31, 2010

109 "We're facing the worst economic crisis since the Great Depression, and John McCain wants us to 'turn the page'?": Asheville High School, Asheville, N.C., Oct. 5, 2008

109 But by the end of the month, Obama was telling voters with a straight face that on election day they "can turn the page on policies that have put the greed and irresponsibility of Wall Street before the hard work and sacrifice of folks on Main Street": Canton, Ohio, Oct. 27, 2008

109 The psychoanalyst Wilfred Bion distinguished between "the language of substitution": W. R. Bion, *Attention and Interpretation* (London: Tavistock Press, 1970)

110 Obama's press secretary, Robert Gibbs, was practicing the language of substitution when he characterized the liberal wing of his party as the "professional Left": thehill.com, Aug. 10, 2010

112 Disapproving the pace of Obama's response to Egypt, the *Newsweek* columnist Niall Ferguson compared him unfavorably to Otto von Bismarck: *Newsweek*, Feb. 14, 2011

115 And what he wrote in 1846 still holds true and has a significant bearing on both Obama's presidency and character: specifically, that when intelligence is valued over all else, ideas replace reality and then become the new reality: Kierkegaard, *Two Ages: A Literary Review* (1846)

116　Kierkegaard said that abstraction "transforms the real task into an unreal trick and reality into a play": Arno Gruen, *The Betrayal of the Self* (Berkeley, Calif: Human Development Books, 2000), p. 30

117　But now his rhetoric has changed, as Mark Klein, who heroically exposed government wiretaps done by AT&T: "Is Thomas Drake an Enemy of the State?" Jane Mayer, *New Yorker*, May 23, 2011

CHAPTER FIVE

119　Inevitably we resist change and turn back with passionate nostalgia to the stage we are leaving: Lionel Trilling, *The Liberal Imagination* (London: Penguin Books, 1970), quoted by J. Turner, "Wordsmith and Winnicott in the Area of Play," *International Review of Psychoanalysis* 15 (1988), 481–496

119　The recurrent configuration is of an explosive force within a restraining framework: Bion, *Attention and Interpretation*

121　As the biracial author Shelby Steele wrote in 2008's *A Bound Man,* "What seems clear is that Barack Obama is a man who truly wants to be black": Shelby Steele, *A Bound Man* (New York: Free Press, 2008), p. 52

121　Richard Wolffe's detailed account of the development of Obama's slogan reveals that the emergence of the phrase was not without resistance: Wolffe, *Revival*, p. 114

122　In his 2011 State of the Union address, Obama presented a vision of change very different from the campaign slogan: State of the Union address, Jan. 25, 2011

129　a pattern rendered with particular detail in Wolffe's account of his writing of his Nobel Prize acceptance speech: Wolffe, *Revival,* p. 40

130　David Mendell's account of following the campaign car during the 2006 Senate campaign and observing cigarette butts being tossed from the rear windows: Mendell, *Obama: From Promise to Power*, p. 294

133　as when he churlishly complained in September 2010 that the Republicans "talk about me like a dog": Milwaukee, Wisc., Sept. 6, 2010

138　he lashes out, most notably in his December 2010 press conference: "So this notion that somehow we are willing to compromise too much reminds me of the debate that we had during health care": White House press conference, Dec. 7, 2010

142　as when he confided to friends in late 2010, according to Jonathan Alter, "All I want for Christmas is an opposition that I can negotiate with": Jonathan Alter, *The Promise* (New York: Simon & Schuster, trade paperback edition, 2011)

CHAPTER SIX

143　The tough mind is sharp and penetrating, breaking through the crust of legends and myths and sifting the true from the false: Martin Luther King, "A Tough Mind and a Tender Heart" (1962), published in *A Testament of Hope* (New York: HarperOne, 1990), ch. 1

143   One notable exception is the work of Dr. George Vaillant, who studied male psychological health by following the Harvard class of 1946 longitudinally: George E. Vaillant, *Aging Well: Surprising Guideposts to a Happier Life from the Landmark Harvard Study of Adult Development* (New York: Little, Brown, 2003)

144   We saw this in his response to the Fort Hood shootings in 2009, when he used his and the nation's anxiety over the tragedy and threat of terrorism forces dividing it to fuel his call for unity: Fort Hood, Texas, Nov. 10, 2009

144   But his ambition is leavened with some measure of humility, as he articulated in his 2006 interview with Charlie Rose (albeit when he was still only a U.S. senator): *Charlie Rose Show*, Oct. 19, 2006

145   On an unconscious level, he projects the damaged parts of his own personality into the nation's less fortunate citizens—the "folks I got into politics for, the reason I'm here": remarks by the president at Laborfest in Milwaukee, Wisc., Sept. 6, 2010

146   But he also consciously presents himself as a emblem of reparation, telling House Democrats during the 2008 campaign that "it has become increasingly clear in my travel, the campaign, that the crowds, the enthusiasm, 200,000 people in Berlin, is not about me at all": Jonathan Weisman, "Obama's Symbolic Importance," The Trail, washingtonpost.com, July 30, 2008

147   He said in an interview in October 2010 with *Rolling Stone* that he considered Fox News: interview with Jann S. Wenner, *Rolling Stone*, Sept. 30, 2010

148   put on vivid display during his February 2011 interview with Bill O'Reilly: interview with Bill O'Reilly, Fox News, Feb. 2, 2011

151   Ironically, by declaring in his announcement about bin Laden that "Justice has been done," President Obama gave the word new meaning: remarks by the president on Osama bin Laden, May 1, 2011

157   In a memorable moment in his Nobel Peace Prize acceptance speech he proclaimed, "Somewhere today, a mother facing punishing poverty still takes the time to teach her child": Oslo, Dec. 10, 2010

158   the Republican pundit and *Wall Street Journal* columnist Peggy Noonan went so far in 2010 as to differentiate between multiple varieties of alienation, describing "the president's rhetorical disconnect": "Slug the Obama Story 'Disconnect,'" *Wall Street Journal*, Jan. 14, 2010

158   In *Obama's Wars* Bob Woodward offered a quote from Obama's aide John Podesta, who said that he "was not sure that Obama felt anything": Woodward, p. 38

158   He admitted as much in the period of introspection that followed one of his first term's darkest moments: interview with George Stephanopoulos, ABC News, Jan. 20, 2010

160   Wolffe describes his very intellectual approach to the often unintellectual task of connecting with voters, in this instance dating back to the primary season: *Revival*, p. 82

162   As the black columnist Melissa Harris-Perry put it in *The Nation*, "The solidarity and creativity of the Obama campaign was quickly replaced by the sober predictability and insularity of the Obama administration": Melissa Harris-Perry, "Politics and the Pleasure Principle," *The Nation*, Feb. 14, 2011

162 This is hardly news to Obama observers; in his review of Jonathan Alter's *The Promise* in *The New York Review of Books,* Frank Rich zeroed in on this trait and added his own two cents: Frank Rich, "Why Has He Fallen Short?," *New York Review of Books,* July 22, 2010

CHAPTER SEVEN

163 People need each other far more than most of us can bear to know: C. Fred Alford, *Psychology and the Natural Law of Reparation* (Cambridge, U.K.: Cambridge University Press, 2011)

163 He must have felt that he had lost the old warm world, paid a high price for living too long with a single dream: F. Scott Fitzgerald, *The Great Gatsby*

171 As the sociological researcher Shelby Steele wrote: *A Bound Man,* p. 53

172 He spoke of the fishermen's prayer that they offered even after this incomprehensible disaster: remarks by the president on the BP oil spill, June 15, 2010

173 He unconsciously said as much when he declared during the 2008 campaign, "We are the ones we have been waiting for": Super Tuesday speech, Chicago, Feb. 5, 2008

175 At a September 16, 2010, fund-raiser in Greenwich, Connecticut, Obama went on a mocking binge: remarks by the president at DNC event, Greenwich, Conn., Sept. 16, 2010.

178 Obama said as much in a 1996 interview for *The New Yorker*: Mariana Cook, "A Couple in Chicago," *New Yorker,* Jan. 19, 2009

179 (Rush later told Obama's biographer David Remnick that Obama was too close to Hyde Park "elites" to be connected viscerally to Chicago's black community): Remnick, *The Bridge,* p. 316

180 He confuses trench buddies fighting a common enemy for community: remarks by the president on Osama bin Laden, May 1, 2011

CHAPTER EIGHT

185 I imagine one of the reasons people cling to their hates so stubbornly is because they sense, once hate is gone, they will be forced to deal with pain: James Baldwin, *Notes of a Native Son* (Boston: Beacon Press, 1955)

185 The second reason that the charge of racism is leveled at patriotic Americans so often is that people making the charge actually believe it: Sarah Palin, newstatesman.com/blogs/the-staggers/2010/11/palin-race-decision-obama, March 22, 2011

185 People who could not spell the word vote or say it in English put a committed socialist ideologue in the White House—name is Barack Hussein Obama: Tom Tancredo, www.cbsnews.com/8301–503544 162–6177125–503544 .html, Feb. 5, 2010

189 Thus we see Rush Limbaugh equating Obama with Hitler and filling the airwaves with discussions of "similarities between the Democrat party of today and the Nazi party in Germany": *The Rush Limbaugh Show,* Aug. 6, 2009

190 Envy of Obama's effectiveness has become so pervasive among Republicans, for example, that John Boehner, on May 10, 2011, indirectly (and somewhat inarticulately) criticized Obama's articulate manner of speech: Boehner interview, *The Today Show*, May 10, 2011

190 Thus Sarah Palin declared in fall 2010, "I think ordinary Americans are tired of Obama's global apology tour": Sarah Palin, *America by Heart: Reflections on Family Faith and Flag* (New York: HarperCollins, 2010), p. 71.

193 In November 2010, Bill O'Reilly said on his Fox News show to his guest Juan Williams, "I'm starting to get even more worried": *The O'Reilly Factor*, Nov. 8, 2010.

195 as heard from the Utah Tea Party Congressman Jason Chaffetz the morning after the 2011 State of the Union address: Fox News, Jan. 26, 2011

195 A comprehensive 2010 CBS News survey of Tea Party supporters revealed much about how the dynamics we've been discussing play out in the group's attitudes and demographics: "Tea Partiers: Who They Are and What They Believe," Brian Montopoli, cbsnews.com, April 14, 2010

198 The psychoanalyst Roger Money-Kyrle wrote that a particular kind of delusional system can develop over time, well after the most intense projections are toned down: Roger Money-Kyrle, *Man's Picture of His World: A Psychoanalytic Study* (London: Duckworth, 1961), pp. 142–167

201 as does Sarah Palin, tweeting after the passage of health care reform, "Commonsense Conservatives and Lovers of America: Don't Retreat, Instead— RELOAD!": Twitter, March 23, 2010

202 As Money-Kyrle wrote, "We are unable to imagine any passion or sentiment in another unless it has been in some degree, either consciously or unconsciously, experienced by us": Roger Money-Kyrle, *Psychoanalysis and Politics* (London: Duckworth, 1951), p. 97

CHAPTER NINE

203 Ethical thought consists of the systematic examination of the relations of human beings to each other: Isaiah Berlin

205 Frank Rich wrote about the puzzling, "enigmatic Obama" in April 2010: Frank Rich, "It's a Bird, It's a Plane, It's Obama!" *New York Times*, April 4, 2010

205 after the 2010 midterm elections, *The New York Times* headlined an editorial "Waiting for the President": *New York Times*, Nov. 12, 2010

205 a year after the Rich "enigmatic" piece, the columnist Paul Krugman declared, "The President Is Missing": *New York Times*, April 10, 2011

207 He appealed to my psychoanalytic colleagues, especially for saying in September 2008 that "we can't steer ourselves out of this crisis if we're heading in the same disastrous direction": Espanola, New Mexico, Sept. 18, 2008

209 On Memorial Day of 2009, Obama said in a speech at Arlington, "This cemetery is in and of itself a testament to the price our nation has paid for freedom": remarks by the president on Memorial Day, Arlington, Va., May 25, 2009

213 *Tikkun* editor Rabbi Michael Lerner saw it early in Obama's presidency when he wrote that pragmatism is dangerous without clear ideology, a sign that he

recognized something that was lacking in this man: Rabbi Michael Lerner, "Obama's Non-Ideological Pragmatism Will Backfire," *Tikkun*, May 24, 2009

213 More vocal disaffected supporters have been emerging, among them Princeton professor Cornel West, who on May 16, 2011, called President Obama "a black mascot of Wall Street oligarchs": interview with Truthdig.com, May 16, 2011

CHAPTER TEN

215 If one just knows how to surprise, one always wins the game: Søren Kierkegaard, "The Seducer's Diary," *Either/Or Part One,* trans. Howard V. Hong and Edna H. Hong (Princeton: Princeton University Press, 1987)

216 But his stance even predates his run for the U.S. Senate: in October 2002, while still a state senator, Obama challenged President Bush. "You want a fight, President Bush?": speech in Chicago, Oct. 2, 2002

218 Speaking on Martin Luther King Day, he went on to say, "The spirit of empathy condemns not only the use of fire hoses and attack dogs to keep people down but also accountants and tax loopholes": University of Chicago, Jan. 21, 2002

220 After announcing that we had killed bin Laden, he said, "On September 11, 2001, in our time of grief, the American people came together": remarks by the president on Osama bin Laden, May 1, 2011

220 Toward the end of the interview he said flatly, "the fact of the matter is, is that we've been able to kill more terrorists on Pakistani soil than just about any place else": interview with Steve Kroft, *60 Minutes*, May 8, 2008

221 He said as much in December 2010 after the Republicans trounced the Democrats the previous month: news conference, Dec. 7, 2010

EPILOGUE

225 Without some self-pity, pity for others is likely impossible, for in pity we echo another's pain: C. Fred Alford, *Psychology and the Natural Law of Reparation* (Cambridge, U.K.: Cambridge University Press, 2011)

226 "My name is Barack Obama, of the Moneygall Obamas": Dublin, May 23, 2011

226 And by "retracing the steps of Presidents Kennedy, Reagan and Clinton," as *The New York Times* pointed out: Mark Landler, "Obama Arrives in Ireland for a Six-Day Trip to Europe," *New York Times*, May 23, 2011

227 by the spring of 2011, some of his most reliable supporters were college-educated white women, 56 percent of whom said they still strongly approved of his performance in an April 2011 Pew poll: Pew Research 2012 Research Survey, April 2011

Acknowledgments

The process of analyzing President Obama was both exciting and challenging. And while his evolution continues, recording my analytic findings had to eventually coalesce in print—despite being in medias res. None of that coming together would have been possible without a great deal of help and support from many people.

First and foremost I owe my gratitude to the subject of this study—a man I never met personally—President Barack Obama. His openness, his consistently thoughtful approach to the toughest of jobs, and his brilliant and moving memoir made my own work that much richer. In *Dreams from My Father* he delved deeply into his own history and feelings with candor one rarely sees outside the consulting room, making my work more collaborative than I ever anticipated.

There are agents and agents, and then there is Gail Ross. Her intelligence and enthusiasm made this book possible. I hope I can justify her generous help. I remain grateful to her colleague Anna Sproul, and to Howard Yoon, who carefully put the proposal together.

My smart and steady editors at Free Press—my astute and effervescent senior editor Dominick Anfuso, and the hardworking Maura O'Brien and thoughtfully meticulous Edith Lewis, who made the book clearer and smarter than I ever could alone.

Research was not easy to come by—at least, good research. Gavrie Kullman introduced me to Sarah Berns, who carried the ball for months, not just by finding requested materials but also by sending me the occasional article she rightly thought would be of interest. Jana Nelhybel organized many divergent ideas so the project could get off the ground. And at my home office I depended on the help and energy of Bea Tolson and Patrice Brown.

I'm grateful for the help and support of many friends: Steve and Karen Scheinman, Marty and Mary Stein, Lou Borgenicht and Jodi Plant, Steve Weissman, Dan Auerbach, John and Kaye Spilker, Steve

Sharfstein, Marilyn Black, Jerry Zupnick, Fred Meisel, Mike and Elizabeth Marcus, Linda and Gerald Stern, Ray and Shauna Wertheim, Spencer Graham and Elizabeth Pressler, Nechy and Tito Pieczanski, Sam Goodman, Jeff and Michele Steinberg, and the two Bobs—Kaplan and King—all friends for at least forty years, many for more than sixty. Thanks also to skiing and fressing friends Richard Miller and Marty Gold. Yaz Boyum tried hard to keep me healthy, while Carlos Campbell kept the beat going in many ways. Sandy Dijkstra—she of the original "on the couch" idea—was positive from the beginning.

Alitta Kullman kept tabs on my progress while offering analytic insights as well; her husband, Uri, presciently recommended that I read Shelby Steele's book on why Obama couldn't win in 2008. Thanks to Jay "the Bump" Schlossberg and Eileen "the Skeptic" Brengle, and the younger set Jenni and Jacob Romanek who were always there in spirit and enthusiasm—along with Mike Decker, Jason Kohn, David Segal, Eric Stern, and Julie Kennedy. I've been lucky to have had so many interesting discussions over the past year. The late Keith Byers often wrote to me on the complexity of political life today; I will miss his sardonic perspective.

Sabrina Cassagnol never stopped giving off her own brand of uniquely positive energy, while the lively Ben Schott—apparently surrounded by a family of neurologists—suggested I look at Anton's syndrome, as it were. Gianna Polacco Williams, Jesse Kornbluth, and Karen Collins kept me from being blinded by my own political frustrations with President Obama. Paul Steinberg encouraged me to look at Jung and Rilke for inspiration. Hannah and Jeff Fox kept asking when they could read the final version, all the while offering trenchant political and psychological insights. Jessica Benjamin is not only smart; she never gives up and insists on thinking clearly about the unclear. Rob Pobi, the thrilling thriller writer, kept encouraging me by telling me to keep my behind glued to the chair. It worked, Rob.

Many friends were kind enough to read and comment on the entire manuscript at various stages in its evolution. My son Abe became my mentor. He was the first person who told me about Obama in January 2002, he helped me clarify my ideas with thoughtful and tough questions, and along with Joe Scott he suggested that I include a glossary of psychoanalytic terms. I thank psychoanalyst Fred Meisel, who said Obama finally made sense, and Gerald Stern, who read while listening to "Ode to Joy." I thank Dr. Anton Obholzer of London's Tavistock Clinic, who affirmed my particular psychoanalytic approach. Pamela Brewer, psychotherapist and incisive radio host of MyndTalk, expanded my thinking about the emotional issues confronting biracial people; Mark Dawes pushed me harder to think about who I thought Obama actually was; Michael Carmichael was generous with both his time and support; Andrea Schultz read the manuscript twice—before and after edits—despite her extremely busy life, and gave me confidence for which I'll always be grateful; Harvey Saferstein read and marked up the manuscript like it was a legal brief; Tony Perram read critically, offering useful suggestions and astute criticism that I took to heart. Connie Kagel's reading both encouraged and inspired. I thank you all.

Nancy Miller and Walter Romanek read with an unflagging enthusiasm that accompanied their astute observations, some of which they will recognize in the book. They deserve their own paragraph.

My book group generously granted me leave, and I thank them all: Don Bandler, Chuck Gustafson, Carole Mason, Walter Romanek (encore), Lois Schiffer, Liz Shriver, Ray Szcudlow, and Tara Wallace. Their support was palpable.

Others who contributed their ideas and support include Michele Kearney, Helen O'Lone, Mitch Liftin, Rosemary McHugh, Susan Samuels, Dr. Jim Herzog (of *Father Hunger* fame), Drs. Qanta Ahmed and Scott Kahan, Sunny Goldberg, Ray McGovern, and cousins Dr. Teddy Rothschild and Nancy Rosenberg. I thank you all.

Culinary support and encouragement came from people who made this process more digestible than ever. Among the support, none tasted as good as from the gang at BlackSalt—the best restaurant in Washington—where the food is as good as the ambience. Special thanks to Rick Cook, the redheaded genius behind the stove; Susan Wallace, who spins sugar finer than any mythic figure; not to mention MJ and Sergio, who kept me in fish exotic or local; and Abdul, Katie, Emilia, Beth, Sarah, and many more. Then there was the stellar staff at the Ritz-Carlton Cancún, who fed me a special

Mayan diet, while concierges took care to make sure the writing conditions were sublime. No culinary support would be complete without the tasty charcuterie and bonhomie of Jamie Stachowski at the Palisades Sunday Market.

My three seminars, composed entirely of talented senior therapists, all helped clarify my clinical thinking while at the same time putting up with my particular analytic approach to the work. Thanks to Janet Black, Allen Du Mont, Janet Finell, Cary Gallaudet, Connie Kagel, Gloria Oviedo, Patricia Slatt, Sharon Alperowitz, Linda Dickson, Jaedene Levy, Micki Penn, Fran Rosenfeld, Linda Schwartz, Denise Shauer, Judy Brandzel, Connie Donaldson, Andrea Feldman; Ann Curtain Knight; Bev Gold, Charlene Goldblatt, Eileen Hunter, Susan Medoff, Margery Rosen, Ellen Rosenzweig, Barbara Shapiro, Kathy Sinclair, and the late smart and sweet Ruth Rapaport.

Of all the people responsible for my learning and growth over the years, however, my greatest thanks goes to my patients past and present. Without them there would be no understanding.

The Perram clan remained positive through it all. Thank you Tony and Shirley and your great daughters Noël, Carolyn, and Elise. And Dave Monahan is a champ. Rich (you know who you are) also kept things in focus.

This book would not have been possible without the hard work of Tom Spain. Not only is he brilliant and extremely organized, but his deep understanding of this project made it flow and grow. He continues to function like my alter ego. Micheline Klagsbrun generously gave her thoughtful support, wanting to be sure I wouldn't be too hard on our president. Ready help was available from my perspicacious sister Ellen and her steadfast husband Steve Dickman. My children Joey, Abe, and Ginevra each and all gave encouragement laced with thoughtful criticism—asking me questions that put me on the spot and pushed me to think more clearly—something they have done since birth. Ginevra not only asked probing questions that challenged my arguments, she also gently helped me keep my nose to the grindstone. Joey offered idiosyncratic approaches to Obama that sharpened my thinking. And Abe carefully read and critiqued the manuscript in its several iterations; the only thing that exceeds my gratitude is my pride in his unique talents—talents that are enhanced by his warm heart. The "significant others" also were there—Maria, Emily, and Vinny—and I thank you all.

Writing is supposed to be a lonely business, but my two dogs Onda and Lilly sat loyally nearby and kept me company, waiting for the next break in the action.

My loving wife Heather's irreverent humor added spice to her consistent love and support that keep me sane.

Thank you all. The help was yours; the mistakes remain mine.

Index

Abortion, 209
Abstract thinking, 116–117
Accommodation, 77–82, 85, 87–89
Achievement, Language of, 109–112,
    115, 219, 243–244
Adams, John, 229
Afghanistan, 63–64, 205
Aggression, 6, 7, 19, 27, 28, 39, 40, 42,
    60, 84, 97, 217, 225, 234
Agriculture, Department of, 111
AIG, 97
Alford, C. Fred, 163, 225
Allen, Thad, 107
Alter, Jonathan, 4, 142, 162
Anton's syndrome, 133
Anxiety
    in infancy, 12, 15
    Obama and management of, 56,
        96, 130–132, 151, 152, 154,
        160–161
Applied psychoanalysis, 8, 186,
    226–227
As-if personality, 79
AT&T Company, 117
Attention and Interpretation (Bion),
    119
Atwater, Lee, 200
Audacity of Hope, The (Obama), 5,
    11, 37, 54, 163–164, 170, 171,
    175, 204
Authority, belief in, 119–120, 162
Automobile industry bailout, 45,
    161–162

Axelrod, David, 121–122
Bachmann, Michele, 57, 191
Baldwin, James, 185
Basketball, 64, 84, 148

Beck, Glenn, 32–33, 189, 191
Benenson, Joel, 108, 122
Berlin, Isaiah, 203
Bernanke, Ben, 171
Biden, Joe, 63, 64, 147, 173
bin Laden, Osama, 2, 7, 27, 28–29,
    45, 59, 61, 84, 89–90, 152, 153,
    161, 162, 180, 189, 190, 202,
    205, 208, 214, 215–222, 225,
    234
Bion, Wilfred R., 109, 115, 119, 208,
    243
Bipartisan cooperation, 29, 71, 85, 87,
    134, 233–234
Birthers, 2, 15, 32, 116, 187, 192, 193
Bismarck, Otto von, 112
Boehner, John, 30–31, 133, 174, 190,
    221, 222, 230, 233, 236
Booker T. Washington High School
    commencement, Memphis (May
    16, 2011), 218, 219
*Bound Man, A: Why We Are Excited
    About Obama and Why He
    Can't Win* (Steele), 121, 171
BP Gulf oil spill, 20, 31–33, 45, 55, 66,
    107, 161, 172
Brandschaft, Bernard, 78–80
Break and repair, 13, 39, 124
Brennan, John, 64
*Bridge, The: The Life and Rise of
    Barack Obama* (Remnick),
    72–73
Brown, Scott, 158
Bryant, Elizabeth, 71
Bush, George W., 2–3, 30, 51, 88,
    90, 120, 132, 151, 152, 195,
    199, 206, 207, 211–213, 216,
    222

Index

Bush on the Couch: Inside the Mind of the President (Frank), 3, 8, 9, 212
Butler, Samuel, 1

Cantor, Eric, 174
Carter, Jimmy, 141, 199
CBS News, 195
Chaffetz, Jason, 195
Change, 31–32, 112–117, 121–129, 131, 137–142, 205
Change We Can Believe In slogan, 121–122
Chu, Steven, 107
Civil War, 229
Clinton, Bill, 51, 160, 226
Clinton, Hillary, 8, 63, 64, 147, 207
Clyburn, James, 56
CNN (Cable News Network), 38, 54
Cohen, Richard, 66
Collaboration, 78
Columbia University, 69, 146, 149, 150, 156
Common (rap artist), 192
Compartmentalization, 208–209, 215
Competition, 78
Compromise and consensus building, 3, 4, 6, 13, 30, 32, 34, 38, 64–65, 72, 78, 85–87, 131
Conflict-avoidance style, 45–46, 140, 234, 235, 238
Connor, Bull, 218
Conrad, Joseph, 26, 152
Constitution of the United States, 33, 34, 58, 148, 212
Containment, 94–96, 98, 241–242
Coretta (pseudonym), 21, 22, 32, 100, 102, 103
Counterprojection, 212
Countertransference, 8, 239, 241

Daniels, Mitch, 190
Death panels, 15–16, 45, 86, 111, 188
DeLauney, Guy, 23
Delusional beliefs, 198–199
Democratic National Convention (2004), Obama's keynote address at, 11, 22, 65–67, 76, 91, 102, 122

Denial, 88, 130, 198, 230, 235–236
Depressive position, 6, 15–16, 28–31, 140–142, 159–160, 202, 245, 246
Detroit, Michigan, 162
Deutsch, Helene, 79
Dickinson, Emily, 91
Dissociation, 14, 44, 130–134, 202, 241–242
Do the Right Thing (movie), 9
"Don't Ask, Don't Tell," 45
Dreams from My Father (Obama), vii, 4–5, 17, 18, 20, 42–44, 49, 55, 59, 67–70, 72–73, 79, 91–92, 97–102, 112–116, 124, 135–136, 146, 147, 149–151, 153–155, 164, 175, 178, 180–182, 204, 211, 227
DuBois, W. E. B., 166, 172
Dukakis, Michael, 200
Dunham, Madelyn Lee Payne (Toots), 5, 16, 24, 42, 49–51, 74, 79, 81–82, 92, 107, 145, 207
Dunham, Stanley Ann
  anthropological fieldwork of, 72, 74, 97
  Barack's childhood and adolescence and, 5, 14, 16, 17, 20, 24, 33, 44, 65, 73–77, 81–82, 115, 127–128, 139–140, 154–157, 163–165, 175, 211, 219, 227, 228, 231, 241–242, 247
  biographer of, 41, 69–71, 76, 81
  breakup with Lolo, 123, 125, 127–128
  death of, 98, 156
  leaves Barack with parents, 20, 40, 72, 123, 125, 128, 154, 157, 206
  meets Barack Sr., 92
  relationships with men, 70–71
  in Seattle, Washington, 13, 67, 164
  second husband of, 17, 71, 72, 96, 125, 127, 153–154
  separation and divorce from Barack Sr., 13, 37, 38, 67–71, 79, 94, 164
  stories told about absent Barack Sr. by, 5, 40–42, 47, 49–52, 69–70, 79–80, 92, 93, 95–96, 97, 106, 126, 146, 165, 166, 174

struggles and sacrifices of, 53, 60, 81, 99, 157, 164–165
Dunham, Stanley Armour (Gramps), 5, 16, 24, 42, 47–50, 67, 74, 79, 81–82, 92, 130, 146, 155, 165, 172, 173, 242
Durang, Christopher, 63

Edwards, John, 120, 207
Egypt, 60, 91, 112, 117, 203
Eikenberry, Karl W., 64
Eldredge, Pal, 24
Ellison, Ralph, 172
Emanuel, Rahm, 46, 173
Eminem, 162
Enron Corporation, 218
Envy, 189–192, 194, 197, 198, 243
Exceptionalism, 188–189, 245

False self, 79, 242
Family romance, 164
Ferguson, Niall, 112
Fire Next Time, The (Baldwin), 185
Fitzgerald, F. Scott, vii, 163
Foreclosure, 117
Foreign Intelligence Surveillance Act (FISA), 205, 207
Fort Hood shootings, 144
Fox News, 57, 147, 148, 193, 211, 222
Frank (old poet), 146, 172, 242
Frank (student), 114
Frank, Abe, 203, 204
Frank, Thomas, 208
Freud, Sigmund, 3, 164, 239
Freudian tradition, 5

Gates, Henry Louis, 58, 116
Gates, Robert, 45, 64
Geithner, Timothy, 167, 171, 173
General Motors Corporation, 45, 161
George Washington University, 77, 110
Georgetown University, 53, 83
Gibbs, Robert, 110
Giffords, Gabrielle, 55, 86
Gingrich, Newt, 135, 189, 236, 237
Good Fight, The (Reid), 108
Grandiosity, 47–48, 102, 132
Great Gatsby, The (Fitzgerald), vii, 163
Gregory, David, 135

Guantánamo prison, Cuba, 114–115, 212, 220
Gun control, 55, 58, 107

Handbook of Industrial and Organizational Psychology (Thomas), 78
Harris-Perry, Melissa, 162
Harvard Law Review, 2, 22, 64, 91, 157, 169
Harvard Law School, 2, 84, 156
Harvard University, 13, 37, 93, 144
Hate/hatred, 6, 7, 26, 30, 52, 86, 141, 142, 185, 187, 190, 192. See also Obama, Barack Hussein, hate/hatred and
Havel, Vaclav, 63
Hawaii, 20–22, 24, 40, 67, 68, 72, 73, 123, 125, 128, 154, 157, 206
Hayes, Chris, 234
Health care reform, 4, 15–16, 27, 31, 45, 46, 47, 77, 81, 82, 86, 112, 131, 138, 140, 141, 148, 191, 201, 205, 237
Hearst, William Randolph, 147
Heart of Darkness (Conrad), 26, 152, 153
Henry, Ed, 97
Herzog, James, 38
Hitler, Adolf, 189
Holiday, Billie, 75, 155
Holocaust survivors, 132
Hoover, Herbert, 199
Horton, Willie, 200
"How the Grinch Stole Christmas" (television show), 42, 70
Hoyer, Steny, 57
Huntsman, Jon, 237
Hurricane Katrina, 120, 172

Idealization, 14, 39–42, 47–48, 103
Indonesia, 4, 17, 23, 30, 71, 96, 114, 124–127, 147, 150, 151, 155, 205–206
Infant psychological development, 12, 13, 15, 94–95, 186–187, 191, 194, 244, 245, 247
Insurance industry, 45, 86
Iraq War, 108–109, 205
Ireland, Obama's visit to, 225–229

Index

Jefferson, Thomas, 229
Johnnie (South Sider), 135–136
Johnson, Lyndon B., 85
Joplin, Missouri, tornado victims, 228

Kamehameha, King, 67
Kellman, Jerry (Marty Kauffman), 167
Kennedy, John F., 91, 226
Kenya, 43–44, 87–88
Kerry, John, 199
Kierkegaard, Søren, 115, 116, 199, 215
King, Martin Luther, Jr., 143, 166, 172
King, Steve, 57
Klein, Mark, 117
Klein, Melanie, 5, 6, 15, 27
Kleinian theory, 12, 28, 195, 245
Kroft, Steve, 27, 29, 215, 220, 234
Krugman, Paul, 138, 205

Language of Achievement, 109–112,
    115, 219, 243–244
Language of substitution, 109–115,
    219, 243–244
Lee, Spike, 9
Left, 28, 80–81, 83, 85, 86, 89, 110,
    111, 116, 151, 174–175, 205,
    212, 228, 241, 248
Lemos, Charles, 78
Lerner, Michael, 213
Letters to a Young Poet (Rilke), vii
Lewis, John, 133
Liberal Imagination, The (Trilling),
    119, 161
Libya, 29, 112, 124
Life magazine, 17–20, 72, 87, 123,
    125, 146
Limbaugh, Rush, 189

Magical thinking, 105–108, 110, 129
Maher, Bill, 116
Malcolm X, 166, 172, 173
Mandela, Nelson, 160, 166
Manning, Bradley, 27, 33, 58
Marcus (student), 101, 114, 152
Margolis, Jim, 122
Mayer, Jane, 117
McCain, John, 11–12, 27, 109, 152
McChrystal, Stanley, 64
McConnell, Mitch, 66, 133, 191

Medicare, 30, 77
Meet the Press (May 15, 2011), 135
Memphis, Tennessee, 218
Mendell, David, 14, 24, 38–39, 44, 130
Midterm elections (2010), 2, 30–32,
    34, 54, 133, 141, 205
Money-Kyrle, Roger, 199, 202
Montaigne, Michel Eyquem de, 11
Mourning, 97
Mullen, Mike, 64
Muslim Brotherhood, 148
MyDD, 78

NAACP (National Association for the
    Advancement of Colored Peo-
    ple), 111
Nation, The, 162
Navy SEALs, 28, 89, 162, 208, 215,
    219, 223
Nazi party, 189
Ndesandjo, Mark Obama, 42
Negative capability, 110, 216
New Orleans, Louisiana, 9, 32, 120,
    172
New York Review of Books, The, 162
New York Times, 205, 226
New Yorker, The, 117, 178
Newsweek, 112
9/11 terrorist attacks, 132, 180, 204,
    220, 240
9/11 workers' health care bill, 45
Nixon, Richard M., 120, 200
Nobel Peace Prize, 2, 129, 157
Noonan, Peggy, 158, 161
NRA (National Rifle Association), 58,
    201

Obama, Ann Dunham. See Dunham,
    Stanley Ann
Obama, Auma, 87–88, 97
Obama, Barack, Sr., 87–89, 102
    abandonment of family by, 5, 13,
    20, 24, 30, 37–44, 52–59, 64,
    67–68, 73, 81, 82, 93, 97, 123,
    124, 132, 136, 137, 156, 159,
    164, 165, 173, 174, 219, 228,
    248
    alcohol and, 42–44, 57, 130, 165,
    166

Ann's stories about, 5, 40–42, 47, 49–52, 69–70, 79–80, 92, 93, 95–96, 97, 106, 126, 146, 165, 166, 174
bar scene and, 48, 134
death of, 37, 51, 114, 166
driving of, 49, 51
education of, 13, 37, 92–93
grandiosity and, 47–48, 102, 132
at Harvard University, 13, 37, 93
in Kenya, 43–44, 87–88
meets Ann, 92
names of, 25
Obama's father figures compared to, 168, 169, 171
physical appearance of, 92
pipe story of, 49–51
racism and, 48–49, 68
separation and divorce from Ann, 13, 37, 38, 67–71, 79, 94, 164
visit to Hawaii by, 21–22, 37, 42, 70, 165, 172
Obama, Barack Hussein
abstract thinking and, 116–117
advisers of, 4, 162, 171, 173, 174, 213
Afghanistan and, 63–64, 205
aggression and, 39, 40, 42, 217, 225, 234
ambition of, 38, 43, 144, 156, 158
anxiety management and, 56, 96, 130–132, 151, 152, 154, 160–161
arrogance, charges of, 160, 161
The Audacity of Hope by, 5, 11, 37, 54, 163–164, 170, 171, 175, 204
automobile industry bailout and, 45, 161–162
basketball and, 64, 84, 148
belief system of, 66
bin Laden raid and, 2, 7, 27, 28–29, 45, 59, 61, 84, 89–90, 152, 153, 161, 162, 180, 190, 202, 205, 208, 214, 215–222, 225, 234
biographer of, 14, 18, 24, 38–39, 44, 69, 179
bipartisan cooperation and, 29, 71, 85, 87, 134, 233–234

biracial heritage of, 2, 5, 12, 16–27, 25, 59, 67, 82–84, 121, 128, 136, 146, 152–153, 170, 171
birth and citizenship issues and, 2, 15, 32, 55, 87, 116, 187, 192, 193
birth of, 2
blind spots of, 3, 4, 32, 47, 66, 133–134, 143, 159, 179, 214, 228
BP Gulf oil spill and, 20, 31–33, 45, 55, 66, 107, 161, 172
calm demeanor of, 3, 6, 20, 30, 126, 196, 228
candidate and president, split between, 4, 8, 12, 27–28, 31, 52, 59–60, 79, 80, 117, 175, 205–207, 212–214, 226, 234
in care of grandparents, 24, 72, 81–82, 97, 123, 128, 165, 206
change, attitude toward, 31–32, 112–117, 121–129, 131, 137–142, 205
change of name by, 25
childhood of. See Dunham, Stanley Ann; Obama, Barack, Sr.
at Columbia University, 69, 146, 149, 150
as community organizer, 22, 24, 64, 86, 112–113, 115, 135–137, 167, 168, 179, 180
compartmentalization and, 208–209, 215
compromise and consensus building and, 3, 4, 6, 13, 30, 32, 34, 38, 64–65, 72, 85–87, 131
conflict-avoidance style of, 45–46, 140, 234, 235, 238
containment and, 95–96, 98, 242
coping mechanisms of, 4, 152–153
Coretta incident and, 21, 22, 32, 100, 102, 103
courtship of Michelle by, 178
depressive position and, 6, 15–16, 28–31, 140–142, 159–160, 202, 246
dissociation and, 14, 130–134, 202, 242–243

Obama, Barack Hussein (*Cont.*)
 Dreams from My Father by, vii,
  4–5, 17, 18, 20, 42–44, 49, 55,
  59, 67–70, 72–73, 79, 91–92,
  97–102, 112–116, 124, 135–136,
  146, 147, 149–151, 153–155,
  164, 175, 178, 180–182, 204,
  211, 227
 drug and alcohol use by, 44, 75, 76,
  130
 economic crisis and, 31, 45, 77, 97,
  109, 151, 152, 235
 education of, 2, 7, 20–21, 24, 25,
  40, 72, 76, 123, 128, 146,
  155–157
 Egypt and, 112, 117
 envy of, 189–191, 193, 197, 198, 243
 as father, 53–56, 59, 61, 98, 200
 father and. *See* Obama, Barack, Sr.
 father hunger of, 166–173
 first two years as president, 27, 77,
  129
 fishermen of New Orleans and, 32,
  66, 172
 Fort Hood shootings and, 144
 on freedom of speech, 33
 friendships of, 176
 Gates incident and, 58, 116
 grandparents of. *See* Dunham,
  Madelyn Lee Payne (Toots);
  Dunham, Stanley Armour
  (Gramps)
 Guantánamo prison and, 114–115,
  220
 gun control and, 55, 58, 107
 hate/hatred and, 7, 15, 22, 32, 47,
  51, 52, 55–56, 90, 132–134, 142,
  159–160, 209, 222, 230–231
 health care reform and, 4, 15–16,
  27, 31, 45, 46, 47, 77, 81, 82, 86,
  112, 131, 138, 140, 141, 148,
  191, 201, 205, 237
 Hitler, compared to, 189
 humility of, 144–145
 idealization of father by, 39–42,
  47–48, 103
 in Indonesia, 4, 17, 30, 71, 96, 114,
  124–127, 147, 150, 151, 155,
  205–206

Indonesia, visit to (2010), 23
infancy of, 5, 12
intelligence of, 24, 144, 147, 149,
  157, 158, 162, 190, 192
interview in *The New Yorker*
  (1996), 178
interview with Bill O'Reilly (2011),
  51, 132, 133, 148–149
interview with Brian Williams
  (2010), 32
interview with *People* magazine
  (2011), 59
interview with *Rolling Stone* (2010),
  147, 161
interview with Steve Kroft on *60
  Minutes* (2011), 27, 29, 89,
  215–216, 220–221, 234
interviews with Charlie Rose (2004
  and 2006), 22, 144
introspection of, 149–151, 155,
  158–159, 207
Iraq War and, 108–109, 205
Ireland, visit to (2011), 225–229
Joplin, Missouri, tornado victims
  and, 228
lack of fear of, 134–137
language, facility with, 3, 6, 60–61,
  96
Language of Achievement and
  substitution and, 109–115, 219,
  243–244
at law school, 2, 84
Left and, 28, 80–81, 83, 85, 86, 89,
  110, 111, 116, 174–175, 212,
  228, 241, 248
legislation passed by, 2, 45–46,
  85–86, 131, 233
Libyan crisis and, 29, 112, 124, 161
life in New York of, 149–150
Life magazine article and, 17–20,
  72, 87, 123, 125, 146
listening skills of, 41, 98, 146–147,
  160, 206
magical thinking and, 105–108, 129
Manning case and, 27, 33, 58
mental health of, 3, 143–146, 226
middle name of, 188, 240
midterm elections (2010) and, 2,
  30–32, 34, 54, 133, 141, 205

mother and. *See* Dunham, Stanley
   Ann
Nobel Peace Prize awarded to, 2, 129
obsessive bipartisan disorder of, 85,
   87, 220, 233, 246
offshore drilling and, 77, 218
Pakistan drone attacks and, 29
paranoid-schizoid position and, 6,
   7, 15–16, 28, 30, 33, 140, 142,
   160, 202, 246
pathological accommodation and,
   78–82, 85, 87–89
payroll tax cut extension and 233
perspicacity of, 206–207
as president of *Harvard Law
   Review,* 2, 22, 64, 91, 157, 169
press conference (December 2010),
   138–139
press conference (February 2011),
   179
press conference (March 24, 2009),
   96–97
projection and, 29, 31, 39, 80–81,
   154, 204, 207, 211–213
prosecution of Bush administration
   members and, 34
public speaking debut at Occidental,
   22, 99–106, 132, 243
rage and, 38, 41, 42, 44–47, 52, 57,
   59, 72, 80, 82–84, 88, 132, 156,
   235
Reagan, admiration for, 89
reelection issue and, 27, 66, 86
reparative drive of, 145–146
Republican opposition to, 7, 15–16,
   30, 46–47, 56, 57, 66, 77, 80,
   82, 84–86, 88–89, 116–117, 131,
   133, 134, 140, 160, 174, 176,
   186, 189–191, 202, 217, 218,
   221, 222, 233–238, 246
research tax credit and, 47
return to Hawaii, 20, 40, 72, 123,
   125, 128, 154, 157, 206
at Rhode Island fund-raiser (2010),
   54, 55
self-analysis by, 154–155
self-hatred and, 19, 20, 105
as senator, 175–176
shame, awareness of, 17, 21, 102

Sherrod firing and, 111
ship's captain metaphor of, 234–235
smoking and, 130
speeches of. *See* Speeches of Barack
   Obama
splitting and, 13, 14, 16, 19, 22–28,
   30, 33–35, 116
stepfather (Lolo) and, 39, 59,
   124–128, 147, 150, 151,
   153–154, 165, 166, 170, 172,
   205–206, 211
Strategic Arms Reduction Treaty
   and, 45
substitution of words for action by,
   107–109, 117
tax cuts to wealthy and, 27, 31, 86,
   107, 129, 138, 173, 179, 221
Tea Party movement and, 7, 29, 45,
   56, 57, 111, 186, 194–202, 244
thought avoidance, attraction to,
   88–89
transference and, 55, 57, 61, 210,
   227, 239–241
Tucson shootings and, 9, 20, 55, 83,
   150–151
Tunisia and, 117
2006 Senate campaign, 130
2008 election and, 2, 8, 28, 30, 59,
   80, 108, 109, 121–122, 137,
   141, 146, 147, 152, 160, 162,
   173, 183, 204–205, 211, 244
2012 campaign, 235–238
uniqueness of, 1–2
unity, pursuit of, 11, 13, 22, 28, 61,
   64–67, 71, 125, 144, 170, 220,
   223
Washington, Harold, and, 167–168,
   173
wedding of, 171
whistle-blowers and, 117
at White House Correspondents'
   Association dinner (2011), 153,
   208
Wisconsin union battle and, 45,
   117, 134
word usage and, 98–99, 104–106,
   108
Wright, Jeremiah and, 145, 167,
   168–171, 173, 176, 180–183

Index

Obama: From Promise to Power
  (Mendell), 14
Obama, Malia, 6, 53–59, 61, 98, 175,
  176, 248
Obama, Michelle, 6, 9, 54, 56, 87,
  171–173, 175, 176, 178, 185, 192
Obama, Sasha, 6, 53–59, 61, 98, 175,
  176, 248
Obama's Wars (Woodward), 14,
  63–64, 158
Objects, 177, 244–245
Obsessive bipartisan disorder, 85, 87,
  220, 233, 246
Occidental College, 25, 69, 149, 243
  Obama's speaking debut at, 22,
  99–106, 132, 243
Oedipal drive, 156, 177
Offshore drilling, 77, 218
Onion News Network, The, 4
O'Reilly, Bill, 51, 132, 133, 148–149,
  193–194
O'Reilly Factor, The, 193
Origins myths, 93, 146
Owens, John, 24

Pakistan, 27, 29
Palin, Sarah, 185, 190–191, 201
Paranoia, 15, 32, 141
Paranoid-schizoid position, 6, 7,
  15–16, 28, 30, 33, 140, 142,
  160, 188–190, 202, 212, 222,
  245–246
Pathological accommodation, 78–82,
  87–89
Paul, Ron, 237
Pelosi, Nancy, 46
Pence, Mike, 57
People magazine, 59
Persecution fantasy, 194
Petraeus, David, 64
Pharmaceutical industry, 45
Planned Parenthood, 209
Playboy magazine, 141
Plouffe, David, 122
Podesta, John, 158
Political slogans, 119–123, 129
Positions. *See* Depressive position;
  Paranoid-schizoid position
Positive father transference, 57

Preconceptions, 216
Presidential election of 2008, 2, 8, 28,
  30, 59, 80, 108, 109, 121–122,
  137, 141, 146, 147, 152, 160,
  162, 173, 183, 204–205, 211,
  244
Projection, 14, 29, 31, 39, 80–81, 154,
  192, 193, 198, 199, 201,
  203–204, 207, 211–213
Promise, The (Alter), 162
Proper Study of Manhood, The
  (Berlin), 203
Psychoanalytic method, 3, 6
Punahou School, Hawaii, 20–21, 102

Racism, 48–49, 68, 71, 86, 134, 186,
  192–195, 197, 208, 217, 222
Rage, 38, 41, 42, 44–47, 52, 57, 59, 72,
  80, 82–84, 88, 90, 132, 156, 235
Ralston, Jason, 122
Ray (student), 99, 114, 172
Reaction formation, 52, 84–85, 240
Reagan, Ronald, 89, 112, 200, 226
Regina (student), 25–26, 99, 101,
  103–105, 114, 152, 178
Reid, Harry, 108
Remnick, David, 4, 18, 24, 69, 72–73,
  179
Reparative drive, 145–146
Repetition compulsion, 57, 129,
  246–247
Repression, 247
Republican opposition to Obama, 7,
  15–16, 30, 46–47, 56, 57, 66, 77,
  80, 82, 84–86, 88–89, 116–117,
  131, 133, 134, 140, 160, 174,
  176, 186, 189–191, 202, 217,
  218, 221, 222, 233–238, 246
Republican primaries of 2012,
  236–237
Republican rage, 235
Research tax credit, 47
*Revival: The Struggle for Survival
  Inside the Obama White House*
  (Wolffe), 46, 54, 108, 121–122,
  160
Rich, Frank, 162, 205
Rilke, Rainer Maria, vii
Robinson, Fraser, 172–173

Index

Robinson, Marian, 200
Rolling Stone magazine, 147, 161
Romney, Mitt, 236, 237
Roosevelt, Franklin D., 139
Rose, Charlie, 22–23, 144
Rove, Karl, 190
Rush, Bobby, 179
Ryan, Paul, 87

Santorum, Rick, 237
Schumer, Charles, 236
Scott, Janny, 41, 69–71, 76, 81
Seattle, Washington, 67, 164
Self-hatred, 19, 20, 105
Sermon on the Mount, 53
Shame, 16, 17, 21, 102
Sherrod, Shirley, 111
60 Minutes, 27, 29, 89, 215–216, 220–221, 234
Social Security, 83
Soetero, Ann. *See* Dunham, Stanley Ann
Soetero, Lolo, 17, 39, 59, 70–72, 92, 96, 114, 123–128, 130, 146, 147, 150, 153–154, 166, 170, 172, 173, 205–206, 211
Soetero-Ng, Maya, 72, 82, 95, 156
South Africa, 99, 100, 105
Speeches of Barack Obama
    at Arlington National Cemetery (Memorial Day, 2009), 209–210
    at Booker T. Washington High School commencement, Memphis (May 16, 2011), 218, 219
    on BP oil spill (June 2010), 161, 172
    in Cairo (June 4, 2009), 60, 91, 203
    campaign speeches (2008), 137, 207–208
    at Chicago church (June 2008), 53
    on defense of Social Security (April 2011), 83
    at Democratic National Convention (2004), 11, 22, 65–67, 76, 91, 102, 122

    at George Washington University (April 13, 2011), 77, 110
    at Georgetown University (April 2009), 53
    inaugural address (2009), 102
    in Kenya (2006), 43–44
    Nobel Prize acceptance speech, 129, 157
    at Notre Dame (2009), 209
    at Occidental College, 22, 99–106, 132, 237
    in Osawatomie, Kansas (December 2011), 233
    on race (April 2008), 83, 105–106, 145, 204, 208, 230
    in response to Republican budget (April 2011), 30
    State of the Union address (2010), 133
    State of the Union address (2011), 33, 122–123
    in Tucson (January 2011), 83, 107, 150–151
    at University of Chicago (2002), 203–204, 221
Splitting mechanism, 12–16, 19, 22–28, 30, 33–35, 116, 195, 198, 201, 236, 238, 247
State of the Union address
    2010, 133
    2011, 33, 122–123, 195
Steele, Michael, 57
Steele, Shelby, 121, 171
Stephanopoulos, George, 158–159
Stranger anxiety, 187
Strategic Arms Reduction Treaty, 45
Strength to Love (King), 143
Substitution, language of, 109–115, 219, 243–244
Sullivan, Andrew, 233
Summers, Larry, 173, 213
Super Bowl (2011), 162
Swaddling, 93–96, 103, 117, 155

Tancredo, Tom, 185
Taxes
    cuts to wealthy, 27, 31, 86, 107, 129, 138, 173, 179, 221
    research tax credit, 47

Index

Tea Party movement, 7, 29, 45, 56, 57,
111, 132, 133, 186, 191,
194–202, 244
Thomas, Kenneth W., 78
Thought avoidance, attraction to, 88–89
Transference, 8, 55, 57, 61, 89, 210,
227, 239–241
Transformation, 112
Trilling, Lionel, 119
Trinity Church, Chicago, 168–171,
176, 180–183
Trump, Donald, 87
Tucson shootings, 9, 20, 55–56, 83,
107, 150–151, 246
Tunisia, 117
Tyson, Mike, 70

Unconscious mind, 120, 247–248
Unconscious repetition compulsion,
57, 129
Unemployment, 117
University of Hawaii, 92
University of Indonesia, 23

Vaillant, George, 143–144, 176
Victim mentality, 188–189, 201
View, The, 161

Walker, Scott, 134
Wall Street Journal, 158
Warren, Rick, 205
Washington, Harold, 167–168, 172, 180

Washington Post, The, 66, 115
Way of All Flesh, The (Butler), 1
Weiner, Anthony, 195
West, Cornel, 203, 214
*What's the Matter with Kansas: How
Conservatives Won the Heart of
America* (T. Frank), 208
Whistle-blowers, 117
White House Correspondents'
Association dinner (2011), 153,
208
White House health care summit
(2010), 11
WikiLeaks, 27, 33
Williams, Brian, 32
Williams, Juan, 193–194
Winnicott, D. W., 79
Wisconsin union battle, 45, 117, 134
Wolfe, Thomas, 43
Wolffe, Richard, 46, 47, 54, 108,
121–122, 129, 160
Woodward, Bob, 4, 14, 63–64, 158
Word swaddling, 94–96, 103, 117
Working through technique, 106
Wright, Jeremiah, 145, 167, 168–171,
173, 176, 180–183, 185
Wright, Richard, 172

Xenophobia, 187

Zetzel, Elizabeth, 176
Zogby, John, 78

About the Author

Dr. Justin Frank, a highly regarded national expert on psychoanalysis with more than thirty-five years practicing psychoanalysis and marital therapy, is a clinical professor in the Department of Psychiatry at George Washington University Medical Center. He is a sought-after teacher and lecturer whose topics range from contemporary films to psychoanalytic theory to revenge and murder in Shakespeare's tragedies to psychopolitical life in America. His numerous publications and media appearances range from articles in popular magazines—including *Marie Claire* and Salon.com—to several book chapters and the *New York Times* best-selling book *Bush on the Couch*. Dr. Frank has three grown children and lives in Washington, D.C., with his wife, Heather, and their two Portuguese water dogs, neither of which is related to Bo.